Christianity after Christendom

Also Available from Bloomsbury

Theological Poverty in Continental Philosophy, Colby Dickinson
The Phenomenology of Religious Belief, Michael J. Shapiro
The Experience of Atheism: Phenomenology, Metaphysics and Religion, Ed. Claude Romano and Robyn Horner

Christianity after Christendom

Heretical Perspectives in Philosophical Theology

Martin Koci

BLOOMSBURY ACADEMIC
LONDON • NEW YORK • OXFORD • NEW DELHI • SYDNEY

BLOOMSBURY ACADEMIC
Bloomsbury Publishing Plc
50 Bedford Square, London, WC1B 3DP, UK
1385 Broadway, New York, NY 10018, USA
29 Earlsfort Terrace, Dublin 2, Ireland

BLOOMSBURY, BLOOMSBURY ACADEMIC and the Diana logo
are trademarks of Bloomsbury Publishing Plc

First published in Great Britain 2023
This paperback edition published in 2025

Copyright © Martin Koci, 2023

Martin Koci has asserted his right under the Copyright,
Designs and Patents Act, 1988, to be identified as Author of this work.

For legal purposes the Acknowledgments on pp. ix–xi constitute
an extension of this copyright page.

Series design by Charlotte Daniels
Cover image: Daniel Domig, "Into the Water", oil on Canvas (2014)
www.currentlynowhere.com

All rights reserved. No part of this publication may be reproduced or transmitted in any form or by any means, electronic or mechanical, including photocopying, recording, or any information storage or retrieval system, without prior permission in writing from the publishers.

Bloomsbury Publishing Plc does not have any control over, or responsibility for, any third-party websites referred to or in this book. All internet addresses given in this book were correct at the time of going to press. The author and publisher regret any inconvenience caused if addresses have changed or sites have ceased to exist, but can accept no responsibility for any such changes.

A catalogue record for this book is available from the British Library.

A catalog record for this book is available from the Library of Congress.

ISBN: HB: 978-1-3503-2263-9
PB: 978-1-3503-2267-7
ePDF: 978-1-3503-2264-6
eBook: 978-1-3503-2265-3

Typeset by Integra Software Services Pvt. Ltd.

To find out more about our authors and books visit www.bloomsbury.com
and sign up for our newsletters.

To Katerina,
Noemi, Elias & Ida

Contents

Acknowledgments ix

Introduction 1

Part 1 Postmodern Ends of Christianity

1 Lost Credibility: Christianity after Jean-François Lyotard's Critique of Metanarrative 15
2 After Deconstruction: Jean-Luc Nancy and the Essence of Christianity 31
3 The Sense of the After: Jan Patočka and the Post-Christian Epoch 47

Postscript to Part I The Questions of After 61

Part 2 The Figures of the After

4 A Secular Christianity of Nihilist Love: Engaging Gianni Vattimo's Atheism 71
5 Christianity Without Religion: Struggling with John D. Caputo's Radicalism 93
6 The Poetics of Anatheist Christianity: Debating Richard Kearney's Universalism 115

Postscript to Part II After Hermeneutics 139

Part 3 Shaken Christianity

7 Christianity Interrupted: A Theological Experiment by Lieven Boeve 151
8 Being Shaken: The After Movement of Christian Life 171

9	The Solidarity of the Shaken: Christian Community after Christendom	193
Conclusion		211
Bibliography		222
Index		234

Acknowledgments

The idea for this book has been growing in my mind for a long time. I could list numerous philosophers and theologians whose work has motivated me to reflect on Christianity and its after, but the central idea was driven home during a relaxed after-dinner conversation with a friend and colleague, a political philosopher and critical theorist who was once a Christian but today has embraced a critical stance toward religion from the perspective of leftist thought. Out of a sincere interest, my friend asked me about my recent project. When I presented him with the main concepts and categories, such as Christianity after Christendom, phenomenologically based theology, and Christianity as a movement of existence, his face went a ghostly white that spoke volumes. That moment of silence, no longer than a couple of seconds, carried a clear message: "But this is impossible." We then resumed the debate as I sought to formulate my argument concerning philosophical theology, Christianity as a truly historical event, and the after of Christianity as not merely an historical-sociological fact but an ontological movement.

That evening, over a glass (or two) of rich, round Italian red wine and in the company of a friend, I learned an important lesson: that the debate we have been having in theology and theologically attuned continental philosophy is, to say it plainly, not remotely self-evident. The goal of this book is therefore twofold. First, to contribute to the debate surrounding theology and contemporary continental philosophy while bringing into the discussion some rather neglected sources of inspiration. Secondly, and perhaps more importantly, to state as clearly as possible the possibilities of a theology which comes after the end of Christendom and which shows that the movement of the after has always been a matter of theological thought.

Now that the project has come to its completion, I think of the many people who accompanied me while I was working on this book. First, my professional colleagues with whom I am in regular contact. I think of Jason W. Alvis, a friend and the leader of the research project that created the conditions that enabled me to work comfortably on this book. Thanks must also go to Kurt Appel, the professor of fundamental theology at the University of Vienna, who secured my teaching position and thus provided me with the stimulating arena in which I could test with my students many of the ideas and arguments included in this book. I do indeed also thank Emmanuel Falque, for his friendship, support, and the time we spent together philosophizing and theologizing.

Then comes a group of people whose assistance can certainly not go unrecognized. I am thinking of those dedicated souls who reviewed my previous book *Thinking Faith after Christianity* (Albany, NY: State University of New York Press, 2020). Written on the highly specific theme of a theological reading of Jan Patočka's phenomenological philosophy, the monograph exceeded all expectations in attracting a wide readership and even being awarded the Book Prize of the European Society for Catholic Theology. Nonetheless, what I found most rewarding was reading the in-depth, engaged, and critical reviews that challenged me and motivated me to think further and to think again. I cannot deny that this current book would be significantly poorer without all the questions raised by Jakub Sirovátka, Erin Plunkett, Martin Ritter, Jan Frei, Marco Barcaro, and Jacky Yuen-Hung Tai. I confess that receiving those reviews while working on this book helped me to reshape what you read here in numerous ways. I still have some doubts as to whether I have succeeded in answering, or at least responding to, all the serious questions addressed to me by the careful readers of my earlier works, but that is for others to decide. One way or another, I am immensely grateful for having such attentive, critical, but generous readers and

I can only wish that this book will resonate in the philosophical and theological communities to the same extent.

I am also immensely grateful to those who commented on previous versions of this text. Chapter 1 is a significantly reworked version of my article "Fighting Hegemony, Saving the Event: Why Theologise with Jean-François Lyotard and Postmodern Philosophy?" (AUC Theologica 7, no. 2 [2017]: 105–27). Chapter 3 is partly based on the previously published "Christianity after Christendom: Rethinking Jan Patočka's Heresy" (Heythrop Journal 63, no. 4 [2022]: 717–30). Drafts of Chapters 7, 8, and 9 were presented as conference papers at, respectively, "The Leuven Encounters for Systematic Theology" (2021), "The International Network in Philosophy of Religion Seminar" in Durham, UK (2022), and "The Danube Institute" in Budapest (2022).

Since editing is a part of writing, thanks must also go to the excellent team at Bloomsbury, especially my managing editor Lucy Harper (née Russell), who makes the process of publishing swift, pleasant, and enjoyable. Above all, I would like to thank Tim Morgan, the careful proofreader of every single line I put to paper. Tim never disappoints in asking pertinent questions that go beyond the mere grammatical structures of my text. Every project on which we cooperate is a true learning process for both of us.

The book was written with the generous financial support of the Austrian Science Fund (FWF) for the project "Revenge of the Sacred: Phenomenology and the Ends of Christianity in Europe" [P 31919].

Last but not least, I must thank my family: Katerina my wife, a fellow theologian and academic who is capable, unlike me, of focusing on detailed problems; my daughter Noemi, who can ask such marvelous questions; my son Elias, a source of unlimited energy; and my daughter Ida, who has come into the world at the very moment of submitting the manuscript for this book. My work would be impossible without you!

Introduction

What Christianity will become in the coming centuries is totally unpredictable. These words belong to Jacques Derrida, the *enfant terrible* of postmodern thought, and self-identified *Jew-Greek* who can't resist speaking in *Latin*.[1] This book accepts the challenge of asking the obvious but nonetheless largely neglected question: What comes after the end of Christianity?

The prolific Christian writer and essayist Tomáš Halík takes inspiration from the analytical psychology of Carl Gustav Jung and refers to the current situation under the rubric of *the afternoon of Christianity*.[2] After the morning, when structures and institutions established themselves and reached their full strength, and after a noontide of idleness and the internal crisis of modern suspicions of religion and its subsequent secularization, a new epoch has been approaching. The afternoon is a time of awakening and reconciliation; it is a challenge to sail to the spiritual depths. The afternoon is a time to become truly spiritual; a time to harvest the fruits of old trees ripened in the course of crises.

I find this metaphor of the afternoon seductive but flawed. People live in stories. For religious people, this is a double truth. Creating comprehensible narratives certainly helps to process spiritual

---

[1] John D. Caputo, Kevin Hart, and Yvonne Sherwood, "Epoché and Faith: An Interview with Jacques Derrida," in *Derrida and Religion: Other Testaments*, ed. Y. Sherwood and K. Hart (New York, NY: Routledge, 2005), 33.
[2] Tomáš Halík, *Der Nachmittag des Christentums: Eine Zeitansage* (Freiburg: Herder, 2022).

upheavals and personal struggles, but (and there is always a *but*) however appealing the language may sound, it is missing something fundamental. The notion of *afternoon* presupposes succession; an easy, all too easy continuation of that which came before. I agree that a certain form of Christianity has come to its end—something this book takes as its point of departure—but I have no intention of looking back in order to reconstruct what caused the shift, nor of exploring what kind of Christianity has been dissolved in order to re-assemble it. Rather, the following pages will focus on the pressing moment of *the after of Christianity*—with the emphasis on the after.

Emmanuel Falque says that "entering with intellectual integrity into the hypothesis of an end of Christianity is probably the sole means of not letting it be condemned to its end."[3] I concur with these words. In my understanding, they suggest that the category of the after does not signify merely or primarily some kind of linear succession. This book is therefore about exploring something radically new, something that has yet to come—something, in Derrida's words, unpredictable. The after is a sign of a *coming future* that is already *present*, but not yet.

The Sense of the After

It is a "truth universally acknowledged" that Christendom has disintegrated and no longer functions as the generally accepted or even generally understood reference point and interpretative framework for that which is. Christianity has ceased to be a compass for the world. Moreover, the postmodern suspicion of grand narratives questions the temptation to create a safe camp of Christian identity exempted from the pluralized and fragmented world. This book will

---

[3] Emmanuel Falque, *The Metamorphosis of Finitude: An Essay on Birth and Resurrection*, trans. G. Hughes (New York, NY: Fordham University Press, 2012), 35.

dedicate much space to the debate surrounding various (postmodern) ends of Christianity and their consequences. Now, however, here at the beginning, what I have in mind is something blunt and obvious: Christianity is not capable of creating a parallel world within the world. Even when we think about the remaining outposts of confessional Christianity, these spaces are also inhabited by plural, fragmented communities that resemble so much of the rest of the world. Almost any suburban parish we cared to visit could be home to a right-wing Christian conservative businessman and a bleeding-heart liberal who enjoys speculating on cryptocurrencies; a vegan with a passion for matcha lattés (made from organic, plant-based milk, of course) and a father of four and grandfather of ten who likes his Sunday steak well done. Radically different persons rub shoulders during worship, sing from the same hymn book, and have roasted preacher together over coffee in the church hall after the service.

Christianity has come to its end yet remains operative. Everyday experience shows that our culture is certainly not-Christian, but the same experience hints to us that it is not yet entirely non-Christian.[4] This makes thinking about Christianity after Christendom a task of some urgency. Nevertheless, the other side of our question points to the problem of essence. As a matter of fact, the situation of the postmodern after of Christianity resembles the earlier historical shock of modernity, which also hit religious life in unprecedented ways. As a response to the ever-present suspicions grounded in rational critique, numerous attempts to define the essence of Christianity in rationally convincing ways appeared on the intellectual map of modernity.

Ludwig Feuerbach's *The Essence of Christianity* (originally published in 1841) triggered a lively debate, especially among Protestant

---

[4] For this insight concerning the difference between not-Christian and non-Christian culture, I am indebted to my friend and colleague Joeri Schrijvers, with whom I have held numerous passionate debates on this topic.

theologians.[5] From Friedreich Schleirmacher, through Albrecht Ritschl, Adolf von Harnack, and Ernst Troeltsch, to Karl Barth and Dietrich Bonhoeffer, we find repeated attempts to address Feuerbach's original critique (and indeed the entire modern suspicion of religion) through a theological distillation of the essence of Christianity.

Sometime later, the so-called *aggiornamento* appeared as the Catholic response to the same historical shock. The struggle with modernity filled endless shelves with the genius of the *ressourcement* and *nouvelle théologie* that culminated in the Second Vatican Council (1962–5), an epochal event for the Catholic Church. Yet all too soon this movement of Christian spirit toward the world lost its way and buried itself in ecclesiastical concerns. In other words, the ethos of searching for a comprehensible and credible version of Christianity incurvated itself into an internal and self-referential debate.

By a similar token, the Protestant debate took the path of de-theologization and developed the narratives of the social gospel, the death of God theologies, and radical theologies without God, eventually morphing into the so-called continental philosophy of religion, which put aside controversial theological baggage in order to be *honest to God* outside of confessional constraints.

By whatever means, Christianity has survived and finds itself in a new radical sense of its own after. The challenge is to repeat the gesture of previous generations and formulate a response. Hence, the intention of this book is not only to understand the present situation of the after of Christianity but also to shed light on the possibilities of Christian life in a culture that is not-Christian but not yet non-Christian.

---

[5] Ludwig Feuerbach, *The Essence of Christianity* (Cambridge: Cambridge University Press, 2011). For a summary of the subsequent debate, see D. L. Deegan, "The Ritschlian School of the Essence of Christianity and Karl Barth," *Scottish Journal of Theology* 16, no. 4 (1963): 390–414.

God after God

There is one unusual aspect to the discussion around the current state of affairs in the postmodern context. Christianity might have come to its end, but the question of God is finding its way back *plus fort*. This is especially the case in the academic arena. The field of philosophy has experienced the return to the religious, the theological turn, and theology's response to philosophy. As a result, the discourse on religion, naming God, religious experience, faith, and so on, has undergone a great reversal. It is no longer theologians who seek to employ the contemporary critical consciousness of philosophy to retranslate, reread, reinterpret, and reconceptualize Christianity to make it more comprehensible, more rational, and more attractive. Now, myriad philosophers, religious and secular philosophers alike, do not hesitate to draw inspiration from the sphere of religion and theology in order to interpret the structures of existence in the world.

The motivations for such philosophical reconsiderations of religion vary, but a general perspective suggests that the religious allows for thinking excess, exploring the impossible; religious thinking offers the possibility of criticizing metaphysics; it provides an alternative to modern objectivism; in short, it provides the other of autonomous reason. Whatever the motivation, the result is obvious: we are confronted with delocalized Christian concepts and even de-theologized theologies that open new horizons for understanding Christianity. The philosophical return to religion has created new symbolical worlds that are not without importance for subsequent theological reflection. Perhaps the most interesting part of the whole movement is the audacious and spirited repetition of Christianity outside the exclusively defined ecclesial body.[6]

---

[6] It is clearly impossible to gather all the philosophers interested in the return to religion under a single umbrella. At best, we can talk about certain family resemblances, as argued

The after of Christianity therefore reveals itself, as a double challenge: *ad extra* vis-a-vis philosophy; and *ad intra* for theology. The former takes the situation of the after as a challenge to thinking and renewing contemporary critical consciousness. The latter is confronted by the after and stands before a challenge of the *recontextualization* of Christian life in the midst of the world. In other words, both Christian and atheist philosophers turn to Christianity and examine its structural thought patterns and lived experiences not with the intention of renewing it, but in order to understand its *modus operandi* after its end. From there, conclusions are drawn about being (in the widest sense of the word) in-the-world-after-Christianity. These philosophical turns provoke—whether they intend to or not—a radically renewed sense of theology; a sense which must, however, be uncovered and tested. The originally philosophical category of the after of Christianity thus puts theological endeavor under pressure and unfolds into a new theological category, that is, a Christianity after the end of Christendom.

From a theological perspective, we find ourselves, paradoxically, in the reverse situation. Whereas the modern masters of suspicion forced theology to develop a new sense of apologetics by pointing to the essence of Christian religion, or by demarcating the path of the *aggiornamento*, the situation of the after offers creatively dislocated and reinterpreted Christian concepts and even suggestions of how to live and experience Christianity after its end. Theology does not need to defend (in the sense of fight). Rather, it is invited to examine

---

in Bruce E. Benson, "Introduction," in *Words of Life: New Theological Turns in French Phenomenology*, ed. B. E. Benson and N. Wizba (New York, NY: Fordham University Press, 2010), 1–12. For a broad but detailed classification, see Colby Dickinson, *Continental Philosophy and Theology* (Boston: Brill, 2018). It is also not possible to reduce the philosophical return to religion exclusively to Christianity. For a discussion of all three major monotheistic religions, see Anthony J. Steinbock, *Phenomenology and Mysticism: The Verticality of Religious Experience* (Bloomington, IN: Indiana University Press, 2007).

the philosophical matter and draw, this time, theological conclusions from there. One way or another, it remains clear how nontheological, historical, and worldly issues are normative for theology and ultimately how they transform Christianity.

The argument of this book will oscillate between the two challenges of *ad extra* and *ad intra*, and will thus attend to the fruitful exchange between two disciplines that are so often seen as radically separate.

The Context of the Argument

I intend to contest and depart from three widespread approaches to Christianity. Two of these are predominantly theological; one is philosophical. As I have already suggested, I find it neither attractive nor accurate to reduce the current crisis of Christian religion to metaphors that tend to reduce the desired theological account to a mere narrative exercise. Although this may appeal to certain groups, both within and without Christian circles, it adds nothing to a rigorous processing of the pressing situation of Christianity after Christendom. Instead of arguments, it remains on the level of emotions, symbols, and propositions. The story goes on and "we" feel well.

The counterpole to quasi-theological narrativity is the conception of theology as an objective and positive science. Many theologians vehemently seek to persuade the audience that their endeavor is no less scientific than the practice of natural scientists. With their claim that theology has axioms, methods of procedure, and scientific terminology, more than a few of these authors then concede to Heidegger who, supposedly, insists that theology is indeed a positive science: "Ha! You see," comes the cry of victory, "even Heidegger acknowledges the scientific pedigree of theology!" Setting aside for a moment such an interpretation of Heidegger (by people who have not read him carefully or perhaps not read him at all),[7] the problem with positive, even positivistic and objectivistic, theology is that it detaches itself from lived experience. Of course, one can research the question of God as a datum and Christian phenomena as objects of experimental examination. However, this theo*logical* attitude easily misses the challenge of the after of Christianity, mainly because this kind of theology creates a self-referential discourse that is remote from actual history. Attending to the unmoving and the ahistorical, failing to recognize any normativity in the question of the after of Christianity, in short, hiding away in an academic ivory tower, is an approach I find even more counterproductive than reliance on metaphors.

Finally, although the argument of this book draws inspiration from continental philosophy, I will not follow the current trend in the philosophy of religion, which seems to be afraid of any explicit engagement with the theological. I will not subscribe to the sometimes declared, sometimes masked, but always detached perspectives of archive, memory, and genealogy. De-theologized perspectives on the very heart of Christian reasoning, concepts, and questions are never the last word. One must not overlook the transformative potential that is inscribed in the very concept at stake. Instead of pretending to write in a one-way register, that is, from the theological through secular reason and ending in a purely philosophical position,[8] I will consider a two-way approach: the theological has the power to transform the philosophical, and the philosophical challenges and advances the transfiguration of the theological.

---

[7] Jean-Yves Lacoste is merciless in attacking what he sees as pseudoscientific avatars of theology. Jean-Yves Lacoste, *From Theology to Theological Thinking* (Charlottesville, VA: University of Virginia Press, 2014), 64–8.

[8] I suggest that paying scrupulous attention to the absolute de-theologization of its agenda plunged the philosophy of religion into an identity crisis. See, for example, Marika Rose and Anthony P. Smith, "Hexing the Discipline: Against the Reproduction of Continental Philosophy of Religion," *Palgrave Communications* 5, no. 2 (2019), http://doi: 10.1057/s41599-018-0207-4 (accessed June 30, 2022).

Rigorous reflection on the after of Christianity must transcend a translation or new inculturation of Christianity. The goal is neither correlation with a particular culture nor opposition to it, which would end in a reactionist yet deeply self-defined creative minority. The ambition of this book, the one to be tested, is to move from a particular experience of a certain end to the normativity and universality of the claim concerning the after of Christianity.

This book accepts the challenge to take seriously the words once uttered by Emmanuel Falque: "To speak and not to remain silent, that is then the first and most necessary imperative of a Western Christianity that does not resign itself to its supposed annihilation."[9] As noted earlier, even though Christianity has come to its end, it remains operative. How can one adequately address this operativity and constant transformation? How do we read Christianity's self-effacement and reappearance? To fulfill the task, this book will make use of contemporary philosophical discourse but will not hesitate to talk in theological vocabulary. On the basis of the presupposed grammar in common—the grammar of the human *per se*—between two autonomous ways of reasoning, two distinct perspectives of asking questions, and two attitudes to "what gives itself" (*es gibt*), I will attempt to do the following: first, to examine what it means to talk about the *after of Christendom*; secondly, to engage with the authors who understand that our situation is *no longer Christian* but not yet entirely *non-Christian*; and finally, to read and interpret (the hermeneutical task) as well as promote, unfold, and develop (the normative task) a credible Christianity after the end of Christendom.

---

[9] Falque, *Metamorphosis of Finitude*, 34.

Part One

Postmodern Ends of Christianity

What is the postmodern condition? The American theologian Colby Dickinson proposes the following: "The postmodern is little more than an internal, continuous dynamic of enlightenment and reformation *within* modernity. It is a fragment of a larger pattern that can never be fully incorporated within some 'whole.'"[1] In this sense, the postmodern critique is an extension of modern critique and as such aims at rethinking ontology (the nature of our being), ethics (the foundation and aims of our agency), and culture (the context of our being-in-the-world).

Modernity was marked by certainty, as if the premodern and particularly solid foundations of existence in religion and metaphysics provoked modern suspicious minds to seek an even more solid grounding in reason and knowledge. The project of modernity was about developing clear and coherent structures of everything that is. In the postmodern condition, reality seems to be fragmented and decentered, including the human subject as the organizing element and the mind behind the grandiose project of systematization, classification, and the technique of theoretical

---

[1] Colby Dickinson, *Theology and Contemporary Continental Philosophy: The Centrality of a Negative Dialectics* (Lanham, MD: Rowman & Littlefield, 2019), 10.

mastery.² The postmodern consciousness rejects abstraction and alienation from the context and deems any universalized concepts problematic. "How can one generalize in a complex world?," ask the postmodernists. And modern rationalists ask back: "Is, then, postmodernity relativistic?" The answer seems to be necessarily dialectical.

The postmodern fragment is relativistic in that it fits everything into relations—in particular those relations in which the subject who is observing, reasoning, and formulating is taking part. However, this lesson has already been taught to us by phenomenology, which at least in Edmund Husserl's conception began as a modern project *par excellence*.³ In answer to the modernists' critique, a prompt and resolute *no* must thus be added: postmodernity is by no means relativistic, at least in the sense that either truth does not exist or truth claims are redundant and impossible. For example, John D. Caputo argues that the postmodern condition rehabilitates truth as an event: truth as something coming (*venir*), though never completely; and thus to come (*á venir*), as an opening to the future (*l'avenir*).⁴ In short, the postmodern condition is the movement of de-objectification and de-possession; it is the repetition of the Nietzschean re-evaluation of all values, although in a gentler mode. The postmodern condition keeps the modern operative but calls for a rethinking—rethinking the power of thought. Or, in the language we will use in this book: the postmodern is continuingly developing an afterthought, or, in fact, competing afterthoughts.

---

² See, for example, Joeri Schrijvers, *Ontotheological Turnings? The Decentering of the Modern Subject in Recent French Phenomenology* (Albany, NY: State University of New York Press, 2011).
³ Edmund Husserl, *Ideen zur einer reinen Phänomenologie und Phänomenologische Philosophie: Allgemeine Einführung in die reine Phänomenologie* (Berlin: De Gruyter, 1994).
⁴ Caputo comments on this Derridean thread and develops it in accessible terms in his book *Truth* (London: Penguin, 2013).

Let us, then, repeat the question: What is the postmodern condition? In its critical and negative form, it is a corrective to modern hegemonies, monisms, and totalitarianisms. No grand narrative is spared from its purifying fire, from the cut of its blade. No solid construction remains unshaken. But does the postmodern spirit speak only in warnings and prohibitions? Is there not also a positive element to the movement? Could the emphasis on openness to otherness, life in heterogeneity, and the possibility of having belief (again) represent a positive feature of the program? Or does the very idea of having a program betray the whole concept? How far does the blurring of boundaries in order to reach beyond clear-cut divisions allow us to go?

This book is interested in Christianity and especially its situation in the postmodern condition. It seems to be taken for granted that for Christianity the postmodern paradigm shift has meant a certain loss: the secularization of (Western) societies; the individualization of life; the declining numbers of those who are (still) practicing religion and dare to use theological language to express their views; the overall disinterest in religion, in Christianity; theology alienated from the real-life problems of the world; suspicion regarding hierarchical religion and the self-referential tone of academic theology—all these are the customs of the day. But is this postmodern? Did it not all start in the good old days of enlightened modernity? Some theologians, at least, are attempting to embrace the challenge as an interruption to Christian tradition, a discontinuity where that which is coming in the future plays a critical-constructive role and complements continuity with the past.[5]

What I will propose is that the *end* of something—which is perhaps a stronger shift than one of mere *interruption*—represents not a closure but an opening. I am convinced that the experience of *after* paves the way for the possibility of thinking (and living) transformation. And

---

[5] See chapter 7, which offers a constructive-critical dialogue with the Flemish theologian Lieven Boeve and his reception of postmodern critical theology from a fundamental-theological perspective.

unlike some postmodern authors of Christian origin, I suggest that this possibility is not impossible at all. Rather, it is the possibility of the possible. Or, to recall Dickinson once again, the postmodern condition reminds us of our vulnerability and prompts us to reconsider the life of Christianity—to reconsider theological poverty, the kenotic tone of theology, which offers the best defense against the poverty of theology in our situation after the end of Christianity. The axial argument of this book is therefore that the postmodern is not to be feared but to be welcomed and taken as an opportunity to address pressing questions concerning Christianity after Christendom.

In what follows, I will not advocate a postmodernism of any particular kind, nor will I develop a new postmodern critical theory. I will focus, rather, on that which could be called the postmodern end of Christianity, or rather, perhaps, the postmodern ends of Christianity, just as there were multiple modern ends. In less paradoxical and perhaps clearer terms, just as the modern remains an operative part of the postmodern, so the end of Christianity does not represent a closure but an opening, a beginning. Guided by the thinking of Jean-François Lyotard, Jean-Luc Nancy, and Jan Patočka I will consider the various senses in which Christianity has been effaced by a growing disinterest in and suspicion of its narrative; I will also explore its self-deconstruction, which has resulted in unexpected reappearances; and, finally, I will disclose the sense of the *after*, which I will argue is part of Christian DNA and thus determines its entire existence.

1

Lost Credibility: Christianity after Jean-François Lyotard's Critique of Metanarrative

"Simplifying to the extreme, I define postmodern as incredulity towards metanarratives."[1] In this single pithy sentence, Jean-François Lyotard defines the postmodern condition. To understand the intellectual richness and critical nature of this definition, it is first necessary to grasp the concept of metanarratives.

Metanarratives play a decisive role in structuring social and political reality. Their principal function is to legitimize "institutions and practices, laws, ethics, ways of thinking."[2] The way we speak and use language, how we decide between the good and the bad, how we reflect on the world around us and even on ourselves is supported or criticized by a narrative, or, to be more precise, several competing narratives. For the sake of greater clarity, we can replace the theoretical-sounding notion of narrative with the word *story*, although I have in mind something rather more complex than simple storytelling. I am thinking of an identity storytelling, that is, a kind of story that has power to convince me and others about the nature of what it means to be a human being, how to build community, how to discern what is true and what is false, how to set goals for individual

---

[1] Jean-François Lyotard, *The Postmodern Condition: A Report on Knowledge*, trans. G. Bennington and B. Massumi (Minneapolis, MN: University of Minnesota Press, 1984), xxiv.
[2] Jean-François Lyotard, *The Postmodern Explained: Correspondence 1982–1985*, trans. J. Pefanis and D. Barry (Minneapolis, MN: University of Minnesota Press, 1993), 18.

and intersubjective agency, and, last but not least, a story that provides a meaningful structure for all of this.

For centuries, religion had been the main agent for providing such a narrative legitimization. Reference to the transcendent reality called God, "as was a custom of the day,"[3] functioned as the argument for or against actions, thoughts, and social norms. However, modernity, and specifically the Enlightenment, challenged religious legitimation in its entirety and thus reconfigured the whole structure of society and determined new means of legitimation in identity construction and the endowment of meaning. This is not to say that the narrative of religion suddenly ceased to function or cast any kind of influence, as the extensive interpretation of the secular thesis would have it. The religious narrative continued to work, adapting itself to the modern situation, and, arguably, growing even stronger.[4] What did happen is that religion lost its position as the privileged interpretative framework of reality, a framework that sought to provide the universal ground and the telos. Modernity became the arena where numerous competing "big stories" battled over the identity of human beings and the meaning of the world, and it is in this sense that Lyotard identifies *grand-récits*—metanarratives or master narratives:

> The metanarratives … are those that have marked modernity: progressive emancipation of reason and freedom, the progressive or catastrophic emancipation of labor, the enrichment of all humanity through the progress of capitalist technoscience, and even—if we include Christianity itself in modernity (in opposition to the classicism of antiquity)—the salvation of creature through

---

[3] Ibid.
[4] Lieven Boeve, for example, refers to the Flemish context in the first half of the twentieth century in which the Catholic Church created a parallel world to such an extent that an individual born into a Catholic family could spend their entire life within the Catholic narrative without ever leaving it. See Lieven Boeve, *Interrupting Tradition: An Essay on Christian Faith in a Postmodern Context*, trans. B. Doyle (Louvain: Peeters, 2003), 44–9.

the conversion of souls to the Christian narrative of martyred love. Hegel's philosophy totalizes all of these narratives and, in this sense, is itself a distillation of speculative modernity.[5]

The taxonomy reveals that Lyotard identifies two modes of master narratives that intertwine with each other: the philosophical-speculative, and the political. Any given metanarrative is always a theory put into practice, or, conversely, a certain practice legitimized by theory. Knowledge, which in the context of master narratives equals the conviction of possessing the truth, is linked to the claim to all-embracing definitions of the good and the just. Theoretical discourse legitimizes political praxis, and, vice versa, political power claims to possess right knowledge. Everything is interconnected: we are going round in a (deadly) circle. Lyotard argues that such grand encompassing theories of everything result in terror because they exclude heterogeneity, difference, and, above all, the most natural element of being, namely, conflict. And the tragic consequences of big modern unifying stories are at the heart of Lyotard's severe judgment and his proclamation that we do not, and perhaps could not, believe in them anymore:

> The nineteenth and twentieth centuries have given us as much terror as we can take. We have paid a high enough price for the nostalgia of the whole and the one, for the reconciliation of the concept and the sensible, of the transparent and the communicable experience. Under the general demand for slackening and for appeasement, we can hear the mutterings of the desire for a return of terror, for the realization of the fantasy to seize reality. The answer is: Let us wage a war on totality; let us be witnesses to the unpresentable; let us activate the differences and save the honor of the name.[6]

---

[5] Lyotard, *The Postmodern Explained*, 17–18.
[6] Lyotard, *The Postmodern Condition*, 81–2.

The Mechanical Structure of Metanarratives

The key to understanding the function of metanarratives is language. And by language we have in mind more than grammar, vocabulary, culturally specific allusions, style, and so on. The key issue is the way we link phrases together: the structure of our speech. Lyotard elaborates at great length on the use of language and language pragmatics, including its totalitarian pitfalls, in his philosophical masterpiece *The Differend*, a book which by his own admission is perhaps "too voluminous, too long, and too difficult."[7]

What happens in language? The question is clear; the answer is decidedly more complicated. For Lyotard, the default situation is that a *phrase* happens; the event of a phrase takes place. Every phrase belongs to a certain *phrase regimen* (e.g., descriptive, prescriptive, interrogative, etc.). Once there is a phrase, it is clear that some other phrase will follow. However, Lyotard insists that it is impossible to predict what phrase will be linked to the preceding one.

What, then, determines these linkages? For Lyotard, it is the *genre of discourse*. In the context of a particular discourse, the linking of phrases is self-evident: "Decisions are easily made because they are regulated in order to realize the goal in the most efficient way."[8] Nevertheless, the default situation of plurality naturally implies that there exist numerous discourse genres with different goals and, therefore, numerous possible rules regarding linking. Lyotard is not interested in all possible linkages but stresses that the *linking itself* is unavoidable. One phrase, following a particular discourse genre, must win and overcome the others.

---

[7] Jean-François Lyotard, *The Differend: Phrases in Dispute*, trans. G. Van Den Abbeele (Manchester: Manchester University Press, 1988), xv.
[8] Lieven Boeve, "J.-F. Lyotard's Critique of Master Narratives: Toward a Postmodern Political Theology," in *Liberation Theologies on Shifting Grounds: A Clash of Socio-Economic and Cultural Paradigms*, ed. G. De Schrijver (Leuven: Peeters, 1998), 300.

The unavoidability of linking causes an expectation—a moment of relative nothingness in Lyotard's terms. The question is, which phrase will win the clash of discourses and according to which rule? The linking repeats itself with each new phrase again and again and provokes conflicts, the situation of the *differend*: "That is the situation wherein one is first of all confronted with a number of possibilities of phrases that can be linked to a happened phrase, and, secondly, wherein one finds oneself without a general rule to decide which specific phrase will follow."[9]

The consciousness of the differend does not deprive the event of a possible phrase of its eventfulness. Neither does it mean that we find ourselves in the situation of resignation or even apathy regarding what is and has to be said. Something must be said! A phrase will happen in any case because silence is also a phrase. Nevertheless, Lyotard attributes much more importance to that which was not said because it could not be said. In other words, the function of the differend is the appeal "not to forget … all those phrases which will never be actualized once one phrase realizes the linking."[10]

The differend is not, however, the only strategy for linking phrases. In fact, we are more accustomed to comprehending language in terms of *litige*. As with the previous case, this term refers to a particular situation of dealing with the conflict of eventual phrases. The litige has an equivalent in judicial proceedings. Applied to language, this presupposes that there is someone, perhaps the judge, who possesses a binding rule which prescribes linking. Practically, this means that one dominant discourse genre, a metanarrative, suppresses the others. The default conflict is abridged. This happens with metanarratives because they exclude everything but the phrases that follow the logic

---

[9] Lieven Boeve, "Bearing Witness to the Differend: A Model for Theologizing in the Postmodern Context," *Louvain Studies* 20 (1995): 370.
[10] Boeve, "J.-F. Lyotard's Critique of Master Narratives," 301.

and goals of their narration. The phrases which will follow and those which will be erased (from memory) can all be predicted.

Master narratives claim to possess the rule for linking: the only correct, objective rule of the game that is plausible in all instances. The problem with this logic is that it excludes any criticism formulated outside a particular narrative because the linking rules either prove the opponents wrong or do not even allow them to speak. A master narrative admits only one voice—its own—which unavoidably suppresses the differend. Master narratives pretend to possess ultimate interpretations of reality while situating themselves above that reality. The storyteller speaks from the position of having a bird's eye view—the Big Brother who surveys all.

Language, therefore, degenerates into a kind of mechanics where the linking is technical, cold, and serves its purpose, and with harmful consequences. The event is mastered, violated, raped. The hegemony of master narratives does not allow anything to happen which is not under their control. The very question of happening is forbidden.[11]

Postmodernism and Christian Exceptionalism

What has all this to do with Christianity? If Lyotard announces that the postmodern condition is characterized by incredulity toward master narratives, and if Christianity is one of those master narratives, then, logically, Christianity should no longer be trusted. The

---

[11] "A 'great story' is a closed unit, in which the sentences are connected in a way that, both for the audience and the storyteller, a liberating whole is created and nothing unexpected can 'happen.'" André Lascaris, "Can I Say 'We'? An Encounter between the Good Samaritan and Three Postmodern Philosophers," in *Who Is Afraid of Postmodernism? Challenging Theology for a Society in Search of Identity*, ed. S. Van Erp and A. Lascaris (Münster: LIT Verlag, 2005), 24. I borrow the concept of language mechanics from Phillip E. Davis, "St Lyotard on the Differend/Difference Love Can Make," in *The Postmodern Saints of France: Refiguring "the Holy" in Contemporary French Philosophy*, ed. C. Dickinson (London: T&T Clark, 2013), 123–6.

disenchantment of the world suggests that theologians, philosophers of religion, and, above all, Christians are called to pay attention to Lyotard's analysis. What is it that lies behind the gradual forfeiting of Christianity's influence in the world? Are Christian truth claims the victims of relativism or of too much certainty? To ask a slightly different and perhaps more challenging question: Can Christianity be considered a hegemonic metanarrative? If we answer in the negative, Christianity escapes postmodern critique; if the answer is affirmative, however, alarm bells will start to ring.

Putting to one side those theological positions that reject Lyotard altogether with the pretentious claim that postmodern theory has nothing to offer reflections on Christianity's place in the world, we see that Christian apologetics shows a warmer yet no less problematic affinity to the father of philosophical postmodernism. The recuperation of Lyotard for the Christian cause proceeds as follows.

The outspoken criticism of modernity and its emancipation narratives, the deconstruction of enlightened rationality as the cause of countless victims and almost unimaginable yet all-too-real catastrophes (wars, totalitarian regimes, genocides), reveals the fraudulent development of modernity. As an ancient and essentially premodern narrative, Christianity stands in sharp contrast to the object of Lyotard's devastating criticism. It therefore not only escapes the postmodern critique of the modern, but also offers a solution to the empty space filled by incredulity and suspicion. Christianity is surely a grand narrative but of a fundamentally different kind from those hegemonic metanarratives responsible for the fragmentation of the world and the fracturing of human identity. A return to Christianity after modernity shows itself to be the saving act, the remedy for the great lack of orientation after the collapse of modernity, and even the source of answers to questions inherited from postmodern theory.

Although the recuperation of Lyotard for Christian apologetics can be associated mainly with Protestant-Evangelical circles,[12] postmodern criticism is also popular among members of the Radical Orthodoxy movement, who find striking connections between Lyotard and their own suspending of secular rationality.[13] One way or another, by these and other groups, Lyotard is re-narrated according to the rules of the Christian narrative as an ally in the polemic against the secular world, while at the same time Christianity is exempted from criticism. Nonetheless, such attempts to re-Christianize Lyotard, even turning him into an exquisite associate of the Christianity identity story, miss the point entirely. Lyotard does not focus on the *modern nature* of metanarratives (and yes, we can agree that Christianity cannot be reduced to being one of modernity's stories). The central point is the problematic nature of any overwhelming narrative structure that tends to rule out or rule over other narratives. In sum, the exceptionalism of Christian apologetics thus paradoxically proves Lyotard's thesis and, moreover, commits the same error—and perhaps even the same hegemonic and oppressive gesture—as language mechanics, while leaving that which has been said forgotten.

The Christian Metanarrative of Love

Lyotard's judgement is resolute and leaves no space for doubt. Although we find scant reference to the subject in his work,[14] Christianity is clearly on Lyotard's mental list of metanarratives. Alongside the criticism of

---

[12] Stanley J. Grenz, *A Primer on Postmodernism* (Grand Rapids, MI: William B. Eerdmans, 1996).

[13] Graham Ward, *Theology and Contemporary Critical Theory* (London: Macmillan, 2000), 133–40.

[14] Lyotard's discussion of Christianity in *The Differend* spans just four paragraphs: §232–5 (pp. 159–161). Other rare references to Christianity can be found in *The Postmodern Explained*, 23–5, and *Postmodern Fables*, trans. G. Van Den Abbeele (Minneapolis, MN: University of Minnesota Press, 1997), 67–101 and 213–14.

modern emancipation strategies that, while promoting their goals, resulted in terror and violence, one can sense why Christianity could and should be counted among those narratives that are no longer credible. Has Christianity not created countless victims in both its distant and its only too recent history? The Inquisition, religious wars, the feudal principle *cuius regio, eius religio*, and the antimodernist crisis and bullying theologians for their opinions are but a few examples of the problem. Moreover, certain (political) theologies have never hesitated to ground political identity narrative on both the societal and the church level.[15] On the other hand, it is not possible to reduce Christianity to just another modern metanarrative. As we have already noted, Protestant-Evangelical theologians and the proponents of Radical Orthodoxy point out that the narrative of Christianity reaches beyond modernity. Jesus of Nazareth and the Apostle Paul, or whoever we deem to be responsible for the creation of Christianity, were hardly modern ideologues. And after all, isn't Christianity—if we accept that it is a narrative, even a big narrative—the story of a great love that transcends all hegemony? "For God so loved the world that he gave his only Son, so that everyone who believes in him may not perish but may have eternal life," says the Gospel of John (Jn 3:16). Someone we assume to be the same author adds: "Beloved, let us love one another, because love is from God; everyone who loves is born of God and knows God. Whoever does not love does not know God, for God is love" (1 Jn 4:7-8). And everything culminates in the Apostle Paul's hymn on love: "Love is patient; love is kind; love is not envious or boastful or arrogant or rude ... Love never ends ... And now faith, hope, and love abide, these three; and the greatest of these is love" (1 Cor 13). Lyotard would agree, and herein lies the crux of the whole problem.

---

[15] In his recent works, Colby Dickinson tirelessly unmasks numerous connections between official—legalistic—theology and political sovereignty. Colby Dickinson, *The Fetish of Theology: The Challenge of the Fetish-Object to Modernity* (Cham: Springer, 2020); *Theological Poverty in Continental Philosophy: After Christian Theology* (London: Bloomsbury, 2021).

The Christian narrative vanquished the other narratives in Rome because by introducing the love of occurrence into narratives and narrations of narratives, it designated what is at stake in the genre itself. To love what happens as if it were a gift, to love even the *Is it happening?* as the promise of good news, allows for linking onto whatever happens, including other narratives (and, subsequently, even other genres).[16]

Lyotard strikes at the very heart of Christianity and identifies the story of love as its oppressive core. Love functions as the principle of legitimation and proves to be even more complex than the modern master narratives. Whereas all modern projects of emancipation aim at some realization in the future (a classless society, maximum profit, the rationalization of all means), Christianity combines the founding event in the past with pursuing an idea concerning the future.[17] However, this complex philosophy of history—a mixture of a mythical foundation in the past (creation out of love) and a story of future emancipation (salvation through love)—is not what turns Christianity into a cunning metanarrative. The key point is the regulative Idea [sic!] of Christianity legitimizing actions, thoughts, and power structures: the *Idea of love*.

Love is at the beginning and love will be at the end: "The obligation of love is decreed by the divine Absolute, it is addressed to all creatures (who are none other than His addressees), and it becomes transitive (in an interested sense, because it is conditional): if you are loved, you ought to love; and you shall be loved only if you love."[18] God (the addressor) is love and addresses the narrative

---

[16] Lyotard, *The Differend*, 159.
[17] Lyotard is aware of the "double legitimation" dynamic of Christianity. For example, in *The Postmodern Explained*, he links Christianity with the past and therefore with a specific form of mythical thinking. Later, however, Lyotard recognizes early flashes of modern modes of thinking in the Apostle Paul and Augustine, especially in their orientation toward the future; see Lyotard, *Postmodern Fables*, 96–8.
[18] Lyotard, *The Differend*, 159.

of love to us (the addressee) and because God is love and loves us we must love God and, as God prescribes, also love one another. It is a vicious circle and there appears to be no escape from the clutches of this metanarrative. All narratives are included, recuperated, and re-narrated according to the logic of the regulative idea of love, which leads to a lack of plurality in discourse genres. Love governs all and what appears as *the other* of love—any other sentence—is suppressed or deprived of its difference.

Christianity is a closed system; the mechanics of language is turned into the mechanics of hegemonic love, which prescribes all linking of the phrases: "Thanks to the precept of love, all of the events already told in the narratives of infidels and unbelievers can be re-told as so many signs portentous of the new commandment … Not only are the narrative instances universalized, but occurrence is problematized."[19] Those who transgress or disrespect the rule of the presupposed linking of phrases, that is, the structure of the narrative and its institutions which hold the key to an authentic interpretation of the regulative Idea, are excluded. The Christian term for exclusion—*excommunication*—says it all. Heretics are expelled from the community and lose any right to speak.[20]

For Lyotard, Christianity is not simply a hegemonic metanarrative that excludes difference, it is the coercive metanarrative *par excellence*: "Christian narration not only tells what has happened, thereby fixing

---

[19] Ibid., 160.
[20] Heresy is perhaps an extreme example. However, the Christian metanarrative of love functions in an oppressive way and produces victims on an everyday basis. For example, the debates on excluding remarried Christians from the sacramental life of the church follow the same logic of an enclosed narrative of love. And although there has been some development under Pope Francis, official documents of the Catholic Church still use the argument of love to justify general exclusion: "However, the Church reaffirms her practice, which is based upon Sacred Scripture, of not admitting to Eucharistic Communion divorced persons who have remarried. They are unable to be admitted thereto from the fact that their state and condition of life objectively contradict that union of love between Christ and the Church which is signified and effected by the Eucharist." John Paul II, *Familiaris consortio*, §84, https://www.vatican.va/content/john-paul-ii/en/apost_exhortations/documents/hf_jp-ii_exh_19811122_familiaris-consortio.html

a tradition, but it also prescribes the *caritas* for what can happen, whatever it might be."[21] Love has been revealed, given, and must be accepted and further conducted. Love has happened and there is no space for a new happening. The Christian metanarrative is an exhaustive reservoir of possible phrases and the regulative agent of their respective linking. It possesses the absolute cognitive claim and is the guardian of the universal knowledge that leads humanity toward fulfillment—all in the name of love.

Forgetting the Event

Through our engagement with Lyotard, it has become clear that the problem of metanarratives—including the Christian metanarrative—is their forgetting or even intentional exclusion of the event *something is happening*. According to a standard definition: "An event is an occurrence beyond the powers of representation, something that the subject experiences but which he or she is unable to comprehend or think through adequately, let alone phrase coherently."[22] Hence, for Lyotard, "the event cannot be presented without losing it."[23] And bearing witness to the event of the *differend* is the point of postmodern criticism.

> An event consists in the perception of an instant in which something happens to which we are called to respond without knowing in advance the genre in which to respond. In other words, events occur in such a way that pre-established genres are incapable of responding adequately to their singular nature.[24]

---

[21] Lyotard, *The Differend*, 160.
[22] Anthony Gritten, "Event," in *The Lyotard Dictionary*, ed. Stuart Sim (Edinburgh: Edinburgh University Press, 2011), 71.
[23] Davis, "St Lyotard on the Differend/Difference," 123.
[24] Simon Malpas, *Jean-François Lyotard* (New York: Routledge, 2003), 100.

In other words, for Lyotard, the event is the interruption of presupposed explanations and conceptual frameworks. It throws any pre-given meaning into a state of shakiness. And in addition to this negative moment, the event has positive effects because it causes astonishment and surprise: the event is the marvel of "that there is" (*il y a*).[25] In this sense, the event calls for a response and demands that we take a position. The event opens the space of new relationships to happening, generates questions and doubts, and initiates challenges. The event motivates us to think in a different way, to think again, and thus unveils new readings of reality. At this point, Christianity fails.

In contrast to the openness of Judaism, argues Lyotard, Christianity closes itself and forgets about the differend. Judaism presents a faithful stance toward the event, which is condensed in its ever-repeating strategy of "read and re-read."[26] Using the example of reading the Torah—the sacred text of Judaism, recorded only with consonants—Lyotard shows there is no binding rule regarding its reading inscribed within the text itself. To let the event happen, one has to take the text and read, give it one's voice. Although there are certain traditions of reading (genres of discourse), the reading is never fixed. The vocalization of the text must always happen anew. In fact, the need to give voice to the text creates the space in which its truth reveals itself.[27] Although the text is always the same, the reading is not. Liturgical reading and re-reading is more than a repetition because the essence

---

[25] Lyotard, *The Postmodern Explained*, 97.
[26] Jean François Lyotard, *The Hyphen: Between Judaism and Christianity*, trans. P.-A. Brault and M. Naas (London: Polity Press, 1999), 10–11.
[27] Consider, for example, Ray Bradbury's dystopian novel *Fahrenheit 451* (London: Transworld, 1967), which portrays a future society in which the reading of books is forbidden. The fire brigade is tasked not with fighting fires but with burning any books that are found and thus preventing people from reading them. The book is seen as a potential danger and reading as a crime because reading opens a possibility of something new to come—something that might be true not in the sense of correctness but as a challenging event.

of liturgy is to let the texts happen as a new revelation, speaking "here and now." In other words, the text is never in our possession and cannot be exhausted.

Hegemonic narratives supposedly seize control over the event and thus possess the desire for total mastery over everything and everybody. In this context, the question *is it happening*? turns out to be forbidden. Instead, metanarrative forces everyone to accept *this is happening*! The question ceases to be a question. It is rather a prerogative statement that determines linking-happening. In Lyotard's own words: "Nothing must happen but what is announced, and everything that is announced must happen."[28] The event must be stripped out. The event must not happen.[29] And because Christianity aims to regulate everything, control all linking of the phrases, re-narrate the happening according to the predefined rules of its discourse, and exclude everything that resists such recuperation, Lyotard concludes that the religion of love is a hegemonic narrative *par excellence*.

Lost Credibility

Christianity, or perhaps a certain form of Christianity, is no longer credible. Nevertheless, following Lyotard, we should add that this is not an outcome of *postmodernism*—a philosophical program often confused with the relativism of *anything goes*. Rather, the incredulity comes out in the context of the logic inherent to the Christian identity narrative—something revealed by the postmodern critique of metanarratives.

---

[28] Lyotard, *The Postmodern Explained*, 90.
[29] "Like theory, which, hypothetically, keeps its head above the water of time, totalitarian bureaucracy likes to keep the event under its thumb. When something happens, it goes into the dustbin (of history, or the spirit)." Ibid.

Lyotard's phenomenological analysis is not without problems. Later, I will further explore the challenge Lyotard addresses to Christianity and its theological reflections. I do not believe that Christianity is an irredeemably oppressive metanarrative that suppresses the event. In Part III, I will challenge Lyotard's hermeneutics—and that of his followers among theologians—through which he insists that Christianity is first and foremost a narrative structure. At this point, however, it suffices to say that Lyotard's observation regarding Christianity, as he interprets it alongside other metanarratives—that is, as a specific combination of the modern and premodern narrative mechanics which suppresses heterogeneity and fails to bear witness to the differend and thus betrays the event of being—raises awareness that Christianity cannot escape postmodern incredulity.

We recognize that the question of the after of Christianity is a serious one and that it is not merely a question about the difficulty of understanding the content of the Christian message in a secular age. The whole problem cannot be reduced to "their problem" and transferred *ad extra* as if the world, culture, and the people were suddenly unable to grasp Christianity because of their own alienation. Lyotard's criticism argues the contrary. Christianity after Christendom is first and foremost a problem *ad intra* that pertains to Christians themselves in a highly concrete form. And the situation of the after does not call simply for better apologetics or for translation into comprehensible language. Rather, the requirement is transformation, that is, bearing witness to the internal differend inherent to the history of Christianity.

2

After Deconstruction: Jean-Luc Nancy and the Essence of Christianity

What does it mean to live *after* something? Intuition directs our thoughts to succession: after the Great War, the political map of Europe was redrawn; since the founding of the European Union, there has (largely) been peace between its members. The same applies to our personal lives: after I finished grammar school, I enrolled in a university; after the publication of this book, I will take a vacation. One state of affairs is succeeded by another. Nonetheless, there is always more than a mere succession. As the examples clearly show, the after-of-something also refers to an interruption and even a rupture: the order of things is changed, shaken, transformed. Nothing is as it was and yet that which was still plays an important role in that which is to come, is coming. There is no clearly visible anticipation. Rather, we are confronted with some pressing questions: "Is there an after? Is there anything that follows? Are we still headed somewhere?"[1]

Jean-Luc Nancy asked these questions concerning the after in the wake of the nuclear catastrophe at Fukushima and challenged a linear understanding of any *post*-situation. Although something is considered as belonging to the past, it still has a bearing on the present and will affect the future—something that will be only too obvious to anyone who visits the town of Pripyat, the former administrative and technological center of the Chernobyl power plant. Yet it is also

---

[1] Jean-Luc Nancy, *After Fukushima: The Equivalence of Catastrophes*, trans. C. Mandell (New York, NY: Fordham University Press, 2015), 15.

possible to draw more general conclusions on the level of theory. For example, *post*-modernism has not left the legacy of modernity behind. However severe the critique of modern reason may be (a critique that is often mistaken for blind rejection of Enlightenment values), modernity is still operative in postmodern theory, as the chapter on Lyotard has shown. Equally, the so-called post-communist countries of the former Eastern Bloc in Europe are still (sad to say) affected by history in ways that complicate their transformation to democratic societies.[2] One way or another, the after is more than a descriptive category—it points to movement.

This chapter will relate these questions concerning the after to Christianity. Do we still believe that the after of Christianity is the kingdom of God? Does the after suggest that worldly reality will be succeeded by a celestial one? Do we (both Christians and those outside Christianity) anticipate any after that may be to come, and if so, from where? Or do we find ourselves in a strange kenotic experience of an empty after—the after of not knowing whether there is any after? The boundary between kenosis and nihilism—two senses of relative nothingness—is thin and dangerous. Not to lose our sense, in this chapter I will take Nancy as our guide. Exploring the after of Christianity naturally leads to what Nancy calls the deconstruction of Christianity. Numerous studies have covered this issue in detail, but most of them draw conclusions regarding a world from which Christianity is rapidly departing.[3] The goal of this chapter is rather to see implications for Christianity and its after, and thus to explore the question: What is the essence of the after of Christianity?

---

[2] See, for example, Ivan Krastev, *After Europe* (Philadelphia, PA: University of Pennsylvania Press, 2017), and, written in a more popular genre with a healthy dose of self-irony, Slavjenka Drakulic, *Café Europa: Life after Communism* (London: Penguin, 1999).

[3] See, for example, Marie Chabbert, "The Eternal Return of Religion: Jean-Luc Nancy on Faith in the Singular-Plural," *Angelaki* 26, no. 3/4 (2021): 207–24; Ignaas Devisch and Aukje van Rooden, "Deconstruction, Dis-Enclosure and Christianity," *Bijdragen* 69, no. 3 (2008): 249–63.

What Is Christianity?

Christianity is the spirit of the West. Whether we like it or not, we live in the shadow of Christian provenance (and sometimes there is much more than a shadow). This is not an echo of Christian apologetics, which copes badly with losing its claim to sovereignty in a secular society. It is the reason behind Nancy's scrupulous engagement with a Christianity that cannot simply be left behind as an artifact from the past. Yet what is Christianity?

Nancy offers a dialectical interpretation.[4] On the one hand, Christianity is the carrier of metaphysical tradition. Metaphysics is understood here in accordance with Heidegger: being (*être*) is represented as being (*étant*) and as being present (*étant présente*). To say that Christianity advances a metaphysical *Weltanschauung* means that it postulates to be a there-beyond, the highest being which is at the same time the ground of being that prescribes the final destination (*telos*) of all beings; the structure which is independent of the world but which structures the world to the finest detail. In short, Christianity is *closure*. On the other hand, Nancy argues, Christianity is also "the demand to open in this world an alterity or an unconditional alienation,"[5] and thus postulates all necessary tools to break with the bonds of metaphysical tradition. The other world—if you will, the kingdom of God—was never the second world, that is, a metaphysical entity, a world behind the world. Christianity spells out the attention to the other of the world, yet from within this world. In sum, Christianity is *opening*—in Nancy's vocabulary, *dis-enclosure*.

---

[4] In what follows, I rely on Nancy's programmatic wittings concerning Christianity: *Dis-enclosure: The Deconstruction of Christianity*, trans. B. Bergo (New York, NY: Fordham University Press, 2008); *Adoration: The Deconstruction of Christianity II*, trans. J. McKeane (New York, NY: Fordham University Press, 2013).

[5] Nancy, *Dis-enclosure*, 10.

Christianity embodies the tension between the closing and the opening. Christianity is the conflict incarnate: it is self-postulation and self-affirmation, but it is also self-critique and self-deconstruction. The cross, Nancy points out, is simultaneously the constitutive element and an undoing.[6] Nancy asks, practically: Where do we find ourselves? Christianity created the West and is its pillar. Even more radically, Christianity *is* the West. Secular Westerners live in Christian provenances. Christianity is not flourishing, it is disappearing from sight, yet it remains with us and in us: "All our thought is Christian through and through," says Nancy, the self-proclaimed atheist.[7]

Is this a dialectic? An impasse? To add more tension, Nancy claims that the major achievement of Christianity is opening to the sense of living in this world as outside the world;[8] a salutation to being in the world outside the world and welcoming another life in the midst of this life, a life that is ultimately marked by finitude.[9]

The Deconstruction of Christianity

The term we require to describe and grasp the dynamic of Christianity is *deconstruction*. A brief examination of the conditions surrounding Christianity suggests Nancy's point. A secular age means, above all, that the world is spread worldwide (*mondial*); that everything is made worldly (*mondaine*); hence, Christianity as a religion based on a metaphysical entity called God no longer carries sense. We can easily postulate at least three layers of Christian effacement.

---

[6] Ibid., 148.
[7] Ibid., 143.
[8] Ibid., 10.
[9] Jean-Luc Nancy, "In the Midst of the World; or, Why Deconstruct Christianity?" in *Re-treating Religion: Deconstructing Christianity with Jean-Luc Nancy*, ed. A. Alexandrova, I. Devisch, L. Ten Kate, and A. Van Rooden (New York, NY: Fordham University Press, 2012), 7.

First, on the societal level, Christianity is no longer the (privileged) organizing principle that structures experience and offers a common and comprehensible framework for interpreting the world. Worse still, except in a handful of regions in the West, Christianity cannot be counted among the competing big narratives (-*isms* in the Lyotardian sense) that claim to structure human life. It is not the case that Christian*ism* would lose the battle. No, none of the modern grand narratives claimed sole right to the empty throne after the death of God. In fact, the death of God is also the death of (divine) omnipotent reason, class struggle, and any other usurper of metaphysical glory. It is just that with Christianity, the state of affairs is easier to see.

Secondly, on the existential level, Christianity ceased to provide a generally accepted orientation for human life. As a direct consequence of this and the societal changes just mentioned, fewer and fewer people are embracing the Christian vision as a meaningful religious grid for reality. Anyone who goes to church twice a day and sits through two sermons will undoubtedly, sooner or later, conclude that compared to what the world has to offer, Christian discipleship represents an unattractive alternative.

Finally, on the metaphysical level, and again somewhat related to the previous point, Christianity ceased to give sense to meaning, as if the clarion call of "anything goes" forced out the true, the beautiful, and the good. The secular world is pressing hard. What remains for/of religion?

Although there may be much truth in this trinity of endings, such a hastily formed judgment concerning the deconstruction of Christianity leads to a fundamental misunderstanding if not an entirely straightforward missing of the point. The deconstruction of Christianity is not a result of external objective forces. Nancy stresses that the deconstruction of Christianity is *subjective genitive*. What does it entail? Paradoxically, the effacing of Christianity is a self-effacement; the world as a site for the deconstruction of Christianity turns out to be the field of Christianity's self-deconstruction. Even more paradoxically, for Nancy, the continuous process of emptying itself reveals the truth of Christianity.

Deconstruction is the Christian mode of self-appearing: "[It] resides essentially in the proclamation of its end."[10] Or as Nancy puts it elsewhere: "Christianity [is] the posture of thought whereby 'God' demands to be effaced or to efface himself."[11] The persistence of closure constantly hits the resistance of opening. Christianity is coming to its end, yet there is the constant possibility of its after. We are still Christian, even though we live after Christianity.

It is obvious that the movement of deconstruction is not shared by the all of Christianity: the objections echo from the religious right, through metaphysically minded neo-Thomists and conservatives, to the evangelicals who are happily embracing postmodernism as a comrade in the war against evil liberal secularism.[12] Nevertheless, I feel that Nancy has a point when he suggests that the process of self-deconstruction is inherent to Christian tradition, just as heresy usually bears witness to an important truth, although perhaps in an exaggerated form.

This conflict within Christianity—between integrality and disintegration, between sure foundations and the opening of the self, between accepting revealed truth and being open to receiving truth—is what Nancy calls the Christian *ipseity*.[13] The recuperation of the metaphysical concept, however, signifies its deconstruction: Christianity is a relation to the self—a mode of being—which embraces the indefinite. The Christian self, as well as the structure of Christianity, exits constantly from the self; it is a movement, an

---

[10] Nancy, *Dis-enclosure*, 149.
[11] Nancy, "In the Midst of the World," 8.
[12] I refer to Chapter 1 and the discussion on Christian exceptionalism and the exemption of Christianity from postmodern critique.
[13] Nancy, *Dis-enclosure*, 146.

infinite movement of faith which discovers itself from within the impassable condition of finitude. In short, the deconstruction of Christianity manifests Christianity's proper historical being.

Essential Incompletion

Nancy holds a mirror to Christian theology by which it can (re)discover its own failures and deconstructive tendencies. On the one hand, Christianity is the worldly criticism of the reign of principle; on the other, there is metaphysics as the reign, sometimes even the terror of principle.[14] This tension is central to Christianity and manifests itself in a number of ways: the Christian criticism of myths, false deities, sacrificial religious practices, and blind obedience to fate versus the mythologization of the Christian message; theological theories that rely on the economy of exchange; the softening of a prophetic faith into a *petit-bourgeois* religion. Nonetheless, for Nancy, this tension between the experience of *being shaken* and the norm offered by the *balance of principle* is seen most clearly in the tension codified by the Gospel itself: *hoc est corpus meum* (principle) clashes with *noli me tangere* (being shaken).

Christianity repeatedly fails to cope with the challenge of its own message.[15] For example, the empty tomb makes present the absence of the body, the body which can be met on the way as the opened body (by wounds) and exposed to the world (in the very sense of taking one's own skin to the world: *exposé* as *ex-peau-sé*) but which

---

[14] Joeri Schrijvers, "Metamorphosis or Mutation? Jean-Luc Nancy and the Deconstruction of Christianity," *Angelaki* 26, no. 3/4 (2021): 162–77.

[15] A coherent discussion of this thought-provoking proclamation regarding the ever-repeated failure of Christianity is provided in Christina M. Smerick, *Jean-Luc Nancy and Christian Thought: Deconstruction of the Bodies of Christ* (Lanham, MD: Lexington Books, 2018).

resists codification. On the other hand, the ever-repeated betrayal of this dis-enclosure and giving preference to defining the real body of Christ as the carrier of the one vision of salvation in one world is a constant temptation for the Christian body—the church. To understand this tension, Nancy uses two terms which he understands as polar opposites: the incarnation and the creation.

The incarnation expresses the dichotomy between the spirit and the body. In line with the Johannine New Testament writings, Nancy interprets the incarnation as the logos principle: the spirit is invested to a particular body as into a shell; the bodies are signified by the spirit, and the spirit, the inwardness, is what matters, and matter can be disregarded. The foundation of the Christian body (the individual, the ecclesial, the political) is its final suspension—something codified in the very saying *hoc est enim corpus meum*, the axial phrase of the West: "Everyone in this culture, Christian or otherwise, (re)cognizes it. ... It's our *Om mani padme* ..., our *Allah ill'allah*, our *Shema Israel*."[16] In other words, Christianity and the entire Western world seemed to be obsessed with the spirit and devaluing the body as the (platonic) prison for the soul. Christianity robs the world of its value.

The concept of creation (outside the Christian meaning) stands as the corrective. For Nancy, the creation does not have any external creator, out there. The creation refers to the self-modification of bodies (the individual, the intersubjective, the political, etc.). In other words, bodies have plasticity, that is, they are capable of movement and transformation. Why is this so? Nancy gives a paradoxical answer: bodies originate *ex nihilo*, from nothing— nothing predetermined, nothing complete. The creation is not something produced from a material cause. Rather, the creation is a movement of modification, matter modifying itself, yet with a certain

---

[16] Jean-Luc Nancy, *Corpus*, trans. R. Rand (New York, NY: Fordham University Press, 2008), 3.

transcendence included in this process, namely the modification of the entire world into something unthought.

Is this critique of Christianity not too schematic?[17] Perhaps. But Nancy balances his position by introducing the concept of a kenotic understanding of the incarnation—the event of the self-emptying God—and of the resurrection, as presented in *Noli me tangere*, as the revelation of no-thing, nothing solid, but openness: dis-enclosure. Despite his previous criticism, Nancy acknowledges a certain corporeal experience inherent to Christianity: the experience of shattered meaning and opening up. In my words, the experience of being shaken.

The leading idea of the deconstruction of Christianity can thus be translated under the rubric of *incompletion*:[18] resistance to rational teleology on the one hand and to excessive mysticism on the other. Questioning Christianity from within mundane existence, from within an engagement with human finitude, means leaving behind a desire for completion and extra-worldly explanations and opposing any sense of a definitive arrival. Nancy's critique therefore challenges Christianity, and especially its theology, to come out from behind its cloud of mysteries. ("We don't know yet. The future will make it clear.") Applied theologically, deconstruction is the exercise of thought—thought open to the coming of completion, a coming that is always opened up again.

Does this not go against the entire Christian tradition and its emphasis on codified doctrine? How could the idea of incompletion, if this is the truth of deconstruction, be accepted as Christian truth?

---

[17] This question is raised, quite rightly I believe, in Peter J. Fritz, "Capitalism—or Christianity: Creation and Incarnation in Jean-Luc Nancy," *Political Theology* 15, no. 5 (2014): 421–37.

[18] Regarding the idea of the *incompletion* of Christianity, I am indebted to Peter J. Fritz, "On the V(I)Erge: Jean-Luc Nancy, Christianity, and Incompletion," *Heythrop Journal* 44, no. 4 (2014): 620–34.

Dogma seems to resist. But what is dogma? Is it petrified truth? Or is it rather the setting of the task of thinking and, in fact, opening up the debate? To be sure, dogma demarcates the borders of theological discourse, but it does not prevent theologians from critical thinking. On the contrary, dogma boosts such thinking. If a solemn dogmatic proclamation decides that this or that is to be thought, the other side of the coin is the important matter of what remains unthought.

Opening the World

Commenting on Nancy's deconstruction of Christianity, Laurens Ten Kate describes the internal dynamics of Christianity as inside-outside dialectics, that is, a play between something that is "inside" Christianity and something that is "outside," and can only be grasped in its coming. This tension between presence and absence, Ten Kate continues, is like the tension between the incarnated Christ of flesh and blood and the kingdom of God which is not of this world.[19] Words, concepts, thoughts, all fall short. Only metaphorical language (of theology) remains. In my view, however, Nancy pushes even harder and fundamentally deconstructs the dichotomy between Christianity and the world. The challenge is not to accept a metaphorical theological language rooted in the world but to accept that there is nothing solid but the earth on which we stand and from where it is possible to think about Christianity. Put differently, what is crystalizing here is a nonmystical, all-too-human Christianity in sheer opposition to the excessive hyperbolic Christianity of the experience of saturation.

In this dis-enclosing Christianity, God alienates Godself from Godself. The death of God illustrates this. The kenotic aspect

---

[19] Laurens Ten Kate, "Outside In, Inside Out," *Bijdragen* 69, no. 3 (2008): 305–20.

of Christianity turns theology into a-theology, and thus the deconstruction of Christianity: God becomes a self-imposed de-theologized atheist, and Christianity, in this respect, provides the ideal exit from religion. Where to? To the world. This seems to be the very nature of Christian monotheism: God is placed outside the world as the singular entity and event which cannot be grasped or mastered. In this sense, monotheism becomes atheism because the world of monotheism is godless—God is present in its absence. For Nancy, this is the core of Christianity, and this is why Christianity is the dis-enclosure of the world.

To reiterate, the deconstruction and indeed self-deconstruction of Christianity reveal and confirm not only that metaphysical narratives are gone but also that the metaphysical guarantee has never been as certain as we may think. Christianity proclaims the message of this negative certainty. The deconstruction of Christianity does not, however, end in a void. It gives way to the world, and there is nothing beyond that which the world gives. Homing in on the subjective genitive of the movement of deconstruction, it becomes clear that the other side of this deconstruction is not secularization but something that Nancy calls detheologization, and which Joeri Schrijvers summarizes as follows: "A secularization of the theological does not attend sufficiently to the demise of Christianity. What Nancy has in mind, with the concept of a 'detheologization,' is rather a complete displacement of all things theological: no longer the valuation of a Transcendent, but rather the absolute value of all things immanent, of the world that is."[20] Or as Nancy puts it himself: "We who are no more than us in a world, which is itself no more than the world."[21]

---

[20] Joeri Schrijvers, *Between Faith and Belief: Toward a Contemporary Phenomenology of Religious Life* (Albany, NY: State University of New York Press, 2016), 58.
[21] Jean-Luc Nancy, *Being Singular Plural*, trans. R. Richardson (Stanford, CA: Stanford University Press, 2000), 17.

The deconstruction of Christianity makes room for the opening of the world, a world without myths, idolatry, or religion.[22] It also makes apparent revelation that is not content-based principles but the figure of dis-configuration, and thus the call that calls for a response,[23] something I propose to name (and will later elaborate as) *interruption*.[24] Finally, the deconstruction of Christianity is an historical movement of opening to the infinite in our finitude, reconsidering transcendence in our immanence, which for Nancy means intersubjectivity and relations,[25] and from which also comes Nancy's concept of *adoration*, the title of his second book on the deconstruction of Christianity. Adoration refers to a state of attentiveness. It is not, however, directed outside the world, but remains firmly within the immanent frame. For Nancy, nonetheless, scrupulous attentiveness—indeed, adoration—from within the world opens up the infinite in the finite, and this Nancy calls *transimmanence*.[26] This confronts the theologian with a cruel message: there is no solid—metaphysical—truth somewhere above us, somewhere in the otherworldly realm. Christianity as the dynamic of self-deconstruction provides, paradoxically, salvation from the temptation to flee from this world: "We are thereby saved from other worlds in order to be restored to the world, to be set into the world anew, as new."[27] The truth of Christianity, if any such thing exists, is the truth of this world discovered and disclosed through Christianity's self-effacement and deconstruction. What, then, comes after the deconstruction of Christianity?

---

[22] Schrijvers comments: "The auto-deconstruction of Christianity therefore consists of the (progressive) disappearance of power, of presence, of the givenness of myths due to the contingent character of its composition and the internal divide on which it draws." Schrijvers, *Between Faith and Belief*, 49.
[23] Nancy, "In the Midst of the World," 20.
[24] See chapter 7 of this book.
[25] Nancy, *Adoration*, 65ff.
[26] Jean-Luc Nancy, *The Sense of the World*, trans. J. S. Librett (Minneapolis, MN: University of Minnesota Press, 1997), 55.
[27] Colby Dickinson, "Ending Christian Hegemony: Jean-Luc Nancy and the Ends of Eurocentric Thought," *Open Theology* 8, no. 1 (2022): 14–27.

After Christianity

We do not live in a post-Christian epoch. Nancy makes it clear that the after of Christianity is not the next step in the linear history of the religion of the West. On the contrary, the after of Christianity manifests the very mode of Christian appearing, that is, the historical nature of the Christian movement in the world. From there, Nancy draws a two-fold conclusion concerning the question of the after: (1) "The only Christianity that can be actual is one that contemplates the present possibility of its negation"; and (2) "The only thing that can be actual is an atheism that contemplates the reality of its Christian origin."[28] Clearly, for Nancy, the question of the after concerns much more than a sociological-historical analysis of the state of Christianity. The after is a movement—a movement of reflection, self-reflection, and constant self-critical deconstruction.

For Nancy, the starting point of this reflection on Christianity and of Christian self-reflection is the world—there is no other place to start. From this point of naked existence, opening to the infinite appears as opening from within the world. Or, as Nancy puts it, the deconstruction of Christianity is also "the opening in the world, which doesn't belong to the world."[29] This category of opening, sometimes described in Nancy as the dis-enclosure of reason, is of central importance because the process of opening is nothing less than a search for meaning. Does the after of Christianity—the result of deconstructive dis-enclosure—suggest that there is something like an authentic core of religion, a pure version of the Christian message which collides with the West? I say absolutely not.

---

[28] Nancy, *Dis-enclosure*, 140.
[29] Jean-Luc Nancy and the editors, "On Dis-enclosure and Its Gesture, Adoration: A Concluding Dialogue with Jean-Luc Nancy," in *Re-treating Religion: Deconstructing Christianity with Jean-Luc Nancy*, ed. A. Alexandrova, I. Devisch, L. Ten Kate, and A. Van Rooden (New York, NY: Fordham University Press, 2012), 307.

What is at stake, for Nancy, is not the meaning of Christianity but a search for the sense of life. It is not a turning back in the usual sense of debating Christianity in philosophical-theological circles, nor the reminiscence of Nietzsche's eternal return of the same, nor the strategy of returning to the fathers (going forward backwards), back to the sources, and discovering the authentic—uncorrupted—core. All these returns tacitly presuppose that time—history—distorts the original, obscures the pure, and destroys the essential. The after of Christianity stands against the illusion of longing for a pure source. What, then, is to be discovered in the category of the after? Nancy replies—and to his credit acknowledges the many predecessors who made the same point: Kant, Hegel, Nietzsche, Heidegger—that the movement of self-deconstruction is a constant historical process: the very movement is essential—the movement of history.

For theology, therefore, danger lurks in any hasty recuperation of Nancy's deconstruction. Like a premature welcoming of postmodern criticism as an ally against modernity and its outcomes, deconstruction can hardly justify a search for the pure core of Christianity. By contrast, Nancy makes it clear that Christianity argues instead for the infinity of its self-effacement, and thus for the impossibility of a pure source.[30]

The after of Christianity is therefore neither exclusively nor even primarily a descriptive project. First and foremost, it is a normative claim. For secular, atheist society, Christianity appears to be given as the task to think again (and again). For Christianity, which may or may not be identified with the church, the task of thinking *qua* self-reflection comes to the fore still more strongly. Secular society comes to see that what is supposedly not-Christian is not entirely non-Christian (Nancy's Christian provenance); the Christian world understands that what is supposedly not of this world is experienceable and thinkable only on the horizon of the

---

[30] Ibid., 318.

world (that is, a completely new de-theologized situation that stands as a challenge to the Christian self-definition).

On the after-of-Christianity, we can conclude with Nancy that the "paradoxical fulfillment of Christianity is its own exhaustion."[31] The after is not an end in itself. It is an opening. What is at stake, for Christianity, is faithfulness to the world and to the human condition of being-in-the-world. The after of Christianity is therefore the detheologization of the world; the removal of the sacred canopy, but with a fundamentally different meaning from the one secular theorists would propose. In this respect, a secular age cannot be explained simply as cloaked Christianity (as if the secular were anonymously Christian).[32] Rather, Christianity retains operativity in its inoperativity: the vanishing presence of Christianity leaves its imprint—it forms our being in the world. It calls for a shaping of being-in-the-world. Nonetheless, it also means that we find ourselves, theologically speaking, in the movement of active autodeconstruction—the after of Christianity.

In other words, we end exactly where we began: we come to understand that the essence of the after, in its pressing presence, its challenges, and its constant calling for a response, is not a mere succession—replacement, progressive improvements, or digress and decay—but the ontological movement of the Christian mode of being.

What remains, then? Can we say with Nancy that Christianity is less about religion and more about an approach to the human condition? This question will stay with us throughout the book.

---

[31] Nancy, *Adoration*, 71.

[32] This interpretation of secularization as a direct outcome of Christianity is presented, for example, by Gianni Vattimo, whom we will discuss in chapter 4. Even more striking, however, is the popularity of some influential theological-philosophical essayists who postulate a version of old/modern Christian triumphalism while asserting liberal points of view regarding secularization as the "child of Christianity." See, for example, Halík, *Der Nachmittag des Christentums*.

3

The Sense of the After: Jan Patočka and the Post-Christian Epoch

Several authors, thinkers, and philosophers come to mind when we are confronted with the end of Christianity. The preceding chapters noted some influential theories that deal with and clarify the problem. From the perspective of traditional theology, however, philosophical (re)considerations of Christianity often appear heretical. Think of Nietzsche's (in)famous proclamation that "God is dead." Although some commentators recuperate Nietzsche's thorny critique as the purification of Christianity—because that which has died is the metaphysical concept of god; the idol has been defeated and the way is cleared for the unspoken icon of a true God[1]—Nietzsche's prophecy is still with us. The death of God is also the death of Christianity.[2] The default human condition, says the modern philosophical heresy, is being without God. In this chapter, I will rethink one further philosophical heresy: that the default condition of Christianity is its after. My interlocutor will be the Czech phenomenologist Jan Patočka.

Throughout his career as a phenomenological author, Patočka perpetrated several philosophical heresies. Perhaps the most intriguing (but most neglected) of these consists in his lifelong

---

[1] For this interpretation, see Jean-Luc Marion, *The Idol and Distance: Five Studies*, trans. T. A. Carlson (New York, NY: Fordham University Press, 2001).
[2] Emmanuel Falque, among others, proposes that Nietzsche's "Death of God" has its equivalent in the death of Christianity. See Emmanuel Falque, *The Metamorphosis of Finitude: An Essay on Birth and Resurrection*, trans. G. Hughes (New York, NY: Fordham University Press, 2012), 30–3.

preoccupation and rapprochement with Christianity.[3] I will proceed in three steps. First, I will provide a context for the already established category of the after of Christianity in Patočka's concept of post-Europe. Secondly, I will explore the meaning of Patočka's thesis that Christianity represents a unique and unsurpassed contribution to the spiritual movement of humankind (although this contribution has yet to be [philosophically] thought through to its end). Finally, I will develop further an afterthought to Patočka's project of rethinking Christianity—a daring afterthought from a philosophical-theological perspective—which leads to a particularly interesting way of answering our initial question concerning Christianity and what it will become after its end.

However, before engaging with Patočka's ideas, let us clarify our use of the provocative notion of heresy. In its traditional sense, heresy is understood as a diversion from orthodoxy, a deliberate choice to contradict established teaching. As such, heresy is an agent of damage, destruction, and division. In what follows, I will use the notion of heresy in a different, more philosophical sense. In fact, the entirety of Patočka's oeuvre can be interpreted as a stream of heretical thinking motivated by his passionate commitment to the most important questions concerning being-in-the-world. In this sense, heresy is indeed a choice, a choice to take ideas and thoughts further, to think creatively, and to think at the limits of the possible. Heresy transgresses borders, pushes ideas beyond limits, and opens new horizons of understanding. Does it sound like a dangerous endeavor? Heretical approaches can, of course, go too far, but not necessarily from any intention to misinterpret the truth. On the contrary, heresy venerates truth, and heretical

---

[3] I devoted my previous book to the theme of Christianity in Jan Patočka's reflection. Martin Koci, *Thinking Faith after Christianity: A Theological Reading of Jan Patočka's Phenomenological Philosophy* (Albany, NY: State University of New York Press, 2020).

thinking fights for a clarification and even transformation of "basic definitions and fundamental concepts while preserving the core of the thought in question."[4] Put simply, heresy is a source of inspiration which reveals something that, for whatever reason, has remained un-thought.

A Post-Christendom Age

The post-European era, a concept widely discussed in Patočka's later writings, can be translated as the post-Christian age. To remind ourselves about the context of this debate, Patočka's interest in *Europa und Nacheuropa* concerns a transgression of the fundamental principles of caring for one's being.[5] In other words, the essence of the European spirit has changed, and this paradigm shift has consequences.

In Patočka's conception, Europe represents the ideal of rational life directed toward truth based on insight. Europe is the culture of insight, of scrupulous reflection on that which appears. Insight is what makes a "spiritual life," "life in truth," or "care for the soul" possible.

Care for the soul means that truth is something not given once and for all, nor merely a matter of observing and acknowledging the observed, but rather a lifelong inquiry, a self-controlling, selfunifying intellectual and vital practice ... The care for the soul—*tes psychés epimeleia*—is thus what gave rise to Europe.[6]

---

[4] Miroslav Petříček, "Jan Patočka and Phenomenological Philosophy Today," in *Jan Patočka and the Heritage of Phenomenology: Centenary Papers*, ed. E. Abrams and I. Chvatík (Dordrecht: Springer, 2011), 6.
[5] Jan Patočka, *L'Europe après l'Europe*, trans. Erika Abrams (Lagrasse: Verdier, 2007), 37–136.
[6] Jan Patočka, *Heretical Essays in the Philosophy of History*, trans. Erazim Kohák (La Salle, IL: Open Court, 1996), 82–3.

Europe was born in Ancient Greece and shaped through Christianity.[7] Philosophy and religion played fundamental roles in the formation of the European spirit, in its success, in the development of modern science, in spreading the European heritage around the globe, and in proclaiming the power of human reason. At the same time, philosophy and religion share responsibility for Europe's decline and fall, for its crises, and, most horrifyingly, for its wars.[8] Nonetheless, the crucial point for our inquiry is that despite Patočka's proclamation that Europe is based on a single, Greek pillar,[9] one passage in his *Heretical Essays* suggests that it was, in fact, Christianity that gave Europe its "care for the soul": "By virtue of this foundation in the abysmal deepening of the soul, Christianity remains thus far the greatest, unsurpassed but also un-thought-through *élan* that enabled humans to struggle against decadence."[10]

The principle of caring for the soul underwent a radical change in modernity. What appears at first to be a paradigm shift in the use of reason and the rise of an entirely rationalistic tendency to exhaust and master the world as a whole[11] is in fact a shift from an interest in understanding Being to a concern for having. Patočka takes Husserl's *Crisis of European Sciences and Transcendental Phenomenology* as the point of departure for his reflections, but Heidegger's concept of *Gestell* is perhaps more appropriate for describing this situation. What does this "enframing"—as it translates into English—mean? In general, *Gestell* is the techno-scientific mentality and thus the hermeneutical key to a world which through this lens appears to be explicable and controllable within the categories—the frame—of

---

[7] Patočka, *L'Europe après l'Europe*, 36–44.
[8] War is the theme of the striking and, as Ricoeur suggests, "frankly shocking" chapter 6 of *Heretical Essays*. Patočka, *Heretical Essays*, 119–37.
[9] Jan Patočka, *Plato and Europe*, trans. Peter Lom (Stanford, CA: Stanford University Press, 2002), 89.
[10] Patočka, *Heretical Essays*, 108 (translation modified).
[11] Patočka deems Descartes and Bacon responsible for this tendency of modernity. Patočka, *Heretical Essays*, 84.

mathematical operations, mathematical sets, and a formal scientific language. The German word *Gestell* comes from the verb *stellen*—to put, to stand. In *Gestell*, everything is a standing reserve and may stand on order. The truth of being(s) is therefore to be found in its purpose, and the purpose of being(s) equals their meaning. Patočka assesses this situation of *Gestell* as potentially dangerous:

> In *Gestell*, the time of universal order, the alienation of humans culminates up to the point that everyone is basically just a function and the performance of this function ... A human becomes one-dimensional, is deprived of its totality, is reduced to an object, in fact, it is not even an object. A human has not become a thing which can further be viewed from a different perspective and complemented ... All this disappears and human beings become only an "object" of the order.[12]

The reason for the serious tone is justifiable. For Patočka, modern techno-scientific theory unties the bounds of reason from ancient *theória*. This shift from the practice of contemplative insight to the techniques of calculation, geometrization, and logical consequential explanation—from *theória* to scientific *theory*—is not a matter of mere wordplay but a radical change in how the world is perceived. Its most serious consequence is abandoning the moment of caring for the soul while grounding and cementing being in technical mastery, manipulation, and the rationalism of means.[13] In the cause of rationalism, the limits of reason are disrespected. According to Patočka, this encapsulates the situation of post-Europe.

---

[12] Jan Patočka, "Čtyři semináře k problému Evropy," in Sebranné spisy Jana Patočky, vol. 3. Péče o duši, III: Kacířské eseje o filosofii dějin; Varianty a přípravné práce z let 1973-1977; Dodatky k Péči o duši I a II, ed. I. Chvatík and P. Kouba (Praha: Oikoymenh, 2002), 390. See also Jan Patočka, "The Danger of Technicization in Science according to E. Husserl and the Essence of Technology as Danger according to M. Heidegger (Varna Lecture)," in *The New Yearbook for Phenomenology and Phenomenological Philosophy XIV. Religion, War and the Crisis of Modernity: A Special Issue Dedicated to the Philosophy of Jan Patočka*, ed. L. Hagedorn and J. Dodd (London: Routledge, 2015), 13–22.

[13] Patočka, *Heretical Essays*, 96–7.

In a fascinating essay on what he calls "supercivilization," Patočka suggests that in its most basic form, the rationalism of *Gestell* excludes the possibility of *vertical thinking* and remains in pure horizontality,[14] a claim which has importance for our dealings with Patočka's reflections on Christianity, the relevant point of which is: Christianity is the principal agent of the tradition of caring for the soul and the driving force of the European spiritual movement. This is so because of the Christian transformation (conversion/*metanoia*) of philosophical life, which is, as Patočka explains, founded upon *sophia tou kosmou*, that is, metaphysics.[15] In other words, Christianity not only challenges Greek philosophy and significantly contributes to the concept of the soul, as we read earlier in the *Heretical Essays*, but most importantly Christianity redirects attention from the truth of being(s) to the truth of Being; that is, from the external (the being of things—*Seiendes*) to the internal (the being of one's Being—*Dasein*). Therefore, the Christian experience of the absolute, which is the term Patočka uses for further unspecified transcendence, transforms the care for the soul.

Now, if the post-European era represents the crisis of caring for Being, it is also the undoing of the Christian spirit that comes to the fore as the great enabler of vertical thinking or, if you prefer, thinking transcendence. Vertical thinking acknowledges something beyond a purely immanent horizon. Put simply, reason is not everything. Knowledge cannot be exhausted by means of objectivistic epistemology. Transcendence has a say. For Patočka, vertical thinking means to think relationally: I (the subject) and God (the other); I and other human beings; I and other beings. By contrast, the horizontal perspective encourages us to think objectively as one object in relation

---

[14] Jan Patočka, *Liberté et sacrifice*, trans. E. Abrams (Grenoble: J. Millon, 1990), 136–7. Patočka's thoughts on supercivilization come to the fore in contemporary debates on his philosophy.
[15] Patočka, *Heretical Essays*, 107.

to other objects. Moreover, it postulates that objective reasoning is the only correct path toward the truth. Although the question of truth would make an interesting debate, it would distract our attention from the main point here, which is the post-Christian age as one of the consequences of or reasons behind the post-European era.

Nevertheless, for Patočka, the crisis of European decadence is not an agonistic, apocalyptic vision. As much as the *Gestell* manifests the post-European era, the end of something, it is also an opening for something new to arise. As much as the post-Christendom age replaces caring for the soul with the care to have and master things, it also carries the possibility of a fresh transformation, a conversion, a reawakening of care for the soul.[16] But what might this new epochal conversion be? The theological origin of the word conversion— *metanoia*—suggests that Christianity can provide us with an answer. But what kind of Christianity should one expect from a philosopher who can by no means be classified as a philosopher of religion and who never hesitated to protect his own discipline—phenomenological philosophy—from "theological imperialism"?[17] After all, it would be paradoxical to seek redemption from the decline—*das Rettende*—in Christianity, as if a step backward could help us to go forward. But this is not the only possible perspective. What if conversion consists in rethinking Christianity after the end of Christendom? What if the issue at stake is nothing less than the sense of the after put into practice? Aware of this possibility, Patočka rethinks Christianity as an important and unavoidable contributor to the spiritual life of caring for the soul. He does not, however, intend to renew religion as a confession. This he has in common with Lyotard and Nancy,

---

[16] I am indebted to Eddo Evink, who presented a paper on the reawakening of the care for the soul in Jan Patočka at the conference "Heresy and Heritage: Jan Patočka on Philosophy, Politics, and the Arts" at Leuven—Brussels, May 3-6, 2017.

[17] Interestingly, one of the first of Patočka's essays to be published (1929) concerned the relationship between philosophy and theology: Jan Patočka, "Theologie a filosofie," in *Sebranné spisy Jana Patočky*, 15-21.

who recognize a certain sense of the after in the postmodern era. The center of gravity thus appears to be the operative after of Christianity in a situation that is not-Christian but not yet non-Christian. Rather, he suggests reconsidering the core of Christianity in the present-day context. In what follows, I will first explore Patočka's heretical idea of Christianity, and from there, in a second step, will draw inspiration for formulating the significance of the sense of the after of Christianity, a sense which emerges in the arena of post-Europe.

Rethinking Christianity

The post-European and post-Christian condition is caused by the rationalism of mastery, which is in turn a consequence of the techno-scientific nature of modernity. Although Husserl and Heidegger teach us that modern science is the culprit for this particular crisis, Patočka broadens the perspective by suggesting that Christianity shares a good deal of the responsibility.[18] As much as Christianity contributed to the emergence of modern science because of its belief in the possibility of a rational understanding about the world, the more practical orientation of modern theology, based on the principle of "having the world" instead of "contemplating it," resulted in a forgetfulness at the core of Christianity.

Nevertheless, Patočka's obsession with the crisis of modernity should not be misread as conservative reactionism triggered by a fear of advanced technology or modern life in general. Similarly, it would be fatuous to search for nostalgia for a previous version of Christianity. Patočka's reflection addresses the internal not the external. The crux is the existential problem of humankind, that is, the mode of being of "modern people."[19] The question is: What is the problem of the

[18] Patočka, *Heretical Essays*, 110.
[19] Jan Patočka, "Le christianisme et le monde naturel," *Istina* 38, no. 1 (1993): 16.

modern mode of being in which Christianity and science are part of the problem rather than necessarily part of the solution? The answer is crude and shocking: *nihilism*.

Patočka follows Nietzsche and Heidegger in understanding nihilism as "the world-historical movement of the people of the earth who have been drawn into modernity's arena of power."[20] Although Patočka does not say it explicitly, he recognizes that after the death of God, a new deity now occupies the throne: the *Nihil*, the lord of all who reigns supreme in the kingdom of boredom,[21] where everydayness, self-preservation, and false self-assertion epitomize this defective mode of being.

Hölderlin cries, "But where danger grows, the saving power also." Heidegger invests his hopes in art; Dostoevsky turns to the world of traditional Orthodox-Byzantine Christianity; Nietzsche ruminates about the eternal return of the same and the rise of the superman. Where does Patočka go? Interestingly, like Dostoevsky, he reconsiders Christianity. But unlike Christian traditionalists, Patočka is not interested in the fossilized heritage of a particular confession. Rather, he turns to what he deems to be the authentic core of Christianity and suggests a repetition of its radical innovative spiritual insight. Nonetheless, what takes place is a Kierkegaardian repetition: not a simple recollection of the past but a repetition as a movement *forward*, an opening to the future. In fidelity to Patočka's vocabulary, the issue at stake is (again) care for the soul: "The soul as that within us that is related to that unperishing and imperishable component of the whole which makes possible truth and in truth the being not of a superman but of an authentically human being."[22] From this perspective, Patočka

---

[20] Martin Heidegger, *Off the Beaten Track*, trans. J. Young and K. Haynes (Cambridge: Cambridge University Press, 2002), 163–4.
[21] Ivan Chvatík, "Rethinking Christianity as a Suitable Religion for the Postmodern World. An Attempt to Reconstruct the Most 'Heretical' Idea of Jan Patočka," *Phenomenology* 4 (2010): 319.
[22] Patočka, *Heretical Essays*, 93.

rethinks the core of Christianity. I will quote the crucial passage from Patočka's *Heretical Essays* at length.

> [In Christianity] there is an implicit notion which has never been reflected upon and philosophically grasped: that the soul is incomparable, incommensurable with all existing things and that this nature of the soul is characterized by its care for its own being. Unlike all other existents, the soul is infinitely interested in its being and an essential part of its structure is responsibility, that is, a possibility to choose what to do and, in this choosing, of arriving at the very core of its own self [to really become what it is]. It is the notion that the soul is nothing present before but only after, and that, in its very essence, it is historical and only in this way can it be rising from the decadence [the fall]. Because of this root in the abyssal depth of the soul, Christianity has been the highest and unsurpassed rise of human being in the struggle with the possibility of fall, but also something which has not yet been thought through to its end.[23]

This enigmatic philosophical confession (without confession) piques the interest of a careful reader of Patočka, who can hardly be described as a philosopher of religion and who stresses that "the philosopher never helps the theologian."[24] Yet this particular place seems to suggest the opposite direction: Christianity transforms philosophical reflection. Although each line gives much food for thought and deserves careful commentary, I will explore three points where the metamorphosis of philosophy by theology, and thus the core of Christianity, is most visible in Patočka's conception.

First, Patočka says that Christianity reveals that the soul is "incomparable and incommensurable with all existing things," and adds that the soul is not "an existent." In other words, Patočka presents

---

[23] Ibid., 108 (translation modified).
[24] Patočka, "Theologie a filosofie," 19.

here his version of the ontological difference between Being (*Sein*)—the soul—and beings/existents (*Seiendes*). This difference is drawn from Christianity, and thus, surely inspired by Heidegger, Patočka transgresses the latter's traditional interpretation and re-Christianizes his major insight. This truly heretical move against both Christianity and Heidegger will become clearer when we move to the second issue, the care for the soul as responsible personhood.

For Patočka, in Christianity as in philosophy, the soul is interested in the understanding of Being. However, what Christianity adds to philosophy is "the structure of responsibility." This is not to say that philosophy (before or without Christianity) would be irresponsible. I propose to read this passage in the way that Patočka weighs the essential intersubjective and interpersonal relationship that lies in the foundations of Christianity. In this sense, the idea of responsibility is not only ethical but ontological: the basis of the Christian mode of being is mutual responsiveness, that is, responding to the other—the other person. As Patočka suggests, Christianity reshapes the movement of caring for the soul by introducing the relationship to a transcendent *personal* agent, that is, God. In contrast to the philosophical life of a sage, who is mostly occupied with his or her subjective and intersubjective relations, Christianity creates a radically new dynamic of human being which is, from this moment, taking into account the gap between humanity and divinity. However, this should not be taken as an obstacle, an unbridgeable asymmetrical relationship between the active giver of life and its passive recipients. Although some asymmetry is undoubtedly involved, the point of the Christian insight, and its innovation, is the reciprocal relationship between a personal God and the human person. The ontological structure of responsibility, therefore, manifests the notion of personhood—*persona*—which emerges with Christianity. Care for the soul is care for the person.

Finally, how are we to understand the paradoxical argument that Christianity "has not yet been thought through to its end"? In *Heretical Essays*, Christianity is presented as the drive of human existence which has not yet been adequately thought. Nonetheless, the question is whether Patočka suggests that we are called to think-through Christianity to its very end at all. By definition, the concept of the un-thought refers to something that has not yet been thought. The un-thought is something forgotten, omitted, something that has not been considered, either through ignorance or through a deliberate act. Alternatively, the un-thought is perhaps something that cannot be thought because of a particular historical situation that constrains its possible appearance. This would mean that our situation, the situation of "modern people," lacks the environment in which the un-thought can be thought. One way or another, we have either lost the sense of openness or are waiting for the openness to come.

However, the un-thought can also be something partially thought—a thought that is not yet finalized, and perhaps never can be. This notion of the un-thought would fit the Christian conception of dogma. A typical way of seeing dogmatic statements is their identification with closing declarations, rigid definitions, irreversible propositions, and the expression of metaphysical truth. However, this perspective fails to think of dogma as a new opening and a call for further thinking and questioning, as a pointer or a sign that something has been thought.

Although these interpretations seem plausible, I argue that Patočka has something else in mind. The previous cases are unsatisfactory because they consider the un-thought to be a provisional state that awaits eventual completion: the un-thought is a lack that must be remedied, a question to be answered, a limited perspective in need of broadening; the un-thought looks for a thought. Against these propositions, I dare to raise (heretical) questions: What if the core of Christianity, according to Patočka, is the very movement of thinking, the moment of thinking again, thinking after, a constant movement of pointing beyond itself? What if Christianity's vocation is to manifest itself as an afterthought? Does the un-thought necessarily look for a thought? I see the key to understanding the un-thought of Christianity in the concept of caring for the soul, a movement that does not search for a final destination, whatever or wherever that may be, but is, rather, "a lifelong inquiry, a self-controlling, self-unifying intellectual and vital practice."[25] In other words, what is at stake is dynamics and indeterminate happening. If Christianity is presented as "the abyssal deepening of the soul," it is hard to imagine that this advancement could mean the replacement of dynamism with anything static. Following the same line of thought, the category of the un-thought, does not then call for a supplement to, or even the completion of, thought. Nor does it suggest a somewhat mystical-gnostic turn that something eternally remains in the clouds of mystery and will never be thought. The point of Patočka's enigmatic statement, I suggest, is an invitation to understand Christianity as the task of thinking. The un-thought does not look for a particular thought. It strives for thinking.

This is not self-evident, however. To stretch the argument further, the "task" we discover in Patočka's text can be retranslated into Christian vocabulary as "vocation": the vocation of thinking through the highest and unsurpassed insights of Christianity in order to understand life as the conflict in Being against a background of everchanging historical conditions. One way or another, Patočka seems to suggest that the present crisis calls for thinking and that this task should incorporate crucial insights from the mode of Christian thinking because this could be a truly transformative experience.

Transformation is close to conversion, a term with explicit religious meaning which we also find in Patočka. In fact, *Heretical*

---

[25] Patočka, *Heretical Essays*, 82–3.

Essays indicates that Christianity has the status of a great conversion with respect to (Greek) philosophy. The point is again ontological and existential and thus has no confessional implications. The first great historical conversion, in Patočka's opinion, happened when philosophy developed from myth and began to criticize the mythical conception and consciousness of the world and the human being. The second great conversion was Christianity, and the extract from the *Heretical Essays* quoted above captures its content.

That said, the notion of conversion that Christianity represents with respect to philosophy seems to suggest that Patočka does not conceive of Christianity merely as one single moment in history. Rather, he points out the dynamism of repeating conversion *qua* caring for the soul of the person, that is, the understanding of Being. In other words, as Patočka mentions in a different context, the task of thinking (something through) is rather *fiens* than a *factum* that might be simply achieved.

In this sense, it also becomes clear that the post-Christendom and post-European age does not refer simply to another step on the chronological, linear development of history. The kernel is the transformation of the ontological status of humankind *after* Christianity, *after* Europe. This means that to describe the conditions of *the after*, one should not think of a single historical phenomenon that occurs after others have occurred. The whole idea of *afterthought* refers to a structurally historical movement. The challenge we now face is to incorporate the sense of the *after* of Christianity and think it through, not to its end, but *beyond* Patočka.

Postscript to Part I
The Questions of After

Which after? Whose after? These questions are central. Where do these questions lead us to? The answers may not be obvious. But the red herring and the key point in the previous chapters is all about emancipation. What kind of emancipation? Emancipating the question of the after of Christianity from the clutches of historical-sociological debates. Charles Taylor's magnum opus *A Secular Age* analyzes the conditions of belief in the so-called immanent frame of the present-day world.[1] His material is unprecedented and its interpretation insightful. Taylor's conclusions are solid, founded on historical data, and explain the relations between causes and effects. But this perspective, however original and groundbreaking, does not represent a comprehensive approach to the question of the after. Sociological-historical analyses are *a posteriori* explanations.[2] The heart of our exploration is different: it is an *a priori* movement, the inherent structure, the internal dynamism of Christianity. In this sense, the question of the after is a philosophical-theological question.

The postmodern ends of Christianity discussed in Part I of this book reveal a change of perspective, a shift in the mode of thinking

---

[1] Charles Taylor, *A Secular Age* (Cambridge: Harvard University Press, 2007).
[2] This is not to say that *a posteriori* perspectives, formulated from historical, sociological, and political points of view are not important. On the contrary, these "outside" perspectives reveal important insights regarding the state of Christianity. See, for example, the excellent book by Olivier Roy, *Is Europe Christian?* trans. C. Schoch (London: C. Hurst & Co, 2019).

which affects the Christian mode of being. Interestingly, philosophers with little or no theological motivation provide us with this *a priori* perspective and help us to understand what is at stake in the question of the after.

Lyotard's reconstituting of *the differend* is an anamnestic lesson—a lesson of remembrance and nonforgetting that there is always an after. The differend bears witness to an afterthought, aftermoment, afterappearance. Put differently, Lyotard leads us to a recollection of history that is more than a cluster of historical—objective—facts to be collected and reassembled in order to offer an explanation. Without denying the importance of such a perspective, the question of the after cannot end there. Christianity must not (to paraphrase Heidegger, although in a different context) forget history, which seems to be its ever-recurring problem, or substitute history with historiography, which is an ever-recurring self-deception.

The lesson from Lyotard is original and telling (as evidenced by the number of theological receptions of the father of philosophical postmodernism),[3] but the claim concerning the end of the grand narrative, including the Christian grand narrative, is formulated from the outside, and it is the claim of this outer world which Christianity needs to be confronted with.

The lesson from Nancy points further. The sense of the after—the after of Christianity—comes to us from the inside. In other words, Christianity is in a constant state of being surpassed. Christianity is not only a self-effacing movement; it is also a movement that constantly points beyond itself. Like Lyotard, Nancy does not intend to reconstitute Christianity or reconstruct its religiosity or, God forbid, its sovereignty. As many commentators rightly observe, Nancy's kinetics is not *retour à* but *retour sur* Christianity, and his

---

[3] Among which the most comprehensive seems to be Lieven Boeve, *Lyotard and Theology: Beyond the Christian Master Narrative of Love* (London: Bloomsbury, 2014).

primary goal is to address the question of sense by reopening the source of the very crux of this question.[4] Christianity is turning from itself and making Christendom disappear, irretrievably. And, Nancy argues, this is important for all of us because we still live in the Christian provenance—under a certain *modus congnoscendi* of the world. Thinking the after of Christianity with Nancy unmasks false dichotomies: modernity and Christianity are not opposites; the return to religion in opposition to the rotten world is a misleading hermeneutical key misused by fundamentalists. Nancy would like to see an entirely different reading of the situation, beyond the atheist/Christian divide, neither Christian nor atheist. The point is to think the fragile nature of the world as the world and from within the world.

The ambition of this book is more modest: How are we still Christian today? How are we atheist, secular, agnostic under Christian provenance? What remains of Christianity? Or, perhaps better, what is Christianity coming to be when reflecting upon itself from within the world and the crude experience of the human condition? Nancy announces the ambivalent end of a Christianity that remains operative. What we can take for our further questioning is the focus on the *modality* not the *substance* of Christianity. Hence, the major goal of this book is to reconsider the sense of Christianity as the everydayness of the Christian mode of being in the world in which God kenotically disappears. Or, to say it straightforwardly with Nancy himself, our interest is "the infinite in the finite. Finitude as an opening to the infinite: nothing but this is at stake."[5]

What has ended then? What is the object of the after? The strong, omnipotent, sometimes violent, but certainly highly (self-)certain form of Christianity is no longer credible and has been deconstructed.

---

[4] François Raffoul, "The Self-Deconstruction of Christianity," in *Re-treating Religion: Deconstructing Christianity with Jean-Luc Nancy*, ed. A. Alexandrova, I. Devisch, L. Ten Kate, and A. Van Rooden (New York, NY: Fordham University Press, 2012), 46–62.

[5] Nancy, *Adoration*, 3.

Naturally, this development has various consequences. The political consequences are among the most visible. The sovereignty of the church, its hierarchy, the power of its words, its transformative potential on a societal level, the escape into moralism, the restorative tendencies, the attempts to draw back from the world into ghettos—these are some expressions of the contested power of Christendom. In what follows, I will consider two direct responses to the situation that pertains after the disintegration of sovereign Christendom: Gianni Vattimo and his secular, nonreligious Christianity (Chapter 4); and John D. Caputo and his Christianity without religion (Chapter 5). And somewhat creatively, I will transpose Richard Kearney's concept of anatheism into a theory of anatheistic Christianity (Chapter 6). Against a backdrop of these radical hermeneutical solutions to the crisis, and inspired by the existential thread of phenomenological philosophy, I will later present an alternative: Christianity as a specific mode of being which has the potential to gather a community of the shaken.

But to return to our question: Can we understand the end of a certain (thus far pre-modern and modern) Christianity as incredulity regarding the monism of ahistorical truth which often functions as a cunning cover for violence, coercion, and hegemonic practices over both the soul and the body of individuals and communities? And is this end—after Christendom—something we should seek to suppress or embrace?

I will explore an answer on the pages that follow, but first I would like to turn our attention to another, more important meaning of the after in the context of Christian existence. It seems to me that the emphasis on the object of the after, that is, the focus on what has ended and why it has lost its relevance, removes the weight from the subject of this after. The danger of missing this fundamental problem is exacerbated by the fact that the object and the subject of the after are, in a certain sense, identical. Christianity does not only experience the challenge of its after; it is also, and perhaps most importantly, the carrier of its own movement of the after.

With Patočka, then, we can ask: Is it necessary to think Christianity—philosophically—*through to its end*? If the historical-contextual understanding of the after in a linear, chronological sense is discarded, a plausible answer would seem to be "No." Rather, the after of Christianity points to a structural tendency—something Patočka deems essential for Christianity. In this sense, Christianity (and what it will become) is neither a religion among religions nor a philosophical program but a certain mode of being: a programmatic sense for a movement of transcendence within immanence; a movement from within the world and history. I will return to Patočka and continue the dialogue with his insightful philosophical heresy in Part III.

To sum up this introductory argument: when we scrupulously focus on the conditions of Christian belief in the present (secular) age, we are not asking the question of the after in the right terms. It seems to me that the main lesson from the prophets of the after, whether Lyotard, Nancy, or Patočka,[6] is that we (human beings) find ourselves in a condition of shakenness, or perhaps, to put it better, a shaken openness. Christianity *is* this shakenness. How can we cope with this situation existentially? How does Christianity address, embody, and materialize this unstable mode of being? These questions concerning the after of Christianity are at the center of this book. In Part II, I will explore attempts to address the shakenness and responses to the need for a credible Christianity. However, because all these attempts appear to be unsatisfactory to some degree, Part III will offer a novel solution: a reading of Christianity as a shaken mode of being-in-the-world.

---

[6] We can, of course, add others whose writings are attentive to the issue. Terry Eagleton's critical debates with the New Atheism movement show that the current ferocious opponents of Christianity target only the objective part of religion, as if the existential—emancipatory—movement were not present at all; moreover, the atheist construction of this objective part is reduced to those unsympathetic currents in Christianity which are often criticized with much more eloquence by Christian theologians themselves. See Terry Eagleton, *Reason, Faith, and Revolution: Reflections on the God Debate* (New Haven, CT: Yale University Press, 2009).

Part Two

The Figures of the After

Christianity after Christendom, the end of Christianity, the after of Christianity; whichever name we chose, the issue at stake is where we stand in the current situation. Externally, a general suspicion of metanarratives, big identity stories, and overarching interpretative frameworks pertaining to the totality of reality forced the Christian religion to reconsider its status in the world. Internally, the deconstruction of Christianity takes the form of autodeconstruction. Turning our attention to this movement reveals that the moment of the after is inherent to Christianity and expresses Christianity's truth of being an historical religion (although this does not apply to the whole of Christian tradition). Nonetheless, one thing has become clear: Christianity, which aims to say something credible in this world, is invited (or forced—depending on one's perspective) to engage with its own after.

It is somewhat surprising that philosophers seem to be more productive than theologians in adopting the task of reconsidering not only the Christian heritage and its archive potential but also Christianity as a specific faith or intellectual tradition that maintains its relevance.[1] However, the argument for this relevance is not presented *despite* the after of Christianity but precisely *because of* it. In other words, the

---

[1] The classic work on philosophy's interest in the continuing relevance of religion is Hent de Vries, *Philosophy and the Turn to Religion* (Baltimore, MD: The Johns Hopkins University Press, 1999). Another important work, written from a more explicitly Christian perspective, is J. Aaron Simmons, *God and the Other: Ethics and Politics after the Theological Turn* (Bloomington, IN: Indiana University Press, 2011).

after of Christianity does not signal the ultimate end of Christianity and thus the need to recuperate its heritage in the secular register, but rather reveals the power of Christianity, despite its weakness in the secular frame, and sheds new light on the meaning of both religion and human existence in the world. One of the most fruitful responses to the situation is hermeneutics—the hermeneutics of Christianity and its after.

Hermeneutics refers to the act of explaining, interpreting, and translating—making sense of a message that has become blurred over the course of history. Hermes was the messenger of the gods who not only transmitted but also explained. As a philosophical discipline, hermeneutics is the art of interpretation, an attempt to bridge the gap between the past and the present. As such, it is most often applied to the reading of a text, whether literary, religious, or historical. Hermeneutics does not end with the text, however. Interpretation, explanation, and translation are required in a much broader cultural, societal, and civilizational sense. No wonder, then, that the shift that has taken place regarding Christianity's position in the world calls for hermeneutical rereadings. The Protestant theologians Rudolf Bultmann and Gerhard Ebeling were among the first to recognize this need to incorporate the hermeneutical moment into theology.[2] After the Second Vatican Council, hermeneutical theologies entered the Catholic tradition, such as in the works of Edward Schillebeeckx and David Tracy.[3] More recently, Paul Ricoeur has become the most significant source of inspiration for hermeneutical engagements with the Christian tradition.[4] All of

[2] Rudolf Bultmann, *New Testament and Mythology and Other Basic Writings*, trans. S. C. Ogden (London: SCM, 1985); Gerhard Ebeling, *Das Wesen des christlichen Glaubens* (München: Siebenstern, 1967).
[3] Edward Schillebeeckx, *Interim Report on the Books Jesus and Christ*, trans. J. Bowden (New York, NY: Crossroad, 1981); David Tracy, *Plurality and Ambiguity: Hermeneutics, Religion, Hope* (Chicago, IL: The University of Chicago Press, 1987).
[4] James Fodor, *Christian Hermeneutics: Paul Ricoeur and the Refiguring of Theology* (Oxford: Clarendon Press, 1995).

these postmodern re-lectures—the hermeneutics of Christianity—attempt to: (1) understand the meaning of the after of Christianity; (2) respond to the after of Christianity by developing it further; and (3) unfold the possibilities inherent to a Christianity after Christendom.

In this second part of the book, I will address three models of the after of Christianity: Gianni Vattimo's nihilist Christianity, inspired by his reading of Nietzsche and Heidegger; John D. Caputo's Christianity without religion, based on his engagement with Derridean deconstruction; and Richard Kearney's anatheism, a third way—*via tertia*—and a counterpoint to mystical nihilism and deconstruction. The three authors have one thing in common: they all address the situation of Christianity after Christendom in terms of a culture that is not-Christian but not yet non-Christian. In this sense, their hermeneutical models share a common motivation, which is to provide a viable and credible interpretation of Christian (and general religious) existence.

The key questions I will ask in what follows are: Do these philosophical-hermeneutical reconsiderations tell us anything valuable about what Christianity might become after its end? And what prospect do they offer for Christianity? Vattimo, Caputo, and Kearney, although indebted to the Christian and especially the Catholic tradition in framing their respective proposals, provide a philosophical path to Christianity, but in all cases seek to appeal to the lives of individuals. Having this in mind, some more questions arise: What is the theological relevance of these philosophies? Does philosophy take the lead in interpreting Christianity? Is, indeed, one result of the after of Christianity the death of theology?

From a methodological perspective, it is important to note that the authors react to one another, although rarely in a systematic way. Kearney critically reacts to Caputo's deconstruction and Caputo offers some answers to the critique; Vattimo and Caputo participated in some joint publications; for Kearney, Vattimo proves to be an interesting partner in the dialogue regarding love, whereas with Caputo, he debates on the hermeneutics of religion.[5] In short, the inter-relations are complex. But although the following pages will occasionally point to some cross-references, the goal is to offer a critical-constructive evaluation of the three hermeneutical approaches one by one—devoting a chapter to each—in order both to draw useful lessons and to point out pitfalls. Disclosure: I approach all three authors with sympathy and value each of their intellectual efforts to take up the challenge of exploring the enigmatic and ambiguous after of Christianity. Indeed, I wish to travel with each of them as far as is possible. My aim, however, is to move beyond the hermeneutics of Christianity to a more profound existential perspective (which we will come to in Part III). The following three analytical chapters will therefore be complemented by the concluding coda to Part II, which is devoted to a critical-constructive synthesis that will pave the way for my own, fundamental-theological concept of the after. Let us interpret.

---

[5] See the recent exchange between Kearney and Caputo: John D. Caputo, "Where Is Richard Kearney Coming From? Hospitality, Atheism and Ana-deconstruction"; Richard Kearney, "A Game of Jacks: Review Essay of John D. Caputo's Recent Works," Both in *Philosophy and Social Criticism* 47, no. 5 (2021): 551–69 and 570–86 respectively.

4

A Secular Christianity of Nihilist Love: Engaging Gianni Vattimo's Atheism

The Italian philosopher-turned-politician Gianni Vattimo explicitly addresses the after of Christianity. His more or less autobiographical book *Belief* and the later collection of essays and lectures published under the title *After Christianity* relate directly to the idea that stands at the center of this book.

Vattimo has written on a wide range of philosophical topics and is well known for his radical leftist politics. His return to the return of religion and even his personal confession *credo di credere* (I believe that I believe) naturally prompted important discussions.[1] Even more, Vattimo presents a somewhat paradoxical thesis that the return of religion, and by religion he thinks primarily of Christianity, is a direct consequence of the death of God proclaimed by Nietzsche and affirmed by Heidegger. For Vattimo, the death of God signals the arrival of a post-Christian situation. However, at the same time, Christianity has not dismissed itself. The truth is that we find ourselves in a society that is no longer Christian but not yet non-Christian. The response to this peculiarity is *weak thought*, which takes seriously the destruction of metaphysics (i.e., a-historical philosophizing)

---

[1] See, for example, Thomas G. Guarino, *Vattimo and Theology* (London: T&T Clark, 2009); Jakob Helmut Deibl, *Geschichte—Offenbarung—Interpretation: Versuch einer theologischen Antwort an Gianni Vattimo* (Frankfurt: Lang, 2008).

and accepts that human existence is irreducibly conditioned by the language structures realized in history. Hence, a one-word summary of Vattimo's general philosophical position and his particular stance on the after of Christianity would read "hermeneutics."

Nietzsche famously said, "There are no facts, only interpretations." Vattimo embraces this notion totally.[2] Interpretation and the subject as the interpreter stand at the center of Vattimo's project. To interpret means to adopt a certain perspective. Meaningful conversation is conditional on awareness of the place *d'où je parle*. One cannot, or perhaps should not, enforce a deemed meta-perspective—a third eye, or, in religion, a God's eye perspective. Such an attitude unavoidably ends in violence, sometimes merely epistemological, sometimes physical, in both cases real. However, Vattimo identifies the default position and fundamental perspective of every interpreter: the world. I see the world from within the world. The subject uses their capacities to know, to represent, to choose, to name—to understand. Understanding is the human capacity that is a result of interpretation. The entire process is indebted to concepts, frameworks, ideas, and language that are all—Vattimo insists—inherited. In other words, human understanding is always historically qualified and culturally determined.

Nietzsche and Heidegger (we could add Gadamer) are therefore Vattimo's guides along the path of philosophical thinking, but they also play crucial roles in his meditation on Christianity. Even more radically, hermeneutics is what Nietzsche and Heidegger realize as the unfolding of Christianity and what Vattimo identifies as the return of religion and the call of Christianity's after.

---

[2] The following commentary is based on Gianni Vattimo, "Toward a Nonreligious Christianity," in *After the Death of God*, ed. J. W. Robbins (New York, NY: Columbia University Press, 2007), 29–31.

The Return of Religion

Vattimo takes for granted that religion is returning. The question is: Why is religion returning? After *what* is religion returning? After secularization, modernization, and atheism? Why has religion not left us? Or, vice versa: Why is the rational human mind unable to leave religion behind once and for all? Why can we not let religion in general and Christianity in particular go?

If we are to find an answer to that first question, we must understand it properly. The return of religion does not imply a return to any previous, historical form of faith. The world has lost its "sacred canopy" (Berger) and is indeed "dis-enchanted" (Gauchet).[3] Neither the return to religion nor, in Vattimo's terms, a renewed interest in Christianity signals a reversal of the transition to a secular world.[4] There is no re-enchantment in sight. The true nature of the question lies in the word *after*: the return of religion *after* what?

According to Vattimo, Western civilization finds itself in a peculiar situation of numerous afters: after scientism, objectivism, positivism; after Marxism, modernism, metaphysics. Like Theodor Adorno, Vattimo senses the resistance to totalizing systems of organization. In almost Lyotardian terms, Vattimo claims that we have lost faith in emancipation narratives. Bright, grand, and prospective projects sound dubious to suspicious postmodern ears. Vattimo is not afraid to call this postmodern epoch an age of either (a) interpretation, or (b) nihilism. (He uses the two terms interchangeably.)

---

[3] Peter L. Berger, *The Sacred Canopy: Elements of a Sociological Theory of Religion* (New York, NY: Anchor, 1990); Marcel Gauchet, *The Disenchantment of the World: A Political History of Religion*, trans. O. Burge (Princeton, NJ: Princeton University Press, 1999).

[4] Gianni Vattimo, *Belief*, trans. Luca D'Isanto (Cambridge: Cambridge University Press, 1999), 20.

It would be inappropriate to jump to the conclusion that Vattimo's nihilism resists all debate. His nihilism is not the liquid ethics of "anything goes." Nor is it the epistemological nihilism of "everyone has their own truth." It is, rather, nihilism as radical hermeneutical ontology. The meaning of nihilism is that universal truth claims have lost their validity, leaving us with an endless flux of interpretations and competing perspectives: "Reality can no longer be understood as a logically consistent system of established facts."[5] Two events bear responsibility for this state of affairs: Nietzsche's proclamation of the death of God, and Heidegger's destruction of metaphysics.

Vattimo does not read Nietzsche as an arch-atheist. On the contrary, Nietzsche appears to be a genuine confessor.[6] How is that possible? Vattimo explains that the key passage from Nietzsche's *Gay Science* cannot be read in the context of classical metaphysics, and therefore as an opinion (a negative one) regarding the existence of God as being. What Nietzsche has in mind, Vattimo explains, is the negation of the objective foundational structure of reality as such. Nothing like that exists: no other-worldly (positive) solution to problems relating to being-in-the-world. By the same token, Vattimo embraces Heidegger's overcoming of metaphysics—the metaphysics that is guilty of forgetting the question of being (*Sein*) and replacing it with the partial problems of beings (*Seiendes*). Nihilism is therefore a deconstructive attack on the thing-likeness of metaphysics. In other words, the God of metaphysics is reduced to a thing among other things; perhaps the highest thing and the ground of all things, but still a thing. This God is dead. Thank God, sighs Vattimo.[7]

---

[5] Erik Meganck, "God Returns as Nihilist *Caritas*: Secularization According to Gianni Vattimo," *Sophia* 54, no. 3 (2015): 364.
[6] Gianni Vattimo, *After Christianity*, trans. Luca D'Isanto (New York, NY: Columbia University Press, 2002), 11–24.
[7] Jean-Luc Marion presents a similar argument by interpreting Nietzsche's "God is dead" as the death of the conceptual idol and the paradoxical liberation of Christianity from the clutches of modern metaphysics. See Marion, *Idol and the Distance*, 27–55.

This shift in thinking God and the emancipation from the bonds of metaphysics have paradoxical consequences. The most important of these, Vattimo suggests, is that the atheistic negation of God's existence becomes obsolete. If we want to look for empirical evidence or logical-objectivist arguments in favor of God, modern critique will remorselessly destroy such a search. But the poetics of the postmodern age of interpretation do not require positivist proofs in order to value something. That which presented an obstacle to progress in modernity reappears in postmodernity as an open option, an invitation, even a calling event.

Secularization

In Vattimo's thought, therefore, postmodernity—this term with numerous competing interpretations—gains a new meaning. It is not an event that fits into any kind of linear historical development, an age that succeeds the disillusionment of modernity. Nor does it represent an affirmation of absolute relativism and an exit from all values. Rather, for Vattimo, postmodernity is a cultural-spiritual condition, the defining feature of which is *secularization*.[8]

If we are to properly understand Vattimo's interest in the after of Christianity, it is vital that we grasp his concept of secularization. For Vattimo, secularization is not a sociological phenomenon (empty churches, the weakened influence of religious institutions), or an historicist theory (the more modern, the less religious society becomes). Neither is it, in other words, an unavoidable result of the modern critical suspicion of religion, nor a necessary consequence of modern development. First and foremost, secularization is a theological-philosophical category and, even more paradoxically,

---

[8] Vattimo, *Belief*, 38–42, 46–8.

a religious experience *par excellence*. It is, indeed, the constitutive aspect of Christianity. Secularization is the truth of the incarnation, and, vice versa, the incarnation sets the movement of secularization in motion. As Vattimo confesses in his aptly titled autobiography *Not Being God*, he is indebted for this fundamental insight to René Girard, the author of the mimetic theory of religious violence.[9] For Girard, because the incarnation and kenosis remove faith from the natural religiosity of mimetic violence, Jesus of Nazareth is the one who interrupts the violent character of natural religiosity based on offering sacrifices to the divine. In Vattimo's opinion, secularization represents an approximation of this process.

For Vattimo, the story of Christianity is the story of the incarnation and kenosis—two terms he uses almost interchangeably. Christianity is not religion according to the Latin *religare*: to bind together by a set of doctrines, laws, or ethics. Christianity is the story of the incarnated God who accepted the contingency of immanence and thus embraced the world—*saeculum*. Referring to the Pauline hymn of kenosis (Phil. 2:6–11), Vattimo views Christianity as emancipation from the myth of religion.

Secularization, as an approximation of kenosis and the incarnation, reveals the original relationship to the sacred—the originary message that has been lost, covered over, and forgotten, even in Christianity. The obvious question is: Why? In looking for a plausible answer, Vattimo points to the usual suspects: metaphysics, violence (both physical and epistemological), dogmatic faith, and, above all, the image of a strong sovereign God—*pantokrator*—the omnipotent governor of everything, capable of all things. In other words, the dogmatic-hierarchical faith organized and controlled by a sovereign-hierarchical institution suppressed true, experiential faith in Jesus,

---

[9] Gianni Vattimo, *Not Being God: A Collaborative Autobiography* (New York, NY: Columbia University Press, 2009), 149–50.

the prototype of the deconstruction of religion and the preacher of autocriticism who embraces the historicity of existence. Secularization is therefore a return to the core of Christianity and is even its more complete fulfillment. Forming a strange alliance, Hegel joins Nietzsche and Heidegger: after the death of the ontotheological (metaphysical) God-who-is-not, the truth of Christianity manifests itself as the confession of the community, the hermeneutical event of the spirit.[10] Secularization is the expression of nonreligious Christianity and as such it is the continual affirmation of God's kenosis established in the historical act of the incarnation. Vattimo's request to move *after Christianity* results in Christianity as a hermeneutical act.

Let us set aside for a moment the problematic nature of Vattimo's linear understanding of the corruption of Christianity. Later, I will critically address this scheme of "original—putrefaction—purification—return to the original" and separate my argument from the all-too-tempting association with Vattimo's thought-provoking vocabulary. For the time being, I will follow him a little further.

To summarize, secularization is a threefold (historical) process of desacralization, demythologization, and deconstruction. First, secularization desacralizes the political power of religion and questions sovereign political power in general. Secondly, it removes all "transcendent, incomprehensible, mysterious, and even bizarre features" of religion.[11] Finally, it deconstructs the absolute a-historical truth and replaces it with a constantly re-examined truth of the incarnation and kenosis. One way or another, secularization results in a kind of purification, a healthy process that returns Christianity to its historical essence: a community of love that confesses Christ, the Messiah and prophet of charity; a community that cares and lays

---

[10] Branko Klun, "Incarnation and 'De-Carnation' in the Hermeneutics of Gianni Vattimo," *Acta Philosophica* 29, no. 1 (2020): 166.
[11] Vattimo, *Belief*, 55.

aside any strong, objective claims. Vattimo's *after Christianity* thus leaves behind, with a sigh of relief, all the natural residues of religion (omnipotence, absoluteness, eternity, transcendence, and so on). The God of metaphysics is dead. But his death makes room for a God of kenosis,[12] and thus for a self-emptied "Christianity of weak thought"; a weak Christianity, which, to echo the Apostle Paul, rediscovers its strength precisely in weakness.

Weak Thought

Some people say, half in joke, that Vattimo produced only one original idea and that this idea is, in fact, decidedly weak. The adjective "weak" appears throughout Vattimo's work—weak ontology, the weakening of being, weak God, the weakening of truth, and indeed weak thought (*pensiero debole*)—and weakness is likewise the core of Vattimo's philosophical project concerning the return and reinterpretation of Christianity.

On the general hermeneutical level, Vattimo seeks to weaken the truth in its modern—metaphysical and objectifying—power. Because knowledge is a certain form of sovereignty, Vattimo suggests that in place of the mastery of being we enter postmodern hermeneutics, that is, the realization of truth in its weakness and powerlessness. In other words, we have here (again) the radicalization of Nietzsche's perspectivism and Heidegger's proclamation of the end of metaphysics. But what is the essence—if one is allowed to talk about an essence in this respect—of weak thought?

---

[12] "The incarnation inaugurated a process of secularization, which [Vattimo] calls *kenosis*." Matthew E. Harris, "Nietzsche's 'Death of God,' Modernism and Postmodernism in the Twentieth Century: Insights from Altizer and Vattimo," *The Heythrop Journal* 62, no. 1 (2021): 58.

One obvious if superficial way to understand Vattimo's central idea would be to identify weak thought with the limits of reason. This is something everyone knows from experience. Our knowledge of something—Romantic literature, quantum physics—is always limited. Mastery of a field is never total. Knowledge is never fixed or finished. There is always the possibility of a new theory or new findings. Scholarship moves on. In this sense, we experience knowledge as something inevitably weak and fragile. The whole of truth is always greater than a particular knowledge of truth (*veritas semper maior*).

Nonetheless, Vattimo does not stop here, and moves his argument beyond the epistemological level to the existential, to weak ontology and the weakening of being. For Vattimo, being is not simply there (the metaphysics of presence). Being is not simply given, nor is it an eternal structure. Being gives itself in occurrence and as an event (*Ereignis*).[13]

The event means that something is happening and that it has an impact on its otherness, unexpectedness, and difference. In his dialogue with Richard Rorty on the future of religion,[14] Vattimo uses the example of the classic to explain the event. The classic could be a particular text that is continually read and reread in history. But this text is not read because somebody prescribed that it should be so. Rather it happens to be an event in intellectual history. Of course, the prime example in this respect is the Bible. The text of the Bible is a material thing, of course, but its essence is not exhausted in the objectivity of its being a thing. In fact, it cannot be grasped objectively as one thing among other things. Although the Bible is an object, it cannot be represented purely as an object. Weakening is nothing

---

[13] Gianni Vattimo, *Of Reality: The Purposes of Philosophy*, trans. R. T. Valgenti (New York, NY: Columbia University Press, 2016), 103–12.
[14] Richard Rorty, Gianni Vattimo, and Santiago Zabala, "What Is Religion's Future after Metaphysics?" in *The Future of Religion*, ed. Santiago Zabala (New York, NY: Columbia University Press, 2005), 65–6.

other than drawing attention to the fact that the being of the Bible is an event. And for Vattimo, weakening is the constitutive character of being.[15]

By the same token, the return to religion by way of secularization must be interpreted in terms of the event. *After Christianity* is still Christianity. The point here is not to disclose the content of Christianity that is returning; rather, the return itself is an event. Hence, weak thought signals the following consequences for Christianity: moving from objective knowledge to the hermeneutics of being; moving from strong universal structures to contextual rationalities; abandoning hierarchical structures in favor of communal living. It is important to remember, however, that this is not an external demand of postmodernity addressed to Christianity. Just as secularization is, Vattimo suggests, by no means an external process but the inherent truth of Christianity, so the weakening of Christianity is a theological truth. For Vattimo, weak thought is the innermost auto-affection and the truly experiential dynamism of Christianity. As such, it is not to be lamented. Quite the contrary. Vattimo urges Christianity to embrace history and historicity in the same way that God in his act of kenosis poured love into the world and adopted the weakness of being by becoming a human being—the incarnation.

Theologically, then, weak thought is the overcoming of a moral God, the God of philosophers. It is the rediscovery of living Christianity, that is, kenosis and love—charity. Nietzsche and Heidegger are two of the greatest prophets who, finally, understood the pure core of Christianity and its constant call for the after. It seems right, therefore, to conclude that Vattimo's weak thought has *epistemo-theological* determination.[16]

---

[15] Vattimo, *Belief*, 35.
[16] Erik Meganck, "*Philosophia Amica Theologiae*: Gianni Vattimo's 'Weak Faith' and Theological Difference," *Modern Theology* 31, no. 3 (2015): 377–402.

After Christianity

In his semi-autobiographical *Belief*, Vattimo confesses that he believes that he still believes. Years later, in the so-called collaborative autobiography *Not Being God*, he states explicitly that he is a Christian philosopher.[17] Nonetheless, Vattimo's vision of Christianity is hardly orthodox or ecclesial: what he proposes is a "non-religious Christianity."

This kenotic and self-critical Christianity stands on three principles centered on the person of Jesus Christ:[18] (1) Christ destroys the metaphysics of the philosophical and religious worlds; (2) Christ abolishes the division between "here" and "out-there," that is, the division between this world and the celestial one; and (3) Christ is interested in the inner part of human being, and thus proclaims that *in interior homine habitat veritas*. And if this is the core of Christ's message, Vattimo argues, it must be at the center of our Christianity (after Christianity).

It is surprising, astonishing perhaps, that the key idea in Vattimo's reconsideration of Christianity is the idea of truth. The ever-repeated rejection of metaphysics is not only an appeal to use a different (more humble and critical) language register but also a challenge to search for more adequate thought patterns regarding our understanding of truth. For Vattimo, Christianity reveals and firmly holds that the classical *adequatio rei intellectum* is insufficient when it comes to spiritual-existential matters. In contrast to the essentialist correspondence theory, Vattimo recognizes Christianity as a true historical movement of salvation and truth.

One way or another, the discourse of *After Christianity* and the later essay "Toward a Nonreligious Christianity" is an exercise in seeking

---

[17] Vattimo, *Not Being God*, 151.
[18] For the following, see Vattimo, "Toward a Nonreligious Christianity," 27–46.

the authentic core, a purified version—the truth in a nonessentialist and nonfoundational sense. Let us examine Vattimo's weakening of Christianity in greater detail.

Vattimo's nonreligious movement after Christianity battles the latent Platonism of the other-worldly and the latent Aristotelianism of inherent essences. Regardless of whether the metaphysical register is preferred, there are consequences on two levels with respect to Christianity. First, on the cognitive level, one is obliged to accept revelation as the true representation of reality. Secondly, on the moral level, one must act according to the accepted knowledge of revelation. It will be no surprise, however, that Vattimo considers such a metaphysical conception of Christianity to be violent and oppressive and suggests that—worse still—such a hierarchical and dogmatic structure of religion misplaces the core of Christianity's liberating message. What is Vattimo's alternative, then?

Again, in reference to what has been noted so far in this chapter, authentic Christianity is hermeneutical. The Christian scriptures represent a flow of interpretations and reinterpretations and as such they perfectly fit Vattimo's diagnosis of the age of interpretation: rather than providing objective knowledge, they represent a constant attempt to understand the person of Jesus of Nazareth, the confessed Christ. And this person, who undoubtedly stands at the center of the Christian narrative, exercised antiauthoritarian power by fighting oppression with weak power, and in so doing, as Vattimo provocatively exclaims, "freed us from the Truth."[19]

How can we prove the validity of such a statement without falling back into metaphysics? How can we sustain the hermeneutical nature of Christianity without betraying it by making an absolute claim? Is

---

[19] Gianni Vattimo, "Nihilism as Postmodern Christianity," in *Transcendence and Beyond: A Postmodern Inquiry*, ed. J. D. Caputo and M. J. Scanlon (Bloomington, IN: Indiana University Press, 2007), 47.

it possible? Vattimo would cry a hearty "Yes we can!" He argues that questions such as these stem from a distorted notion of truth, a notion damaged by metaphysics and modern science in their search for the total mastery of objectivity. In *The Transparent Society*,[20] Vattimo uses the example of the media to illustrate his argument. The media present a form of reality, but this presentation is always an illusion and, in fact, a distortion of the whole of reality. The media pretend to present reality objectively but in fact they blur any such supposed objectivity. As observers (consumers) we have a problem understanding that media coverage is an interpretation because we are infected with the notion of objective truth—the truth of that which is represented. Vattimo's hermeneutical claims are therefore seen as a new kind of objective foundationalism because they are understood against a background of the previous perversion of truth.[21] In short, in Vattimo's opinion, metaphysics and its heir, modern science, created a false claim regarding objective reality.[22] Unfortunately, we cannot help but see truth through modern lenses and thus miss the point that there are no facts, only interpretations; and that this is also an interpretation.

To return to our main concern, Christianity supports Vattimo's thesis. If we take the scriptures and read the biblical text, Vattimo argues, we will easily realize that what we have before us is not a representation of objective facts. We are confronted with inconsistencies, illogicalities, and primitive understandings of reality. In short, the Bible is far from scientific and even quite alien to the modern rationalist mind. At the same time, Vattimo believes, only a few readers would have problems accepting that the scriptures are a

---

[20] Gianni Vattimo, *The Transparent Society* (Cambridge: Polity Press, 1992).
[21] For a more detailed account of Vattimo's concept of truth and the debate surrounding it, see Frederiek Depoortere, "Gianni Vattimo's Concept of Truth and Its Consequences for Christianity," in *Theology and the Quest for Truth: Historical—and Systematic-Theological Studies*, ed. F. Depoortere, M. Lamberights, et. al. (Leuven: Peeters, 2006), 241–58.
[22] This is the underlying tone of Vattimo's *Of Reality*.

true testimony. The key to understanding this tension is to distinguish the truth of objective knowledge from a witness to the truth. In other words, Vattimo concludes, the Christian truth is not external but must be understood from within the person. The Christian truth is the inner truth of making (*facere veritatem*) and not the objective fact of knowledge.

We have now arrived at the destination of Vattimo's argument: Christianity is the driving force behind the unmasking of false epistemological pretensions. It advances secularization and reveals itself as weak thought, and in this sense is nonreligious and antimetaphysical. To define it positively, Christianity is an existential imperative pertaining to the inner sphere of human beings. What remains after Christianity is not dogmatics but ethics and spirituality: "The future of Christianity, and also of the Church, is to become a religion of pure love, always more purified."[23]

Charity—*caritas*—is the only principle. To borrow from Derrida, love/charity occupies the position of the undeconstructible. Where does Vattimo's position lead us? What is the ultimate meaning of charity, and figuratively of Christianity, in the situation of the *after*? The answer is twofold: (1) To embrace love means to renounce every reference to external normativity and objectivity. In other words, love excludes metaphysics and the sacral aspect of religiosity because love pertains to the internal. Love happens as an event; (2) The event of love advances conversation and continuous interpretation, that is, the praxis of love as the praxis as such. The ultimate consequence, or meaning, of *after Christianity* is that God disappears and only love remains. God-talk becomes love-talk.

We saw while discussing Lyotard's postmodern critical theory that the narrative of love could turn out to be a dangerous or even violent thing. Does Vattimo escape from the clutches of the master narrative?

---

[23] Vattimo, "Toward a Nonreligious Christianity," 45.

The biblical proclamation that God is love (1 Jn 4:8) is replaced in postmodern faith by Love is God. For Vattimo, love is certainly not sentimental. Love is more than a nice feeling. Erik Meganck summarizes the content of Vattimo's proposal in three points: (1) Love is the praxis of the weakening of objective truths for it values more the subjective; (2) love is the deconstruction of the metaphysical destination of both philosophy and religion; and (3) charity is the orientation of history—the principle of all principles for an age of interpretation.[24] Charity does not completely abolish truth but redirects attention to the real *locus* of truth, that is, "a historical socio-ethical immanence."[25] Charity therefore represents a shift in the *how* of thinking. Similarly, *after Christianity* is a recontextualization of Christian praxis. The return to religion is the return to the origin. However, this origin must not be understood a-historically, metaphysically, or, to borrow from Heidegger, in terms of ontotheology. The origin is not the ground of being, the foundation of everything that is. Vattimo's Christianity of pure love returns to the originary event—the event of love poured out into the world through Christ's kenosis. In the perspective of charity, kenosis becomes the sense of history—an ever-repeating act of interpretation without end or final destination.

One is tempted to include Vattimo's project in a large group of other authors who propose nonreligious forms of Christianity or nonmetaphysical approaches to religion in general. Think of dialectical theology and philosophical theologies of the wholly other. Karl Barth's severe rejection of religion and Dietrich Bonhoeffer's idea of nonreligious Christianity stand on one side; Emmanuel Levinas and Jacques Derrida can be found on the other. Protestants and Jews appear to join company with the Catholic Vattimo. Nonetheless, although at first sight some similarities appear, a more detailed

---

[24] Meganck, "God Returns as Nihilist *Caritas*," 372–3.
[25] Ibid., 373.

examination reveals much greater discrepancies. With dialectical theologians, Vattimo shares the critique of natural sacredness, but he objects to the notion that revelation (the central category for Barth, for instance) does not come to us from above, from the transcendent sphere. Revelation is an historical interpretation of historical experiences and as such it was given to past generations and is now given to us. In other words, revelation is the challenge of a constant after, a challenge always to see ourselves and the world in a new way, but always from within history. To the group of Jewish philosophical theologians who project an ever-open and indeterminate appeal of messianism to come, Vattimo replies that as a Christian philosopher,[26] he follows the concrete image of Jesus of Nazareth as the Christ, the Messiah. Messianism without a Messiah, a constant *to come* oriented to the future, is for Vattimo not only unbearable but also dubious. Anyone who is extraordinary or charismatic enough can then claim the empty throne of the savior of the world. Christianity as the incarnated reality of kenosis moves *after* this.

Vattimo therefore rejects the leap of faith and the wholly other (be it given revelation or a constant future orientation). *After Christianity* urges us to embrace experience here-and-now and to interpret it. Vattimo's gospel is the praxis of charity as the principle that is materialized in continuous dialogue. Vattimo believes that he still believes in love as the foundational event—the originary pure event— of which Jesus of Nazareth is the prototype. However, if Vattimo

---

[26] I have already mentioned Vattimo's self-identification with Christian philosophy, but it is important to note that he formulates his "Christian" confession as an explicit and direct self-differentiation from Derrida and Jewish (postmodern) philosophy (Vattimo, *Not Being God*, 151). Meganck even presents the thesis that Vattimo understands Derrida as his main adversary in the fight for Heidegger's legacy. See Meganck, "*Philosophia Amica Theologiae,*" 392. Klun, on the other hand, claims: "Vattimo's notion of weakening is largely interchangeable with Derrida's notion of deconstruction, and both share the same ethical criticism of strong metaphysical thinking." Klun, "Incarnation and 'De-Carnation,'" 164.

believes that he still believes, then the Messiah who kenotically poured love into the world is not only the example par excellence of this love, but also, surely, its ontological determination.

The Weak, the Spiritual, and the Idealistic

Secularization is the (hi)story of weak thought. We have ceased to search for God, or objective truths, which are supposed to set us free. Rather, Vattimo insists, we need to revisit the praxis of solidarity, love, and self-critical irony. The question is, however, whether this form of radical kenotic Christianity is not in fact *too* weak. Paraphrasing Nietzsche's mad man: Who gave us the right to wipe out the horizon? How credible is the word of charity when God must remain in his tomb?

The good message—indeed, the only valid gospel—*after Christianity* reads: there are no facts, only interpretations. And, as Vattimo promptly adds, this is also an interpretation. Truth, if the word is still worthy of its name, is purely worldly; a matter of consensus without an external referent, be it philosophical-metaphysical or religious-sacral. In the movement of kenosis, Christianity removes itself from the eternal origin, that is, from transcendence. Logically, only ethics remains. The principle of love—charity—seems to replace the Kantian categorical imperative. The originary event of the cross urges us to forget the distance between "being-in-the-world" and "out-there." In fact, there is no "out-there," no unchangeable truths, only "being-in-here" and interpretations. The ultimate meaning of Christianity is therefore brought to light in secularization. Secularization is not the adversary of Christianity and by no means brings an *after* of Christianity. The after of Christianity is secularization. And this after signals the return of religion, that is, Christianity: our culture is perhaps not Christian, but it is by no means non-Christian, and Vattimo wants to show that after Christianity it is (again and still) Christian, though differently.

After Christianity is an epistemo-theo-logical category. Epistemologically, Vattimo deconstructs the truth and announces a postmodern nihilism—an age of interpretation. Theologically, he reframes the question of God in terms of kenosis and secularization. Now, the question is whether this postmodern hermeneutical project is theologically plausible. Is there in fact any question of God? Or are we left, willingly or not, with an immanent Christianity? Let us recapitulate: secularization as the ultimate truth of Christianity (what a metaphysical claim!) consists of an endless withdrawal from transcendence. The result is remembrance of the Nothing beyond—Nihilism. What matters is the internal, that is, love as the ethical principle. This love is taken from a particular narrative of Christianity, but it seems to be universalized as the general foundation of the future nonviolent well-being and dwelling in the world. Two problems can immediately be detected. First, Vattimo somewhat biases his open postmodernism with a clear preference for one particular and very specific notion of love taken from Christianity. Secondly, Vattimo's interpretation of charity is philosophical and, paradoxically, excludes the theological. As Meganck suggests, Vattimo converts philosophy from *ancilla theologiae* to *dominatrix*.[27] In other words, Vattimo's *after* Christianity is equally *after theology*.

This lack of genuine theological awareness leads, I suggest, to the gravest problem with Vattimo's reinterpretation of Christianity. The deliberate preference for an hermeneutical approach, even more radically, for understanding Christianity as the foundation of hermeneutics and as a hermeneutical act *par excellence* throws Vattimo into irredeemable idealism. "There are no facts, only interpretations,"

---

[27] Meganck, "*Philosophia Amica Theologiae*," 388.

he confesses. The incarnation—the center of Christianity—is also not a fact but an interpretation, the interpretation of a confessing community, something we called earlier the hermeneutical event of the Spirit. In other words, the incarnation of Jesus Christ and God's kenosis is a narrated story that provokes an ongoing interpretation and makes Christianity utterly hermeneutical (which, for Vattimo, means standing in opposition to anything metaphysical). However, it should be noted that this rendering of the incarnation is spiritualized, metaphorical, in Vattimo's words, weakened, and thus deprived of all its historical materiality and physical concreteness (which in my opinion is the real scandal of the Christian narrative of Jesus of Nazareth). This "hermeneutical reduction of Christianity"[28] stands, in Vattimo's view, for the liberation of Christianity. From a theological perspective, however, Vattimo turns the Johannine message upside down: the Word became flesh is turned into the flesh became the word. As a result, Vattimo's after Christianity is dis-incarnated. Vattimo's gospel of charity—the message of incarnation—is a universal spiritual prophecy that can do without the particularity of a flesh and blood Jesus of Nazareth.

What we have, therefore, is that Vattimo, a self-proclaimed Catholic philosopher, seems to repeat the gesture of the earlier modern theologians (both Protestant and Catholic) who attempted to reconcile Christianity with the secular age. In so doing, these theologians often run the risk of an immaterial, spiritual, and too-idealistic form of Christianity, although one that is liberated from the clutches of religiosity.[29] Vattimo appears to me to arrive at the same cul-de-sac. In his vigorous struggle with the metaphysical violence of religion, he eliminates the flesh from the incarnation and arrives at a violent

---

[28] Klun, "Incarnation and 'De-Carnation,'" 170.
[29] Frederiek Depoortere observes something similar in his *Christ in Postmodern Philosophy: Gianni Vattimo, René Girard, and Slavoj Žižek* (New York, NY: T&T Clark, 2008), 31–2.

spiritualization of Christianity. And although Jakob Deibl attempts to redeem Vattimo's dis-incarnated philosophy of Christianity by pointing out the materiality of the text in the hermeneutical process, and thus attempts to understand the grappling with the biblical legacy as a profound engagement with the materiality of the incarnation,[30] I have to ask: Where is the body (of Christ)?

In Vattimo, there are certainly thought-provoking insights in the great and necessary tradition of the masters of suspicion. There is an ever-valid warning to be aware of the danger of the metaphysical violence of what Vattimo calls dogmatic-hierarchical faith. Vattimo justifiably demands an act of difference on the part of Christianity, that is, to think through again and again what Christian existence means. Yet, ultimately, he comes to the nihilist *caritas* as the principle of all principles and its particularity and specificity. Otherwise, he in fact holds this charity as empty. In which case, it seems to me that Vattimo idealizes Christianity by making it entirely kenotic, and thus empty, like his attempt to idealize communism by making it hermeneutical.[31] In my view, which will be unfolded in Part III, Christianity contains a real conflict, a real fight for truth, a real struggle for existence in-the-world, and, last but not least, for a real body/flesh. I see Vattimo's *after Christianity* as far removed from an attempt at a consoling discourse of love. On the other hand, as Heidegger's *Dasein* is rightly criticized for being without the body, Vattimo's caritas must be charged with an inappropriate dis-incarnation. In its hermeneutical nature, kenosis, as put forward by Vattimo, remains an intellectual principle—a purely intentional affection. Theologically, however, Christ's kenosis was a highly physical phenomenon, or in Vattimo an *event*, which took place in history. Vattimo's philosophical project weakens this

---

[30] Jakob Helmut Deibl, *Menschwerdung und Schwächung: Annäherung an ein Gespräch mit Gianni Vattimo* (Vienna: Vienna University Press, 2013), 184.

[31] Gianni Vattimo and Santiago Zabala, *Hermeneutic Communism: From Heidegger to Marx* (New York, NY: Columbia University Press, 2011).

theological aspect that should certainly be considered in any attempt to address the after-of-Christianity.

Perhaps ... Christianity has something hermeneutical in itself; something that could help us retain the belief that we still believe in emancipation (because this is what Vattimo really means when he says *credo di credere*). Thus, Vattimo urges his readers to embrace Christianity in its pure form. This purified mode of Christian being bears a provocative name: nihilism. In other words, nihilism—as conveyed by Nietzsche's "God is dead" and by Heidegger's announcement of the end of metaphysics—reveals the truth of Christianity. Nihilism throws us into a post-Christian age, an age of interpretation. For Vattimo, this Christian history—our history—simply must be accepted. My point, which I will develop later, is somewhat the reverse: we need to accept history and that Christianity is historical. The issue at stake is not Christian history but history as the proper mode of the Christian being and being Christian.

5

Christianity Without Religion: Struggling with John D. Caputo's Radicalism

John D. Caputo is a prolific writer whose critical mind covers a wide range of topics, among which religion occupies the central position. As he confesses in *In Search of Radical Theology*, it all begins with Heidegger and his deconstruction of the idolatrous metaphysical god, a caricature of God not worthy of the name.[1] However, then comes Jacques Derrida, who further complicates the matter. Caputo embraces the theological side of Derrida's deconstructionism, which helped him find his own voice—a voice which sang the critical song of the philosophy of religion under the rubric of radical hermeneutics, thus closing the circle on the most recent, mature period in which Caputo has been developing a new sense of theology, a radical theology that is hermeneutical in nature.[2]

In this chapter, I will examine Caputo's concept of "religion without religion" as a particular instance of the after of Christianity. In the footsteps of Derrida, Caputo identifies himself as a postmodern

---

[1] John D. Caputo, *In Search of Radical Theology: Expositions, Explorations, Exhortations* (New York, NY: Fordham University Press, 2020). Indeed, one easily notes that Caputo's early writings were dedicated to a comparison of the Christian theological tradition and the philosophy of Heidegger. See, for example, John D. Caputo, *The Mystical Element in Heidegger's Thought* (Athens, OH: Ohio University Press, 1978); *Demythologizing Heidegger* (Bloomington, IN: Indiana University Press, 1993).

[2] Justin Sands makes a compelling argument for reading Caputo's work principally as radical theology. See Justin Sands, "Confessional Discourses, Radicalizing Traditions: On John Caputo and the Theological Turn," *Open Theology* 8, no. 1 (2022): 38–49. Most recently, a volume dedicated to the reception of Caputo's thought bears the subtitle *Radicalizing Theology*: Joeri Schrijvers and Martin Koci (eds.), *The European Reception of John D. Caputo's Thought: Radicalizing Theology* (Lanham, MD: Lexington Books, 2022).

pilgrim on the road toward faith, hope, and love. Deconstruction opens the path that leads toward a certain kind of weak theology, the practice of Christianity without belief.

My question is whether Caputo's version of deconstruction can tell us anything about the after of Christianity. Does Caputo propose (in addition to his severe criticism) that theology has something (anything) positive to contribute to a credible vision of Christianity in the postmodern era? Is there any attempt to present us with something similar to Vattimo's (Nietzschean-Heideggerian) Christianity of love? Is a (Derridean) Christianity without religion an option? The following pages will explore whether Caputo's variation on the after of Christianity is restricted to a discourse of warnings and prohibitions or is capable of providing a positive program; in short, some hope for postmodern pilgrims.

The Theopoetics of Deconstruction

Caputo's radical theological trilogy *The Weakness of God* (2006), *The Insistence of God* (2013), and *The Folly of God* (2016), more recently complemented by *Cross and Cosmos* (2019) and *In Search of Radical Theology* (2020), testifies to his gradual transformation—*metanoia*—from a self-proclaimed philosopher of religion to the kind of theologian that is not so much interested in the nature of doctrine as in developing Christian practice: a theological life—*vita theologica*—materialized in faith, hope, and love. To put it differently, Caputo's interest in radical theology could be translated as insistence on a radical recontextualization of Christian practice. To use the vocabulary of this book, Caputo is searching for the after of Christianity. However, to understand this move in its proper context, we must follow Caputo's postmodern pilgrimage through some crucial milestones, of which the philosophy of deconstruction is perhaps the most decisive.

"Deconstruction is a passion for transgression, a passion for trespassing the horizons of possibility," says Caputo.[3] Caputo was originally drawn to Derrida and the notion of deconstruction because of his fascination with the striving for justice in Derrida's philosophy. Probing the foundations of our traditions, politics, communities, institutions, and, last but not least, religion, deconstruction has the power to crack open petrified concepts,[4] revealing problems with the words, language, and modes of behavior that have become unquestioned and indeed unquestionable. Deconstruction is *the* postmodern critical theory, a hermeneutics of reality. Most importantly, it revives the art of questioning.

However, the question of deconstruction is not purely philosophical and intellectual. It does not primarily concern rationality, but aims, rather, at the heart of existence, questioning the very being in the world. In this sense, Caputo argues, deconstruction comes close to the religious notion of transcendence for it is a movement of excess which transgresses stable boundaries. Although Caputo never fails to remind his readers that Derrida rightly passes for an atheist, he is quite insistent that "deconstruction repeats the structure of religious experience."[5] This thread of Caputo's thought is what interests us most.

In a somewhat declaratory manner, Caputo informs us that deconstruction is religiousness *without* religion in its concrete historical forms. It is a messianic expectation *without* the determined historical messianism. Deconstruction is the gospel of the "without." On the one hand, Caputo relies on the mystical tradition and apophatic theology, which both resist determinism

---

[3] John D. Caputo, *The Prayers and Tears of Jacques Derrida: Religion without Religion* (Bloomington, IN: Indiana University Press, 1997), xix.
[4] Caputo has written a readable and elucidating introduction to Derrida's deconstruction: John D. Caputo, *Deconstruction in a Nutshell: A Conversation with Jacques Derrida* (New York, NY: Fordham University Press, 1998).
[5] Caputo, *Prayers and Tears*, xxi.

in religion. Angelus Silesius's "rose without the why," and Meister Ekhart's prayer that seeks to banish God are paradigmatic examples of religious deconstruction *avant la lettre*.[6] On the other hand, Caputo suggests a practical reason for promoting the "without" as the central element of deconstruction with respect to religion. He believes that "*sans* [without] the concrete messianism of the positive religions that wage endless war and spill the blood of the other," and that without those who by "anointing themselves God's chosen people are consummately dangerous to everyone else who is not so chosen,"[7] the world would be a better, that is, more just and hospitable place. Deconstruction is a passion for impossible justice, something that is promised in religion but obscured in certain religious traditions.

Caputo's dialectics also suggests that deconstruction is a passion for God, but we will not rush to identify this God with any particular tradition. The concern here is not a being that is supposed to be God, but the mystery, as Karl Rahner put it, that we call God. Thus, almost immediately, Caputo adds the qualification that deconstruction is also a passion for the impossible: "For the passion for the impossible is precisely not to be quenched. The one who is coming, the just one, the *tout autre*, can never be present. He [sic!] must always function as a breach of the present, opening up the present to something new, to something impossible."[8] Deconstruction does not proceed by knowledge but by faith. It repeats the structure of religious experience and reactualizes the passion of faith, albeit a faith of the without: *sans savoir, sans avoir, sans voir*.[9] A less metaphysical, more philosophical faith, perhaps?

---

[6] John D. Caputo, *Hoping against Hope: Confessions of a Postmodern Pilgrim* (Minneapolis, MN: Fortress Press, 2015), 24–30, 102–22.
[7] Caputo, *Prayers and Tears*, xxi.
[8] Ibid., xxiv.
[9] Ibid., xvvi.

It is not easy to dismiss the charges that Caputo piles up against religion. Regardless of whether religious wars started for political aims, as William Cavanaugh argues in *The Myth of Religious Violence*,[10] it is an indisputable fact that it was still religious people of different confessions who were killing each other, often with holy zeal. Speaking of more recent times, Caputo often uses the example of the American religious Right, whose clear and distinct image of God and Christian values causes considerable hostility and injustice in society instead of promoting the opposite. Caputo suggests that deconstruction can not only prevent these pitfalls but also contribute to a reconsideration of religion.

Caputo likes to provoke, and one of his major provocations is directed against theology: "Nobody trusts theology ... and with good reason."[11] Caputo dismisses theology as a self-referential game of words. In his opinion, theologians pretend to hold a monopoly on the truth. In fact, they pretend to have the Truth and back themselves up with premises, assumptions, and presuppositions which only infidels or heretics could possibly contradict. Caputo sees all this as stemming from an attachment to a strong, sovereign God. Will deconstruction become a new theology, one that is capable of rethinking itself, opening its horizons, and (re)turning to a passion for the impossible as conveyed in the mystical tradition?

Although Caputo claims that deconstruction has the structure of religious experience, deconstruction is not a theology. Caputo argues that deconstruction comes as the *after* of theology. To put it even more radically, Derrida's deconstruction "saves theology from itself."[12] Following this creed, Caputo wants to replace the strong, violent, and

---

[10] William T. Cavanaugh, *The Myth of Religious Violence: Secular Ideology and the Roots of Modern Conflict* (Oxford: Oxford University Press, 2009).

[11] John D. Caputo, "The Sense of God: A Theology of the Event with Special Reference to Christianity," in *Between Philosophy and Theology: Contemporary Interpretations of Christianity*, ed. L. Boeve and C. Brabant (Farnham: Ashgate, 2010), 27.

[12] Caputo, *Prayers and Tears*, 61.

sovereign theology of a great God with a weak theology, sometimes called a theology of the event.

Weak theology is not concerned with the question of a highest being, a God located somewhere outside this world and time. It is not interested in whether God is accessible through reason or through revelation. Rather, it adheres strictly to the principal premise of deconstruction: everything that is constructed can be deconstructed. As Joeri Schrijvers puts it: "Whatever theory that is constructed about such a highest being is a construction in space and time and therefore *as contingent as* anything else in the world, so that no discourse, neither 'Christian faith' nor, perhaps, religion without religion is safely sheltered from 'the postmodern critique of metaphysics.'"[13]

Caputo is clear: "The real interest of theology is not God."[14] Deconstruction therefore makes theology aware of its metaphysical, ousiological, and hyperessentialist travesty. This is difficult vocabulary—for professional theologians and all the more for practitioners. Put into other words, Caputo's deconstruction redirects theology's attention to the foundational question: "What do I love when I love my God?"[15] To ask this Augustinian question in a postmodern way is to allow the idea of praying without destination, having faith without faith, and believing without knowledge. Asking the question about love means that God, indeed, becomes *nothing* for theology.[16] God is saved from God. Naming God is no longer subordinated to metaphysical violence. Faith is redeemed from cognitive procedures: "Deconstruction takes the form of a general or non-determinable faith in the impossible."[17]

In consequence, Caputo retranslates theology into *theopoetics*, emancipating the discourse about God from the realm of logos, that is,

---

[13] Schrijvers, *Between Faith and Belief*, 145.
[14] John D. Caputo, *The Folly of God: A Theology of the Unconditional* (Salem, OR: Polebridge Press, 2016), 1.
[15] Caputo, *Prayers and Tears*, 61.
[16] Caputo, *Hoping against Hope*, 47.
[17] Caputo, *Prayers and Tears*, 64.

from the doctrinal-metaphysical attitude of a strong theology rooted in its ecclesial-hierarchical setting. Instead of promoting the theoretic attitude with regard to *what* one believes, Caputo suggests returning to the matter itself, or, as phenomenology would have it, *die Sache selbst*. Indeed, phenomenology and its suspension—the reduction of the supernatural attitude—is a direct source of inspiration here. For Caputo, what matters is lived experience interpreted through narratives, the founding figures of religion. In other words, theopoetics is the hermeneutics of the religious experience; it is the practice of deconstruction. The act of poetics is coming to terms with the event of religion: revelation, challenges, questions, new ideas; the relationship to the icon of god: "[Theopoetics] is not about making propositional claims but about being-claimed, not about proposing but about being-exposed to something that is beyond the reach of propositions."[18]

Finally, we are coming to see what, according to Caputo, constitutes the religious, theological, or, better, theoretical side of deconstruction. It is a dialectical repetition in the Kierkegaardian fashion, that is, a constant affirmation of faith without having firm ground at one's disposal. It is a call to remain faithful.[19] Thus, applying Caputo's thought theologically (because Caputo, as much as Heidegger, is still drawn to write theology occasionally), "Deconstruction is something like a *fin de siecle* faith, but *without*."[20]

The question is: Without what? In answer, the without functions as an ever-open variable. We can replace it with dogma, or hierarchical institution, or sacrificial exchange. In sum, deconstruction in the context of religion functions as the movement of purification: let faith be faith, not knowledge, and certainly not triumphalism. Deconstruction resituates faith, relocates it; it brings faith out to the

---

[18] John D. Caputo, "The Theopoetic Reduction: Suspending the Supernatural Signified," *Literature and Theology* 33, no. 3 (2019): 251.
[19] Caputo, *Prayers and Tears*, 65.
[20] Ibid., 56.

desert (*khora*) as its new home. But a positive definition is also possible: deconstruction is an apology for the impossible. Deconstruction brings us to the field of religion without religion.

Religion without Religion

So, Caputo insists that deconstruction is structured like a religion, the religion of a messianic prayer crying *oui, oui, viens, amen*, the religion of faith in something "to come"; religion without religion. This concept stands at the center of Caputo's philosophy, including his rereading of Christianity.

Caputo's motivation for rethinking religion using Derrida's deconstruction is the present historical condition. Where does religion find itself? For Caputo, the hermeneutical key is to be found in Derrida's *Faith and Knowledge*: "A traditional faith finds itself locked in an embrace with the uprooting, delocalizing, decorporealizing, detraditionalizing forces of teletechnological science."[21] Technology has been transplanted into the body of religion. The pope has become a TV celebrity. Religion is transplanting itself onto the internet—the all-powerful, all-encompassing worldwide web. For Caputo, this is the same old song of global mastery, but his point is not so much to comment on the state of hi-tech society, but to explore the processes taking place in religion, and in Christianity in particular.

Again, Caputo finds Derrida to be a helpful companion, this time with his concept of autoimmunization.[22] Christianity, for Caputo,

---

[21] Ibid., 152.
[22] Derrida develops the concept of autoimmunity in "Faith and Knowledge: The Two Sources of 'Religion' at the Limit of Reason Alone," in J. Derrida, *Acts of Religion* (New York, NY: Routledge, 2002), 79–82, and mentions the concept on many instances in *Rogues: Two Essays on Reason*, trans. P.-A. Brault and M. Naas (Stanford, CA: Stanford University Press, 2005).

has suppressed its immune system, that is, its antagonism toward technology, and has thus activated the autoimmunity that negates the protective powers (its own natural immune system) that would otherwise evict the alien object—technology—from the body, thus allowing the alien to achieve mastery over body, soul, and spirit.[23] This travesty has a simple explanation: technology provides the power to proclaim the truth of religion and give it a new, almost mythological expression that can reach everyone on the planet. Yet, for Caputo, religion is not something external, a system of beliefs. In his substantial essay *On Religion*, his attention is turned to the internal, to the existential inside every human being:

> The impossible is the very quality that also defines religion for me ... [I argue] that there is a fundamentally religious quality to human experience itself, whether or not you have the blessing of the bishop or the rabbi, whether or not you subscribe to one of the institutional faiths at all, whether or not you believe in the "God" of one of the traditional confessions, whether or not you are an "atheist" vis-a-vis the several theisms. There is a deeply religious element within us all, with or without religion.[24]

Caputo goes on to define the axioms of religion without religion: undecidability, questionability, and love.[25] The truly religious element inherent to every human being defies the possibility of giving a definitive answer to the ever-present question of whether I believe in God. On the contrary, the religious experience is aware of continual doubts regarding what it is that I have faith in. Only in this sense, Caputo claims, does the *act* of religion—love—prevail over the *concept* of religion. From these axioms, we can see the nature of the problem

---

[23] Caputo, *Prayers and Tears*, 153.
[24] John D. Caputo, *On Religion* (London: Routledge, 2002), 109.
[25] Ibid., 132–4.

with religion *with* religion. Instead of pondering on the undecidable question, the answer is suddenly available and disposable. The unquestioned presuppositions deprive religion of its fundamental call—the call of the event.

Caputo is interested in the event, and religion is one of its many instantiations, perhaps the one that creates the best opportunity for welcoming indeterminacy, freedom, and openness in the human life. For what matters in Caputo is not allegiance to one confession or another but openness to the event, the experience of otherness, disruption, the disclosure of the always insufficient—the impossible. This, in Caputo's opinion, is a truly religious mode of existence.

Naturally, such religiousness without any propositional content announces the end of metaphysics. After the dismissal of metaphysical fantasies and speculations concerning the essence of God, after the poetical turn in the philosophy of religion, the field is open for the coming of the event. As human beings no longer need to escape this world, having a religious vocation means "to make ourselves answerable to the world, to the voices that call us in and from the world, from within the world."[26] A religion of the impossible but without religion resists any reductionism with respect to the world, human beings, the divine (if there is such a thing) because none of these could simply be rendered as a thing-present-at-hand, and thus to the objectifiable.

In order to find religion without religion, Caputo suggests embarking on a pilgrimage, but not to Santiago de Compostela or Guadalupe. The postmodern pilgrim of religion without religion has no map. They will reach their destination by being on the way, and this way leads through the desert called *khora*, a concept drawn from Plato's dialogue *Timaeus*. In Caputo, it comes via Derrida, for whom

---

[26] Caputo, "The Sense of God," 36.

khora is a way of naming radical otherness, is something that resists the sensible and the intelligible. Hence, for Caputo:

> [Khora is] neither present nor absent, active nor passive, the Good nor evil, living nor nonliving. Neither theomorphic nor anthropomorphic—but rather atheological and nonhuman ... Khora has no meaning or essence, no identity to fall back upon. She/it receives all without becoming anything, which is why she/it can become the subject of neither a philosopheme nor a mytheme. In short, the khora is *tout autre*, very.[27]

How can we speak of khora? We can only say that there is (*il y a*) khora. Khora gives and promises nothing. Rather the khora is an act of promising, the moment of the "to come" of absolute otherness. Is khora God, then? Caputo's answer is "no." Khora is a posture, a mode of coming through something that might be described as the difference of deconstruction, that is, the differentiating of all beings. Khora is undecidability, the silent experience of the desert. In defense against the oft-raised criticism that khora leaves us in a nihilist void without even "nothing,"[28] Caputo is quick to clarify that undecidability is not indecision.[29] The opposite of undecidability is not a decision but programmability. In fact, the experience of khora calls for a decision, but one without predetermined rules: "Without khora," Caputo argues, "we would be programmed to God."[30] To put it differently, we would be without freedom, responsibility, and faith with respect to our religion. Khora nudges us toward a passion for the impossible.

---

[27] Caputo, *Prayers and Tears*, 36.
[28] This critique of khora as an empty, miserable place is raised, for example, by Richard Kearney in *Strangers, Gods and Monsters: Interpreting Otherness* (London: Routledge, 2005), 202–3.
[29] John D. Caputo, "Richard Kearney's Enthusiasm: A Philosophical Exploration of the God Who May Be," *Modern Theology* 18, no. 1 (2002): 87–94.
[30] Ibid., 93.

One way or another, Caputo constructs a kind of an-khoral religion according to the model of the postmodern desert father and anchorite Jacques Derrida. This religion is something older and more authentic than the religion drawn from the Latin *re-ligare* (holding the bond and being bound with the divine). It is also different from the religion of *re-legere* (being respectful of what is given in the sacred). The an-khoral religion is, perhaps, the original structure of religious experience; it is religion without religion, messianicity without messianism, ground without ground: One without name.[31]

Religion without religion does not concern God. It concerns the longing for God. It addresses the question of God while leaving aside arguments about God's existence. Instead, Caputo suggests that we talk about the *insistence* of God. God insists, that is the creed of religion without religion. For Caputo, this posture is more verbal than nominal. Religion without religion is therefore a proto-religion without the origin. Interestingly, Caputo's project to be open to what has yet to come returns us to the originary. The condition of the after reveals what is at the very beginning: the without.

The question we must now ask is whether Christianity, as a still existing and insisting phenomenon in this world, could be remodeled according to the proto-structure of religion without religion.

Christianity: The Poetics of the Without

To reiterate: according to the principles of deconstruction, everything that is constructed—culture, traditions, institutions, practices, beliefs, and so on—can be deconstructed. So far, we have been pursuing deconstruction as the imperative of history, historical contingency, and the finite state of being. However, Caputo insists that there is

---

[31] Caputo, *Prayers and Tears*, 159.

also a greater call; namely the call of the undeconstructible.[32] One is tempted to interpret this as the trace of metaphysics in Caputo, but our author sees things differently.

Caputo introduces the concept of the unconditional as the equivalent of Derrida's notion of the undeconstructible. Consider the pair *law* and *justice*: the latter is a principle for which the former is a manner of realization. The problem is that laws are always provisional, open to change. Moreover, laws are not always adequate for the demands of justice. Therefore, laws must be continually deconstructed in order to be reconstructed. The deconstruction of any given law opens the path for justice to come. However, justice will never be present exhaustively. Every law falls short when compared to justice, yet the striving for justice cannot be abandoned. In other words, the undeconstructible does not pertain to this or that theory of justice. Rather, the call of justice is what can never be deconstructed. In contrast, laws constructed as the provisional attempts to capture (some aspect of) justice need to be deconstructed if one is to be faithful to the call of the undeconstructible. In this sense, the undeconstructible is also the unconditional.

As we have seen, for Caputo, there is something of religious experience in deconstruction. So, what of religion without religion and the undeconstructible? Caputo provides one of his books with a telling subtitle, *A Theology of the Unconditional*, but even in the first chapter dissolves any unsolicited presumptions that in the realm of theology the unconditional is God. Forget it, says Caputo. The major interest of theology is not God, or the question of the essence and existence of God. God insists. This means that God, or, even better, naming God remains an ever-open question. And this open question, this proto-religious posture, this modality of indeterminate faith without the determinate content of belief, this is the unconditional with respect to religion. To say it as clearly as possible, Caputo does

---

[32] Caputo, *Folly of God*, chapter 2.

not propose deconstruction in order to dismantle idolatrous images (the Feuerbachian anthropomorphic projection) of God. In fact, Caputo criticized, for example, Marion's *God without being* for exactly this and for safeguarding a good-old-God as the highest excess of being. Rather, Caputo argues for deconstruction because he wants to renounce any talk of God as the supreme being. Deconstruction thus repeats the truth once noted by mystics of the Christian tradition for whom the journey to God was its own aim. Deconstruction opens our eyes to see that we do not see. In this sense only, deconstruction as a certain religious experience reveals the truth of the undeconstructible, that is, undecidability, indeterminacy, and the impossible. The unconditional is the benchmark for measuring any closed and totalizing system, which religions tend to create quite often. The undeconstructible is a worldly revelation that describes the truth of the human condition, namely the condition of being lost but also being on the way. This is how Caputo also sees the tradition that was once his own and which, in a radically hermeneutical manner, continues to be engraved in his thought—Christianity.

> I treat the New Testament as an "archive," a depository of memories, which presents a certain way to be, a certain "poetics"—not a politics or an ethics or a church dogmatics—that I like to call a "poetics of the kingdom," which lays claim to us and which calls for a "transformation of existence."[33]

Is Christianity a mere memory, a useful intellectual archive instrumental in pinning down the undeconstructible element of religion without religion? Schrijvers summarizes: "Christianity, for Caputo, is but a name for a historical set of beliefs that is always but a historical construction (and therefore subject to change and to

---

[33] John D. Caputo, *What Would Jesus Deconstruct? The Good News of Postmodernism for the Church* (Grand Rapids, MI: Baker Academic, 2007), 33.

deconstruction)."³⁴ Such an interpretation is certainly possible. But perhaps we should ponder a little longer Caputo's position and allow for a more benevolent reading. In addition to the notion of archive, Caputo also speaks of a poetics of the kingdom and the transformation of existence. These should not go unnoticed because both pertain to the fundamentals of (religious) existence.

Arguably, Caputo proposes another Christianity. It goes without saying that the institutional shall be deconstructed: the right approach to the kingdom is captured in *viens!* Not metaphysics but poetics; not escaping from this world but the community in this world. Caputo's Christianity is a play of differences and "the kingdom of God, Who is love, not (just) (Greek) Being."³⁵ What hides behind plentiful metaphors is "the without." Caputo's Christianity adopts the structure of "the without religion." What shall be deconstructed and removed from this, as Caputo says, "slightly de-Paulinized and more Jewish Christianity that turns away from the economics of sin and redemption, and turns on the notions of giving and for-giving, of for-giving and for-getting"?³⁶

As I see it, Caputo's Christianity is without myth, the metaphysics of being, dogma, hierarchy, sacrifice in terms of the economy of exchange. Surprisingly, Caputo's Christianity is not without the church.³⁷ For Caputo, the church happened quite unexpectedly. The disciples expected the kingdom soon-to-come but the church came instead. This maxim is often ascribed to the condemned theologian Alfred Loisy. Caputo, nevertheless, gives a completely different reading to this phrase: the fact that no one expected something like the church to come indicates that the very happening of the church is an event; and hence, the event of the church is something inherently provisional. In a certain way, the church is the institutionalized

---

[34] Schrijvers, *Between Faith and Belief*, 133.
[35] Caputo, *What Would Jesus Deconstruct?* 229.
[36] Ibid., 222.
[37] Ibid., 34–5.

movement of deconstruction that exists to make the room for the undeconstructible. In this and other respects, Caputo's project seems like a longing for the pure origin of Christianity. As Schrijvers summarizes: "One would need to bracket and reduce the *entire* tradition and its beliefs in order to come to this pure faith."[38] Caputo's Christianity, if authentic, is without religion.

Now, the question is: How do we cope with the particularity of the Christian Messiah—Jesus of Nazareth, proclaimed the Christ? Like Derrida, Caputo is skeptical of the Hegelian-Christian model of the incarnation, which is "the phenomenalization of the infinite in the finite, making the infinite palpable, visible, letting it shine as the *Erscheinen* and *Schönheit* of infinite *Sein*."[39] Caputo sides with Kierkegaard, who claims that the divinity remains completely invisible. In other words, like Derrida, Kierkegaard wants to preserve the total otherness/alterity of *tout autre*. From there comes Caputo's preference for theo-poetics over theology—"Theo*poetics* is incredulity about theo*logy*"[40]—as if the poetical account could redeem the postmodern, Lyotardian incredulity toward the system of logics. And, Caputo adds, the founding narrative of Christianity, the narrative concerning Jesus of Nazareth, has the form of a poetic rather than rational account: "In the New Testament, Jesus is a poet, not a theologian."[41] The story of Jesus resists the temptation to rationalize, to objectify. Poetics preserves the event, keeps the system open.

Jesus bears witness to the event—this is clear for Caputo. Yet he asks: What about the incarnation?[42] Caputo explains that Derrida, of course, rejects the possibility of identifying the messianic with a particular individual: the event must be preserved, and Hegelian hegemony resisted. For Caputo, this does not deprive the narrative

---

[38] Schrijvers, *Between Faith and Belief*, 142.
[39] Caputo, *Prayers and Tears*, 244.
[40] Caputo, *Folly of God*, 95.
[41] Caputo, "Theopoetic Reduction," 250.
[42] Caputo, *Prayers and Tears*, 247.

of its exemplary importance. Jesus of Nazareth, or Yeshua as Caputo prefers to call him, became the icon of God. After the death of this preacher-prophet from Galilee, the tiny community of his disciples recognized in him an event: a parable of God and his physical flesh became the iconic body. Caputo assures us that "[this] is not an attack upon the Incarnation but a more persuasive rendering of it."[43] Nonetheless, one comes to suspect that he is, in fact, masterfully avoiding a head-on encounter with the question of the incarnation. At least, he avoids commenting on the singular person of Jesus as the Messiah who has already come and yet is still to come.

Caputo sees another way of responding to the question of the incarnation. In the essay *What Would Jesus Deconstruct?*, he discusses what may be desired of Christianity in terms of a practical contribution to the world. In the context of a critique of the religious Right, Caputo makes a strong case for a socially engaged church that cares for the poor, accompanies those on the margins, and serves people not according to their faithfulness but according to the imperative of the sermon on the mount.[44] This practical aspect finds support in Caputo's conviction that the kingdom is always expressed in "the future present."[45] The incarnated Christian community works under the principle of *semper reformanda* (a theological antecedent of deconstruction), reacting *hinc et nunc* to those who are in need. In short, Christianity is always incomplete and tries to name God and itself inappropriately. In other words, Caputo remains faithful to his religion without religion. For him, it is not so important whether one confesses Jesus to be the Christ because church dogmatics says this is who Jesus of Nazareth is. Rather, Caputo insists that the true meaning of the incarnation is *facere veritatem*—doing the truth.

---

[43] Caputo, "Theopoetic Reduction," 252.
[44] Caputo, *What Would Jesus Deconstruct?* 89ff.
[45] Caputo, *Prayers and Tears*, 223.

The incarnation is less about "word becomes flesh" than it is "flesh becomes word": the poetic narrative which lives in the form of tradition (*tradere*—to carry on) in the historical community that we call the church. Yeshua died on the cross but could not remain dead because he was resurrected and elevated into theopoetic space and time, which is, Caputo argues, above flesh and blood: it lives on as a love poem.[46]

There is an obvious question we must ask: Is this move toward poetical Christianity merely technical, or does it contain fundamentals? I am utterly sympathetic to Caputo's struggle against all forms of fundamentalism and triumphalism, but I fear that reconfiguring the crucial Christian doctrine or narrative of the incarnation to the spirit of community, despite all its insistence, runs the risk of a hermeneutical reduction that is not dissimilar to the one we identified with Vattimo's charity-oriented Christianity. We have seen that Caputo claims to find inspiration in phenomenology and its reduction of the supernatural attitude. However, phenomenology, unlike Caputo, does not start with the moment of understanding (Yeshua is a poet, Yeshua is the icon of God, Yeshua is not a metaphysician) but with the moment of embodiment, with crude experience. Caputo does not leave this experience completely behind, but he does seem to spiritualize it, as if the factual actuality of embodied experience— its phenomenological occurrence—has no role to play, at least not a primary role. Incarnated love is reduced—hermeneutically—to a language-event; the narrative of the community; the spirit of love. Moreover, Caputo is critical of Vattimo's Christianity of love, which is also hermeneutical, for not being radical enough. In Caputo's opinion, Vattimo still prefers the Christian heritage over other traditions and, in consequence, reintroduced a strong metaphysical sentiment into

---

[46] Caputo, "Theopoetic Reduction," 253.

his concept of the after of Christianity.[47] Caputo gives preference to Christianity without—without myth, metaphysics, transcendence—that is, a Christianity of the event, the call, insistence.

In sum, rather than love for the necessary, Caputo's Christianity is aporetic love for the impossible; rather than adherence to the system, it is undecidability. In this sense, Christianity seems to approach the undeconstructible. Like justice and hospitality, like the gift, Christianity is to come. The repetition of the theo-poetics of the kingdom is a creative repetition; something that is arriving, but also something which might be lost. Christianity is something that is arriving when it embraces weakness and powerlessness; it loses itself when it is strong, powerful, and sovereign. Christianity is presenting a future without knowing its destination; it is a conversion rather than a recollection. Christianity is without religion.

With or Without?

It is easy to be taken in by the spiritual drive—the mystical twist—of Caputo's radical perspective on Christianity. We may also, however, be justified in accusing this radical undecidability of unbearable lightness.

The first problem is with Caputo's reading of Derrida. Do the two positions, Caputo's and Derrida's, really correspond? Derrida, for his part, never searched for a pure faith. David Newheiser contests this (mis)reading of Derrida and explicitly criticizes Caputo for drawing from him an indeterminate spirituality.[48] Derrida's interest was

---

[47] John D. Caputo, "Spectral Hermeneutics: On the Weakness of God and the Theology of the Event," in *After the Death of God*, ed. J. W. Robbins (New York, NY: Columbia University Press, 2007), 77.
[48] David Newheiser, *Hope in a Secular Age: Deconstruction, Negative Theology, and the Future of Faith* (Cambridge: Cambridge University Press, 2019), 10–12.

always real, incarnated faith. Of course, Derrida's is a faith without confessional belief, a prayer without destination. However, as the autobiographic *Circumfession* clearly shows, it is more an existential than a conceptual struggle—more existential phenomenology than radical hermeneutics.[49] I agree with Schrijvers that for Derrida there is indeed no such thing as a pure faith: faith is always accompanied by belief.[50] In my opinion, Caputo presents premodern and modern beliefs as something stabile, as if they were monolithic, univocal structures—something that the postmodern mind must question and deconstruct as nonpermanent and oppressive. The response to historical contaminations of faith is then radical hermeneutics, a passion for the Impossible, love for the kingdom, theopoetics; you name it. Nonetheless, Derrida never describes religion in terms of an opposition between the pure and the contaminated (for which read original faith in contrast to impure beliefs). Rather, Derrida's interest is in the structure of the experience of faith which is coming to itself, losing itself, and thinking-through itself (regardless of its premodernity, modernity, postmodernity). Caputo is perhaps paradoxically closer to the Hegelian system—the synthesis of the absolute future—than he wished to be.

The second problem is with the notion of *without*. For Caputo, any religion worthy of its name must surrender the sovereign *with* that makes the infinite available, disposable, the victim of propositions and historical contaminations. In contrast, religion *without* religion is disturbed by radical unknowing. Caputo's argument runs as follows: (1) the severe critique of deconstruction informs (2) the particular (religious) identity regarding its historical contamination and incompleteness while exposing it to (3) the undecidability, the

---

[49] Jacques Derrida, *Circumfession*, trans. G. Bennington (Chicago, IL: The University of Chicago Press, 1993).
[50] Schrijvers, *Between Faith and Belief*, 182–3.

powerlessness of differential thinking from the perspective of radical hermeneutics. In sum, religion without religion is the negotiation between the unconditional appeal of the (pure) event and its worldly conditions of appearing, but with a clear preference for the impossible of the event. Derrida, I believe, stands on the other side, that is, on the side of the world. The fact that he rightly passes for an atheist means that he confesses to be faithful to the world and the human condition *without* recourse to excessive and hyperbolic events. Perhaps Caputo's religion without religion throws us into a hyperbolic metaphorical version of Christianity which dreams about its core in terms of "the *indeterminate but indefinitely determinable structure of foi*, as a kind of archi-faith which goes to the heart of the human heart, and [on the other hand] the variously determinate and historically concrete *croyances*."[51] My argument in this book runs contrary to this search for a postmodern proto-religion, an arch-faith inherent to Christianity. The category of the after of Christianity aims to show that there is nothing like a stable core (an undeconstructible which is also impossible), but that the Christian movement is always historical and worldly. As I see it, Caputo's Christianity without religion—a passion for the impossible—is an ahistorical revelation of its own kind, a beautiful and inspiring poem that dreams of a different kind of world. I suggest that we, however, are called to live in *this* world.

---

[51] John D. Caputo, "Only as Hauntology Is Religion without Religion Possible: Response to Hart," in *Cross and Khôra: Deconstruction and Ethics in the Work of John D. Caputo*, ed. M. Zlomislic and N. DeRoo (Eugene, OR: Pickwick Publishers, 2010), 112.

6

The Poetics of Anatheist Christianity: Debating Richard Kearney's Universalism

After the horrors of the Holocaust and the gulags, after the turmoil of modernity manifested in wars, genocides, starvation, dictatorships, violence, mass migrations, and unspeakable suffering, it is an insult to speak of God. After all of this, atheists claim, no one can hold onto their belief. Theists object that nothing remains *but* belief. What stands at the heart of Richard Kearney's project in the field of philosophy of religion is the struggle between (1) the death of God, the incredulity of metaphysics, and the loss of any hope that the world can be ordered in a meaningful way, and (2) the return to religion after the death of God. It bears the name *Anatheism* and Kearney proposes it as a third way, an alternative to (conceptual) theism and atheism. Anatheism is a wager on God *after* God, a God "who may be, rather than a metaphysical God who is, a God as a concept, *causa sui* which can die."[1]

The cornerstones of anatheism are to be found in Kearney's earlier trilogy "Philosophy at the Limit," which explores the three major themes of his intellectual project, namely imagination, otherness, and God. This all comes to us in the hermeneutical register (inherited from his mentor Paul Ricoeur) informed by the Catholic tradition (from his context as an Irish philosopher) and the tradition of continental philosophy (in a constant struggle with the imposing figures of Levinas

---

[1] Richard Kearney, *Anatheism: Returning to God after God* (New York, NY: Columbia University Press, 2010), 3.

and Derrida and in dialogue with contemporaries such as Caputo, Marion, and more recently Falque). This all indicates that anatheism is not a new analytical theory of religion; rather, it is a hermeneutical endeavor to understand the possibility of religious experience. And although Kearney would loudly protest that his anatheism should not be considered as theology or a theological tradition,[2] we turn to this philosophical-existential concept with the following question: Could anatheism stand as a model of the after of Christianity?

Openness to the Possible

Richard Kearney is a philosopher of wagers. His voluminous output includes dealings with aesthetics, identity, nationalism, the ethics of intercultural encounters, and hospitality. Nevertheless, one of the most provocative risks he is willing to take is his wager on religion. And it is necessary immediately to add that far from being a detached observer applying a third-eye perspective, Kearney is a highly engaged thinker for whom religion functions as an embodied aspect of his thought. Anatheism, therefore, is not merely a word on the state of religion; it is a wager to bring the divine, God, faith, and religious experience back into serious debate.

The notion of wager is crucial. Blaise Pascal once challenged his contemporaries to wager on God.[3] The rationale behind Pascal's position is simple: If I accept the religious faith (meaning Christianity) and there is no God, I will still lead a virtuous life without being much bothered with the result after the death. If there is a God, however,

---

[2] Michael Barber does not hesitate to label Kearney's anatheism "a kind of philosophical theology," although Barber himself approaches Kearney's thought quite critically. Michael Barber, "Richard Kearney's *Anatheism* and the Religious and Theoretical Provinces of Meaning," *Revista Portuguesa de Filosofia* 2, no. 3 (2020): 973.
[3] Blaise Pascal, *Pensées*, trans. A. J. Krailsheimer (New York, NY: Penguin, 1995), §418.

I will enjoy the life eternal. On the other hand, if I choose to reject faith and it turns out that God exists, I will be damned. In other words, Pascal believes that those who opt for faith cannot lose, whereas nonbelievers put themselves under an unnecessary risk.

Shortly before his installation as Pope Benedict XVI, Joseph Ratzinger proposed a modified version of Pascal's wager. In a lecture given on the day he received the Saint Benedict Prize, he invited all people of good will, regardless of their religious affiliation, idleness, or even atheism, to act *as if* God existed.[4] Again, the rationale was to motivate people to act for the good, and thus to make the world a better place.

What is Kearney's wager about? For Kearney, anatheism is a third path. It is not about mitigating risk but about taking a risk. It is not a dialectical synthesis of opposites. Anatheism does not grow out of the thesis of theism and its atheistic antithesis. Rather than overweighting the aspect of being a "third," Kearney stresses the default situation of being on the way: anatheism is an adventure, a drama. It is also a movement containing a call, a promise, and a possibility. And although this may all sound highly poetic and abstract, Kearney is convinced that anatheism is above all a practice. Hence, the nature of the anatheistic wager is an encounter with the other and his or her otherness *qua* otherness. The anatheist gesture prefers the risk of hospitality and openness over hostility and rejection. The figure of the stranger opens the space of anatheism—exposing us to the possible, but without advance knowledge of the results. In this sense, there is no foundational act of anatheism, just an ever-unfinished event, an ever-present risk, and the need to wager again and again.

Kearney builds the central thesis of anatheism with inspiration from and in the context of: (1) Levinasian interiority, (2) Derrida's

---

[4] Joseph Ratzinger, "Europe in the Crisis of Cultures," *Communio: International Catholic Review* 32, no. 2 (2005): 345–56.

nameless messianicity, (3) abandoning determinism with respect to the divine (echoing Derrida's voice again), and (4) a general hermeneutics of suspicion regarding religion in dialogue with a more religiously attuned hermeneutics (drawn from Ricoeur). Three French philosophers—two of them Jewish, one a Protestant—pave the way for the Irish Catholic Kearney to formulate his concept of anatheism. Each of Kearney's holy trinity of mentors embraces, in his own right, certain aspects of the anatheist gesture. Levinas's critique of classical theism and his preference for a *contre-Dieu* that allows an *á-Dieu* (in the double sense of departing from God to be able to return) opens the question of otherness in the mode of welcoming. Derrida's later works on religion show the struggle to tackle metaphysical determinism regarding the divine—God's name—while rightly passing for an atheist. In the mode of deconstruction, Derrida shows that all words related to the divine fall short. Finally, Ricoeur, the master and mentor of Kearney from the time of his studies in Paris, presents his Christian faith as a constant question vis-á-vis the atheist critique which both purifies and challenges faith.[5] Ultimately, the French forefathers lead Kearney to depart from metaphysics, or, more precisely, to research the possibility of a return of God after the collapse of the metaphysical (ahistorical) narrative. In such a context, Kearney struggles with the concept that would allow the possibility of a return of God.

The question is: Who is this God? What is the experience of anatheism all about? Is it just a rhetorical game, a trick, a seductive religious strategy to bring God back into the discussion while using some clever wordplay developed by a trio of enigmatic French postmodern philosophers? What are the consequences of leaving the God of the past, the deemed conceptual idol who is dead? One constant question in this book concerns whether the various returns of God

---

[5] Richard Kearney, "Ana-theism: God after God," in *Phenomenology and the Theological Turn*, ed. J. McCurry and A. Pryor (Pittsburg, PA: Duquesne University, 2012), 8–11.

and returns to religion are somehow instructive for (re)discovering the meaning of Christianity after its end. As we have already noted (several times), a certain Christianity has come to its end, and we find ourselves in a peculiar situation which is "not-Christian" but "not yet non-Christian"—something I call "the after of Christianity." Does Kearney's model of religious experience, described under the rubric of anatheism, shed new light on the nature, meaning, and destiny of Christianity?

To elucidate this point, we must turn to Kearney's earlier work *The God Who May Be*, which bears the appropriate subtitle *A Hermeneutics of Religion*. Kearney opens his book with the statement: "God neither is nor is not but may be."[6] He later qualifies: "The God of the possible [is] a God who refuses to impose on us or abandon us, traversing the present moment while opening onto an ever-returning future."[7] To understand the issue at stake, Kearney leads us through a philosophical exegesis of one particular biblical pericope: the revelation of God's name in Exodus 3:14.

Kearney juxtaposes two competing interpretations of the text: the onto-theological and the eschatological. The former emphasizes the centrality of the *esse*—being as God's name—while the latter focuses on the revelation of the name as a future event: in other words, we have a Christian versus a Jewish hermeneutic.[8]

God is *Is*: Christian tradition favors this clear metaphysical understanding of Exodus, from Augustine, through Aquinas, to neo-Thomist realism. Anselm's *fides quaerens intellectum* finds an answer in a providential marriage with Greek metaphysics (to borrow the language of Ratzinger), something Heidegger would later call

---

[6] Richard Kearney, *The God Who May Be: A Hermeneutics of Religion* (Bloomington, IN: Indiana University Press, 2001), 1.
[7] Ibid., 22.
[8] We are reminded here of the discussion in chapter 1, where Lyotard distinguishes the Jewish open-ended reading from the Christian fixation on the text as it is.

ontotheology, with the pejorative meaning of reducing God to a being (*ein Seiendes*), albeit the highest being above all other beings. The eschatological reading favors translating the tetragrammaton as "I shall be what I shall be": God's name is revealed as a mission and an invitation to respond, a narrative and a promise for the future. In short, God enters history and makes room for relationships: God is a God to come.

Kearney agrees that the ontotheological, ahistorical reading misses so much of the original historical perspective of Hebrew thought. The God who comes and is coming is a God of covenant rather than a God of conceptual metaphysics. For Kearney, this signals a need to revise philosophical categories and to turn—to convert—from the perspective of *sub specie aeternitatis* to *sub specie historiae*. In sum, Exodus 3:14 reveals a transcendent God who resists the logocentric immanence of onto-theology.

Kearney does not, however, want to be as one-sided as it may first appear. The eschatological reading runs the risk of subscribing to a radical negative theology—the impossibility of saying anything about God. Too much transcendence, we may say, disqualifies the subject—the person—from relating to God. Be it apocalyptic mystical postmodernism or the pure givenness of God, Kearney is uneasy with these concepts and seeks an alternative—*metaxological*—middle, mediating way between metaphysical absolutism and apophatic relativism: a poetics of the possible God.

What is the nature of the possible? Kearney raises the question and reviews several philosophical options in order to disperse the (flawed but possible) accusation that his thinking is merely part of an elaborate metaphorical discourse.[9] First, Kearney acknowledges the important tradition of the metaphysics of the possible. Whether it be the realist version (Aristotle and Aquinas), the representationalist

---

[9] Kearney, *The God Who May Be*, 80–100.

(Leibnitz, Hegel), or the vitalist (Bergson), these approaches have one fundamental feature in common: that in metaphysics, the category of the possible functions as a subcategory of the real. In other words, the possible is already present in reality but not yet actualized.

To illustrate, I will return to my early years of philosophical studies, especially my introduction to metaphysics. Everything pre-exists in God's mind. It is all there in all its aspects. For example, I cannot foresee my fourth child. I have only three children, but a fourth is possible, and if the possibility exists, the child is already present in God's mind as a possibility. Hence, the actualization of this possibility is the materialization of the pre-existent presence in God's mind now actualized in reality—ergo, the possible is a subcategory of something already real.

Secondly, Kearney highlights the post-metaphysical interpretation of the possible which is associated with phenomenology. Husserl outlines a teleological possibility—the possible as a reason that leads to an end. This end, or aim, is not present. On the contrary, the present moment signals that it is absent and orients the expectation to the future. The possible, then, is a future that interrupts the present. Kearney nonetheless stresses that Husserl's point of view should not be misread as a kind of progressivism. Neither epistemological positivism (we are gaining more and fuller knowledge in order to know absolutely) nor political emancipation (we are building a better society) is at stake. For Kearney, the teleological perspective of phenomenology bears witness to transcendence: the possible is an invitation to set foot on the path and to remain, constantly, on the way. In Kearney's assessment, Heidegger understands Husserl's intuition and takes it forward.

The third option in approaching the possible is therefore the Heideggerian ontological reading. "Possibility stands higher than actuality," proclaims Heidegger in *Being and Time*:[10] possibility is the manner of revealing being. In other words, being reveals itself in possibility. Kearney even introduces the language of love—love for the possible and loving as possibilizing (which is how Kearney translates the German *mögen* and *vermögen*). Being possibilizes thinking, and being a conscious thinking being possibilizes being. Kearney thus sees a double belonging of loving-possibilizing: "The loving-possible is for Heidegger something that surpasses the understanding of both metaphysics and logic. It is nothing less than the giving of Being [*sic*!] itself."[11]

Fourthly, and finally, Kearney turns to Derrida's elaboration of Heidegger. Derrida's deconstruction clearly favors the notion of the possible: "*peut-être*" is a precondition of all experience. This *perhaps* possibilizes an event, that is, the coming of the future as the future—otherness, strangeness, indeterminacy. The event can never be predicted. It is impossible. Therefore, deconstruction speaks of the impossible possibility, which is not a negative theology or an apophaticism of the mind. Rather, Derrida wants to save the event of the possible (which can be whatever). The event happens as something that is both possible and impossible to anticipate. Derrida sees the interplay between the possible and the impossible as the structure of experience.

Kearney is sympathetic to each of these philosophical approaches to the possible. As we will see, his goal is not simply to repudiate metaphysics as something redundant, even though he clearly favors postmetaphysical readings. Being postmetaphysical does not necessary entail a militant antimetaphysical sentiment. Indeed, Kearney's goal is to reconsider a certain tradition of religious experience, even the tradition of Christian experience. Kearney

---

[10] Martin Heidegger, *Sein und Zeit* (Tübingen: Verlag, 1993), 38.
[11] Kearney, *The God Who May Be*, 93.

believes that the philosophical pathway leads to religious praxis and creates the conditions of possibility for the One-Who-May-Be to appear. To be precise on this point, Kearney turns to Nicolas of Cusa, whose *posse esse* (or, possibly, the neologism *possest*) seems to stand in the background of Kearney's concept. For Cusa, God is everything that is possible to be: there is nothing other than God because God is prior to all being. Cusa thus challenges the metaphysical tradition by privileging possibility over actuality. However, Cusa's *possest* is an absolute concept in which Kearney sees a totalizing category, as if everything had been predescribed from the beginning. In fact, Cusa offers a fresh language but remains locked in a metaphysical reading. Kearney suggests that this is not entirely wrong and refuses to set a binary opposition between *posse* and *esse*. Rather, like Cusa, he believes that the possibility is inscribed within being. The difference is Kearney's view on historicity. Instead of an archeological approach, that is, *posse* as a principle, Kearney suggests an onto-eschatological perspective: *esse* finds itself in the possibility of being transfigured. Combining the traditional and the postmetaphysical, Kearney comes to the conclusion, or rather the challenge, "to open ourselves to the loving possible by acting each moment to make the impossible that bit more possible."[12]

It should be clear by now that Kearney's philosophy of the God-who-may-be is not about a catchy metaphor that is responding to the unfortunate spiritual condition of our time. Nor can it be reduced to a pastoral adjustment of language appropriate to a world without traditional religious referents. The God-who-may-be is primarily a struggle with the challenge to thinking. Kearney scrupulously struggles with the question: Who comes after the God

---

[12] Ibid., 111.

of metaphysics? His notion of possibility is indeed postmetaphysical, but it is by no means antimetaphysical.

In an explicitly Christian manner, Kearney interprets the God-who-may-be by pointing to the figure of Christ. Christ opens himself to continual interpretation because his story, as both the transfiguration and the resurrection attest, cannot be closed. In this respect, Kearney positions himself in proximity to aspects of Vattimo's hermeneutical vision of nonreligious Christianity. The two philosophers are united in rejecting the wishful thinking that seeks to pin down the pure core of an historical Jesus.[13] The danger of originary purity returns in Vattimo as the avatar of love. Kearney seems to be more balanced in this respect and carefully avoids returning to anything in the past. For Kearney, it is all about the imperative of contemporary experience. And to be faithful to this experience, one needs to move from the intellectual to the carnal. Therefore, when Kearney thematizes love, he never fails to remind his readers that love is always carnal, and points to the biblical example of *The Song of Songs* as proof.[14]

The Embodied Persona

Kearney's most recent work stresses the primacy of the body, touch, and materiality.[15] For the argument here, the important lesson is to acknowledge the embodiment of religious experience, that is, the incarnated reality of everything that Kearney attempts to describe.

---

[13] Jeffrey Bloechl argues that Kearney focuses on "the Jesus of the transfiguration and not necessarily the Jesus of the transubstantiation, the passion, the crucifixion, or the resurrection. Kearney's Christology, let us then note, does not need Jesus to have actually died in order to fulfill its role within his eschatology." Jeffrey Bloechl, "Christianity and Possibility: On Kearney's *The God Who May Be*," *Metaphilosophy* 36, no. 5 (2005): 737.
[14] Kearney, *The God Who May Be*, 53–60.
[15] Richard Kearney, *Touch: Recovering Our Most Vital Sense* (New York, NY: Columbia University Press, 2021).

In this respect, Kearney radicalizes the Levinasian notion of face and turns it into his own (Christian) category: each person has the capacity to make the divine possibility incarnate and living; each person is capable of responding to the possibility of transcendence. Kearney calls this embodied faculty *persona*.[16]

The category of persona functions as a privileging of ethics, action, and experience (following Levinas) over onto-theology and metaphysics (taking a lesson from Derrida). The persona embraces the good over being and thus prefers the (eschatological) relation of one-for-the-other to the onto-theological relation of one-for-one, or the one-for-itself-in-itself.[17]

The importance of persona to the issue of anatheistic Christianity is clarified by Kearney himself when he addresses the biblical scene of Christ's transfiguration. The basic thesis is clear: "The infinite persona of Christ is not exhausted in the finite figure of Jesus of Nazareth."[18] The transfiguration functions as an interruption that holds and subverts the continuity between Jesus of Nazareth and Christ (the Messiah). Jesus Christ is the way, not a terminus. His transfiguration reveals the eschatological core of faith. We can call it *openness* toward the Messiah and his kingdom to come (which in contrast to Derrida is somewhat informed by the incarnated reality of Christ, but in accordance with Derrida is not determined by the metaphysics of presence). Hence, the transfiguration leaves us with a choice between openness (eschatology) and fixation (ontology). It provides an opportunity to discover the persona within the person or to lean toward the reduction of the person to a being among beings. Applied to the person of the transfigured one: either we look at the Christ icon who is indeed present yet is to come, or we seek to master the fetish of Christ.

---

[16] Kearney, *The God Who May Be*, 9–19.
[17] Ibid., 15.
[18] Ibid., 42–3.

In a masterful play with the intellectual heritage of Levinas, Ricoeur, Derrida—and indeed Marion—and their respective concepts, Kearney achieves a fresh, anatheistic synthesis of competing ideas by repeatedly thinking them through. However, as the concept of persona shows, Kearney proposes something original. In contrast to the deconstructive-critical movements, Kearney does not welcome the leap into radical otherness which results in "rightly passing for an atheist." *Tout autre est tout autre* leaves us with a God without a name. Kearney applauds the otherness of the other, but persona enables him to understand the excessive otherness of the other as ever firmly embodied/incarnated in concrete persons. In other words, the otherness of the other is always the otherness of someone with an identity. Once again, and this time more poetically, the other has a story, a narrative, from which we can learn about this other, from which we can guess, sense, and experience who this other may be: "Persona is the infinite other in the finite person before me."[19]

The figure of persona presents a hermeneutical phenomenology of transfiguration which sees the other as both present and absent. In short, not only the face but the persona of the other "always exceeds the limits of our capturing gaze [and] transcends us."[20] A total picture of the other—an idol, fetish, object—ruins the persona within the person. Persona creates a space, a space where we meet otherness, and where—perhaps even more importantly—the other mirrors my own otherness.

Kearney's theoretical concept of persona in his earlier work on the hermeneutics of religion is, I suggest, later translated into anatheism—an attempt to conceptualize a universal experience with the divine; an experience stretched between concrete otherness and universal sharing. The concept of persona is the trace of anatheism.

[19] Ibid., 17.
[20] Ibid., 11.

A Wager on Openness toward Otherness

As we said at the start, anatheism is a wager. Kearney explicitly calls it "a movement of return to what I call a primordial wager, to an inaugural instant of reckoning at the root of belief."[21] Yet, this return must be qualified. It is not a Platonic anamnesis. It is not a return to the premodern state of religion that was consumed by the fire of critical suspicions and postmodern liquidity. Nor is it a search for originality, anything particular in the past. Nothing could be further from Kearney than the presupposition of a paradise lost, an original mystery that would reunite everything into a coherent and rational-logical system. Kearney deals with this train of thought in his novel *Sam's Fall*, in which he dedicates much time and many pages to critiquing the quest for pure language—a universal grammar.[22] He also brings to light the tragic consequences of participating in this quest. Kearney prefers to follow Kierkegaard's repetitions that move us forward and open the new.

The "ana" of anatheism, meaning once again, repetition, does not chronologically follow atheism and theism. Anatheism as the path of return returns to the originary: "Pure attention. Vigilance. Receptivity. What Rilke calls 'the open.' The *ana-* is letting go of something, of all that you think you know, in order to open yourself to the possibility of something novel and strange."[23] Once again, this is not a search for the original but the discovery of the originary. The issue at stake is not the content of anatheism but its movement. In this sense, anatheism is a return to the condition of the possibility of faith and nonbelief: "Why is there God rather than no-God?"[24]

---

[21] Kearney, *Anatheism*, 7.
[22] Richard Kearney, *Sam's Fall* (London: Spectre, 1996).
[23] Richard Kearney and Emmanuel Falque, "Anatheist Exchange: Returning to the Body after the Flesh," in *Richard Kearney's Anatheistic Wager: Philosophy, Theology, Poetics*, ed. C. van Troostwijk and M. Clemente (Bloomington, IN: Indiana University Press, 2018), 91.
[24] Ibid., 91.

From the perspective of our main argument, Kearney's concept must be tested as the avatar of the after of Christianity. The subtitle of the book *Anatheism* reads "Returning to God after God," which Brian Treanor translates as "Recovering Faith after Faith."[25] Could we also transpose it to "Reconsidering Christianity after Christianity"?

> [Anatheism] is not an end but a way. It is a third way that precedes and exceeds the extremes of dogmatic theism and militant atheism. It is not some new religion, but attention to the divine in the stranger who stands before us in the midst of the world. It is a call for a new acoustic attuned to the presence of the sacred in flesh and blood. It is *amor mundi,* love of the life-world as embodiment of infinity in the finite, of transcendence in immanence, of eschatology in the now.[26]

Over the course of this book, we have certainly encountered similar appeals to turn away from sociological, historiographical, and purely theoretical concepts in favor of philosophical-existential movements. Kearney is clear that the existential has preference over the theoretical, but the anatheistic gesture contains two interrelated components.

First, speaking philosophically, anatheism repeats itself, for example, in a Socratic not-knowing Augustine's question about the self which becomes the question itself, in Cusa's *docta ignorantia*, and even in Husserl's epoché, which is a specific exercise in openness while bracketing prejudices and deemed foreknowledge. In short, anatheism leaves the object of a divine whose existence requires proof (theism) or refutation (atheism) and favors the moment of experience and suggests that the question of the divine is beyond all conceptualization. This leads Kearney, secondly, to the

---

[25] Brian Treanor, "The Anatheistic Wager: Faith after Faith," *Religion and the Arts* 14, no. 5 (2010): 546–59.
[26] Kearney, *Anatheism*, 166.

lived-existential aspect of anatheism, which finds its concentration in an encounter with an uninvited guest and thus with a choice: hostility or hospitality; rejecting or welcoming the other. In this decision regarding opening up or closing down the horizon of the person, faith can be born. The stranger—otherness—puts us on hold and challenges us to think anew and once again.

Ana—to think again—is *the differend* in practice, something we encountered earlier in Lyotard. Kearney recovers narratives and their credibility without absolutizing any one of them. Every narrative has a right to be heard. Every narrative must be reflected upon. This is the nature of dialogue—to think through otherness. But to be able to do this, we need to possess the faculty of imagination, that is, the ability to imagine different possibilities.

Reimagining Christianity

Anatheism as the practice of imagination is a logical continuation of Kearney's lifelong project of philosophical poetics. In *On Stories*, Kearney says: "Every life is in search of a narrative."[27] Telling stories, inventing stories, sharing stories—a communal act *par excellence*—is what makes our condition human. However, the major aspect of narratives is their performativity—the ability of an imaginary breakthrough. Narratives offer us a "newly imagined way of being in the world."[28] They allow us to see things differently. They give rise to the idea that the world can be otherwise (without necessarily knowing what this otherwise will be).

Narrative-telling is in crisis, however. Our media culture has replaced the call to say something meaningful with the need to say

---

[27] Richard Kearney, *On Stories* (London: Routledge, 2002), 4.
[28] Ibid., 12.

something now. Right now. And the crisis of imagination—our failure to tell stories, missing the point of our narrative identity—is behind the crisis of religion.[29] The power to re-create possible worlds within the world seems to have been lost. The narrative is both a world-making and a world-disclosing process, and thus there is never absolute objectivity in (hi)story. But nor is there any absolute relativism. In other words, we must search for truth even though reaching totally objective truth is impossible.[30] Being stretched between the desire for the possible truth and the impossibility of mastering it returns in Kearney's anatheism—it is the canonized experience of being religious.

Hence, talking about imagination does not mean talking about fantasy, consoling stories, or fairy tales, even though, as all parents know, these have their own powerful truth in themselves. To understand Kearney's point properly, we must read imagination as a faculty of *thinking*, that is, as a posture of being open to the possible future which may become present; being open to thinking anew. In *Anatheism*, Kearney refers to the Annunciation in the Gospel of Luke: "Mary was troubled and pondered" (Lk. 1:29). Of course she was troubled: she could not imagine that what the angel had told her would be possible. Yet she pondered and gave it all some thought. This act of thinking, naturally, is closer to the artistic *phronesis* than to the scientific *theoria* as pure abstraction.

Imagination—as living, experiential thinking—is an indispensable faculty in the realm of religion and the divine. Anatheism incorporates imagination and reactualizes it. Returning to the question of the after of Christianity, we see that anatheism issues a call not only to think again but also to reimagine Christianity. And it does not stop there. We must not forget that imagination is "an open-ended invitation

---

[29] Ibid., 130.
[30] Ibid., 149.

to ethical and poetic responsiveness."[31] We are called from thinking toward action, from thinking Christianity to living Christianity. "Or, to put it in another way," in Kearney's words, "how do atheists in a secular age respond to the question: What is to be done?"[32]

The Ethics of Anatheist Christianity

Anatheism represents the tension between the secular and the sacred—the world and religious experience. Anatheism is a crossroads, a meeting point between the secular self and the sacred other. Concern for this relationship stands at the heart of anatheism. Kearney identifies three figures of otherness—strangers, gods, and monsters—and suggests we have two ways of dealing with otherness: first, the attempt to understand, to open ourselves up, and to accommodate the experience of the other; secondly, and in contrast, the tendency to reject otherness, to close ourselves off, and to expel the other. The latter approach often wins.[33] Anatheism represents a commitment to the former: to hospitality rather than hostility.

Anatheism is not absolute openness, however, but a discriminating, reflective openness. To be "just" open, meaning tolerant or even relativistic, is not enough.[34] And here again it is imagination that plays a crucial role in solving the problem. A relationship to otherness, the very possibility of encountering the stranger, presupposes that one self establishes a relation to another self. The encounter, sometimes described in terms of diacritical hermeneutics in Kearney, is twofold: first, recognizing oneself as another; secondly, seeing the other as

---

[31] Ibid., 156.
[32] Kearney, *Anatheism*, 133.
[33] Kearney, *Strangers, Gods and Monsters*, 2–4.
[34] Ibid., 77.

another self.³⁵ This two-edged dynamism allows, later, for welcoming the other to become a part of my self, in other words, hospitality.

What functions on the individual level, also functions on the communal level. How would Christianity look after a transposition of Kearney's diacritical hermeneutics? Originally developed as a critical reaction to postmodern theory, mainly to Lyotard, Kearney sets in motion three principles: (1) phronetic understanding; (2) working through; and (3) pardon. Each of these principles seems to find its way into the concept of anatheism, or, better, becomes a part of the anatheistic gesture. Phronetic understanding is the exercise of practical wisdom, a call to reflection. Working through the situation is the *ana* of anatheism, that is, pondering the challenge again and again. Finally, pardon opens the possibility of change, the possibility of opening up that which previously was closed. Diacritical hermeneutics is all about discernment: trying to say the unsayable, that is, *saying* and using images, ideas, and narratives because they are important features.³⁶ The void of deconstruction and radical otherness is not an option. Anatheism is not the external power of overwhelming experience but the embodied experience of the self in relation to otherness. And otherness always comes to us in this world. In other words, a potential anatheistic Christianity is Christianity which is a hermeneutic of existence; a hermeneutic with practical consequences for both thought (thinking again) and action (the ethics of hospitality).

Kearney thus comes to the conclusion that the crucial and very concrete element of the anatheist way of life is the pre-emption of love.³⁷ After imagination and discernment comes a commitment—to love the other. And love is always concrete—not an abstract principle but the major issue that points to the *worldliness* of anatheistic

---

³⁵ Ibid., 80.
³⁶ Ibid., 229.
³⁷ Kearney, *Anatheism*, 47.

practice, which in turn leads to constituting community. As Kearney reminds us, Jesus did not say that his kingdom is not of *the* world, but that it is not of *this* world.

Anatheism is another name for *amor mundi*—faithfulness to the world and the challenge to contribute to truth, beauty, and the good. It should have become clear by now that Kearney's anatheism wants to be a positive (although not positivistic) concept—an alternative to the deconstruction we discussed in the preceding chapter. Anatheistic Christianity is not, therefore, a religion without religion, a radical openness to the wholly other (*tout autre*). Rather, anatheistic Christianity retains a narrative identity and therefore functions as the poetics of life: a vision of the infinite other but within the finite limits of being in the world.[38]

Anatheism concerns experience, and the very heart of religious experience. Anatheistic Christianity is therefore a form of faith that pays little attention to the content of faith. Anatheism is not a doctrine but a modal perspective. The question is: Can we consider anatheism a viable and credible mode of Christianity?

There is little doubt that for Kearney the Christian tradition serves as the privileged—but not exclusive—*locus* of anatheist religious experience.[39] Christianity is the principal reference point for all three major components of the anatheistic gesture, namely, its attempts to overcome (1) the divide between theism and atheism, (2) the concept of a radical deconstructive faith, and (3) a static, metaphysical concept of God. For Kearney, Christianity incorporates both the atheist and theist side of anatheism. Christianity goes beyond contentless deconstructive formal messianism. Finally, Christianity allowed the

---

[38] Kearney claims to borrow this phrase from W. H. Auden, but cites it from Arthur Kirsch, *Auden and Christianity* (New Haven, CT: Yale University Press, 2005). See Kearney, *Anatheism*, 189, footnote 15.

[39] Kearney discusses religious traditions other than Christianity, especially Judaism and Islam, in which he tries to point out the same anatheistic dynamic that can be applied to his vision of his own tradition, namely Christianity.

death of the God of static religion and metaphysics: a conceptual idol without existential relevance.

Christianity, in its anatheist gesture, is *the call to think* and to think again and to think of a God to come (onto-eschatology). This expectation does not, however, neglect the narrative identity of the Christian tradition. To adopt the task of thinking and to be open to what might come from this does not contradict a certain narrative thickness. Rather, it brings into play openness as a wager—the risk of hospitality—which is based on the conviction that the self finds itself engaged with the other. Analogously, Christianity that allows for new paths of thinking about its fundamental experiences comes to itself. In contrast to the authors who favor negative theological movements and recurses to the unspoken mystery, the gesture of anatheism is a worldly—incarnated—perspective. Anatheistic Christianity, or perhaps we should talk about the anatheistic component of Christianity, is therefore firmly rooted in the world and history. It is a Christianity in the world—it starts from the world and acts in the world. Kearney thus provides us with a modest perspective which suggests that the world does not exist for Christianity, but Christianity exists through the world. Anatheism is not a new master narrative but a storytelling with an open end. This end is not empty, however, but is constantly reformulated in dialogue with the tradition of thinking about the divine via imagination and interpretation.

Too Universal? Too Particular? When Poetics Fall Short

It is pleasing to engage with Kearney's thought, especially after the deconstructive and in many ways disturbing concepts of Vattimo's nihilism and Caputo's Christianity without religion. After these negative theologies, Kearney's positive proposal provides a balm for the open wounds poignantly brought to the light but now in need of care and a cure. I am convinced that Kearney's project helps us to dwell better on earth and to experience the diversity of the world as something that demands our respect. Nevertheless, does it help us to grasp the essence of Christianity after the fall of Christendom? If anatheism bears witness to God after God, will it keep carrying the message of Christianity after Christianity?

God beyond God; a God who may be; a returning God—this is powerful imagery. It raises awareness that God is given to us as a constant task of thinking; that we are never finished with the question of God. Kearney's poetical language with its overwhelming metaphors is eye-opening in this respect. Credible speech about God cannot return to the metaphysical language and dogmatic systems of propositions. Nor can it become lost in deconstructive tendencies for deconstruction's sake—a secular negative theology without God, without religion, is equally unacceptable. God is the other. And the other of God is greater, but not a kind of otherness to be completely lost within.

Confronted with Kearney's rhetorical finesse, we must not avoid a question of high theological significance: Do we expect, and are we willing, to welcome a radically different God—a stranger to come? Are we capable of assuming the risk? The anatheistic wager is neither Pascalian (because I do not have the answer, I should bet on the possibility of its being true) nor Ratzingerian (I shall act *as if* because it will make me a better person and the world a better place). Anatheism is a commitment. Or is it just a rhetorical trick? Is God after God really another God—the icon of a stranger? Or is this God another idol created according to our image? Does an anatheist God, and a poetic anatheist Christianity, really come from openness to the future, from the realm of indeterminacy and eschatological openness? Or is anatheism another attempt to return to the origin and the original purified image of God (and therefore something that comes not from the future but from a supposedly forgotten past)? What are the consequences of leaving God behind and waving *á-dieu* while welcoming God again *hors-dieu*?

The poetics of anatheistic Christianity manifests itself in a particular historical moment as an invitation to think about God once again, and from there it draws the ethics of being in the world. Anatheistic Christianity and its commitment to love—*amor mundi*—thus appear as a genuine historical process, that is, a religious experience traceable in the past (the history of Christianity), but also in general culture (poetry and literature) and even in other religious and thought traditions (in Abrahamic religions and beyond).

Indeed, Kearney makes it clear that anatheism is not Christianity but a universal experience. He even confesses:

> I would say that if I hail from a Catholic tradition, it is with this proviso: where Catholicism offends love and justice, I prefer to call myself Judeo-Christian theist; and where this tradition so offends, I prefer to call myself religious in the sense of seeking God in a way that neither excludes other religions nor purports to possess the final truth. And where the religious so offends, I would call myself a seeker of love and justice *tout court*.[40]

In other words, anatheism is a general experience; something to be found across religions and cultures—a universal point, a firm point that can move the entire cosmos toward striving for justice, righteousness, and hospitality.[41] Consequently, anatheistic Christianity is, for Kearney, perhaps a privileged but still a general experience.

No wonder Kearney hears numerous critical voices which accuse his anatheistic narrative of not respecting the particularity of religious

---

[40] Kearney, *The God Who May Be*, 5–6.
[41] Kearney is quick to remind us that the "golden rule of hospitality towards the Stranger" is not only to be found in the major religious traditions but is central to all religious and spiritual pathways. See Kearney, *Anatheism*, 150.

traditions.⁴² Is an experience which looks similar indeed the same experience? Paradoxically, Kearney comes close to the so-called pluralist position in the theology of religions which suggests that there is one and the same divine occurrence (in his case anatheism) albeit embodied in concrete traditions. Anatheism is therefore a general experience distilled from the patchwork of the religious world. Christianity bears witness to anatheism but does not exhaust it.

This critique is pertinent and addresses a weak point in Kearney's concept. In my opinion, however, one can also formulate a reverse critique: despite Kearney's tireless efforts to show that it is something universal, the centrality of love and hospitality in anatheism clearly originates in his Christian or Judeo-Christian—biblical—background. *Amor mundi*, hospitality toward the stranger, is heavily supported by biblical imagery in Kearney. In this sense, anatheism is indeed a form of Christianity: a transfigured Christianity of an ethical commitment to love. In this case, Kearney is less religious pluralist than he is open-access particularist.⁴³ This means that through Christianity and its anatheistic gesture—Christianity as the exemplary manifestation of anatheism—we can see anatheism elsewhere.

Whichever way we look at it, a universal anatheist and an anatheistic Christian run into the same problem: the others are deprived of their particularity; heterogeneity is wiped out—we are all anatheists, let's have a dialogue. This is reminiscent of a famous critique of Karl Rahner's concept of anonymous Christians to which Buddhists reply with a thesis about "anonymous Buddhism"; and all other traditions

---

⁴² See, for example, Lieven Boeve, "God, Particularity and Hermeneutics: A Critical-Constructive Theological Dialogue with Richard Kearney on Continental Philosophy's Turn (in)to Religion," *Ephemerides Theologicae Lovanienses* 81, no. 4 (2005): 305–33.

⁴³ I am indebted to Gavin D'Costa, the author of the category of *open-access exclusivism*. Originally formulated in the field of the theology of religions, I recontextualize this as open-access particularism in the context of philosophical theology. Gavin D'Costa, *Christianity and the World Religions: Disputed Questions in the Theology of Religions* (Oxford: Willey-Blackwell, 2009).

can fire back likewise. Kearney seeks to convince others that they can meet on the plain of anatheism. But they can rightly reply that they are not interested in this, in a concept founded on the Christian/ Judeo-Christian tradition, or that they do not recognize their own particularity mirrored in this universal concept.

I am convinced that Kearney would protest against being labeled a Christian open-access particularist. There is a clear desire, on his part, to find something religiously universal—the desire itself; the desire for God and anatheism as the return to this *beginning*. The *ana* of anatheism is therefore not only about "to come from the future" but also about "to come from the origin."[44] This makes Kearney even more vulnerable to the criticism of neglecting particularity. Kearney thus joins Caputo in the search for some kind of pure faith; a purer Christianity; a more originary religious posture which is universally sharable.

The question of universality is indeed an issue in our discussion of Christianity after Christendom. Late Christendom pretended to be universal and ended up in colonialism, oppression, and violence. Kearney is desperate not to repeat this mistake yet wants to retain the sense of universality. I applaud this decision but find his suggestion problematic. In Part III, I will employ the lessons we can take from Kearney but will present an alternative argument for the universal, without, hopefully, neglecting heterogeneity and particularity.

---

[44] Kearney, *Anatheism*, 99.

Postscript to Part II
After Hermeneutics

We have engaged with three extraordinary thinkers, prolific writers, and philosophers of the Christian, and specifically Catholic background, who courageously venture into the border zone between theology and philosophy. We have met their respective—postmodern—perspectives on Christianity in its present and its future. Sometimes agreeing, sometimes competing, the proposals of John D. Caputo, Gianni Vattimo, and Richard Kearney prove to be of some significance for the argument developed in this book. The after of Christianity has many facets.

Vattimo presents his project explicitly in terms of *After Christianity* and his wording is undoubtedly closest to the language and concepts in this book. Although Kearney's *anatheism* is not limited to a single religious tradition, his project certainly nudges us toward rethinking Christianity. Finally, Caputo's tireless deconstructive efforts and his *Prayers and Tears* are clearly about seeking out an "after Christianity" that is focused on its futural "to come."

Nonetheless, what at first looks broadly similar can often contain even more significant dissimilarities. This is certainly true of all three philosophers when we compare them one with the other, as well as when we relate their respective thoughts to the conceptual variations on the after of Christianity that I suggest in this book. Where do Vattimo, Caputo, and Kearney agree? On what do they disagree? What are they searching for? And how does it all differ from my position?

From a temporal perspective, Vattimo is firmly rooted in the present-day situation he calls secularization. Interested in the here-and-now, Vattimo does not align himself to unfulfilled visions and projects; rather, he analyzes the meaning of where-we-are. By contrast, Caputo and Kearney share a futural orientation, that is, a quasi-eschatological vision of religious experience in general. For Caputo, deconstruction leads to the ever open, the nondetermined, the new; something always "to come." For Kearney, hermeneutics leads to a wager on openness—welcoming and embracing the other despite the risk associated with such actions.

Regarding principles, Vattimo and Caputo are both implacable adversaries of metaphysics. Both subscribe to Nietzsche's word that God is dead and adopt Heidegger's interpretation of the event in terms of the end of an ontotheological conception of a supreme being. For both Vattimo and Caputo, metaphysics violently opposes the asking of questions because it already has the answers. In this respect, the death of a metaphysical sovereign God means emancipation. Although at one point, Kearney confesses that neither does he believe in God as a supreme being,[1] he allows for a certain possibility of metaphysical thinking: reading Nicolas of Cusa and reinterpreting his metaphysics of the *posse* in the hermeneutical gesture; even, in Kearney's opinion, the irreducible category of *persona*; the affirmation of the Trinitarian dynamism in God—this all suggests that his *God who may be* is not antimetaphysical but postmetaphysical. And just as the modern remains operative in postmodernism, so the metaphysical lingers in postmetaphysics. After all, Kearney identifies his position as onto-eschatology.

It is perhaps for this reason that Vattimo and Caputo seem to be at odds with Kearney's interpretation of kenosis. The temporary lowering

---

[1] Richard Kearney, "Anatheism, Nihilism, and Weak Thought: Dialogue with Gianni Vattimo," in *Reimagining the Sacred: Richard Kearney Debates God*, ed. R. Kearney and J. Zimmermann (New York, NY: Columbia University Press, 2015), 143.

of God, even to the point of his own death, even though it stands in service of a later majestic rising, remains a strong metaphysical concept in the eyes of Caputo and Vattimo. In contrast to Kearney, Vattimo and Caputo favor weak thought and weak theology.

However, where Caputo and Vattimo seem to be united in their passion for weakness, a great discrepancy cries out. Vattimo concentrates exclusively on Christianity. Christianity is his tradition, his story—a story/history that also, in his opinion, makes a general history possible. Even more radically, for Vattimo, Christianity is not an abstract, philosophical concept but the incarnated reality represented by the church. This sort of particularism is alien to both Caputo and Kearney, who also come from the Catholic milieu but who in their respective philosophical writings adopt a far more radical distance. Caputo and Kearney aspire to say something about religion in more general terms. Anatheism purports to disclose the general, universal, trans-traditional structure of religious experience. Christianity without religion searches for what lies *before*, or perhaps better, *beneath* religious experience.

Who are these three philosophers, then? Caputo, unlike his mentor Derrida who rightly passes for an atheist, says that he passes for a Christian (although a highly unorthodox one). Surprisingly, it is Kearney who appears to be more of a religious universalist. In his works on hospitality, however, Kearney seeks to retain more particularity than, for example, Caputo. When confronted with the other, Kearney argues, we are what we are, but we suspend our firm identities to be more welcoming and more hospitable. Caputo, in contrast, sees his Catholic origin as fully deconstructible. His identity is an historical contingency which cannot be wiped out from his language completely but equally has no essential meaning. Ultimately, I believe Vattimo to be the fairest of the three. He does not hide his Catholic-Christian identity, and confesses: Thank God, I am an atheist who believes that he still believes.

What really unites them is love. Not love for one another (there is a lot of tension), but love as a concept. When all is said and done, Caputo, Kearney, and Vattimo are practically oriented: the community of *caritas*, the hermeneutics of the kingdom, hospitality. Everything leads to the ethical. When it comes to the question of how to do a thing—*facere veritatem*—how to practice the truth in a postmodern world, Caputo and Vattimo are united in preaching a gospel of social justice. For Caputo, faithful to deconstruction, ultimate justice is undeconstructible, forever out of reach, always "to come," but this does not stop him foregoing the magnificence of bells and smells in favor of more service on the part of the church as a visible Christian community. For Vattimo, a socially oriented Christianity does not care so much about what is "to come." Rather, echoing his own engagement with practical politics as a member of the European Parliament, it cares in the here and now and delves into questions relevant to today. His down-to-earth approach nonetheless has difficulty formulating a positive program. As he himself acknowledges, he is by nature an anarchist: always *against*.[2]

Kearney's wager on hospitality does better in this respect. The carnal aspect of the anatheistic gesture is indisputable[3] Anatheism thus integrates a certain deconstructive action, as proposed by Caputo, with a set of practical consequences, as demanded by Vattimo, all woven together in a positive program of openness toward the other.

So, we may ask, what are these three upstanding seekers ultimately seeking?

Vattimo is a progressivist who does not subscribe to an illusionary future and who abandons the search for an originary Christianity. He wants to remember the forgotten and improve the present. Caputo,

---

[2] Vattimo, "A Prayer for Silence," in *After the Death of God*, ed. J. W. Robins (New York, NY: Columbia University Press), 113.
[3] Kearney develops this aspect in his *Carnal Hermeneutics* and, most recently, in his mini-book *Touch*.

in contrast, searches for a pure origin, although not in the modern version of this myth, which seeks to distil an authentic Christianity (or religion) from some of its primitive or earlier constitutions. Caputo embraces the postmodern way of going deeper—going beneath—yet without propositional content. Caputo affirms the affirmation pure. Finally, Kearney is looking for a concrete, universal experience "beneath," but affirms that this anatheistic experience is incarnated in multiple traditions in its own right.

Where do these authors lead us on the question of the after of Christianity? Kearney's Christianity is a poetics of the possible; the anatheist gesture of the ever-open wager on rethinking-through again and again. Caputo's ideal Christianity is undeconstructible, but the Christianity of the present is never fixed and is always in need of deconstruction, of autodeconstruction: it must not lose sight of the "to come," because the "to come" is more important than Christianity. Vattimo's Christianity is historical. It is history and historicity, and thus an unequivocal affirmation that a particular historical moment matters. For Vattimo, the Messiah came and is now gone. That is the message of Christianity: to embrace history and remember the weak whom we tend to forget.

Caputo's messianism leaves us without the Messiah. Kearney would perhaps most likely confess that the Messiah "may be." Kearney is an anatheist. Caputo has a passion for the impossible which oscillates between asking "Who do I love when I love my God?" and refusing to name God. Vattimo is a Christian atheist whose nihilism no longer sees a need for God but who believes that he still believes in the legacy of Jesus of Nazareth who came as the Messiah. In sum, Kearney is poetical in a hermeneutical fashion; Caputo is deconstructively theo-poetical; Vattimo is radically and kenotically down to earth.

All three proposals are in some way seductive. Each offers its own rereading of Christianity. Each proposes a highly attractive vision of—how should we say it—a better, purer, more authentic Christianity, one that pays attention to the weak, fights for justice, cares more about *doing* than *thinking* (and all this without neglecting the rich intellectual tradition of Christian thought). One way or another, all three authors declare allegiance to existing traditions. They have discovered nothing new. Their efforts could tentatively be described as a thorough anamnesis of what Christianity used to be, can be, and should be. As has already been noted, anatheism, Christianity without religion, and the after of Christianity are all seductive concepts. After all, everyone wants to be on the right side—the side of a better, more open-mined, more favorable Christianity.

The important lesson from reading Vattimo, Caputo, and Kearney is that despite relentless secularization, our cultural and intellectual tradition may be not-Christian anymore, but it is not yet entirely non-Christian. From the midst of these philosophical prospects, the question arises: Is a hermeneutical approach enough? Do these (and some other) philosophies of Christianity provide a new credibility for the Christian narrative and identity? Do these "heretical" perspectives also propose a viable alternative to a strong theological tradition? What is the theological relevance, if any, of these challenging and unorthodox relectures?

I fully appreciate the genuine attempts to take the existential aspect of being Christian and/or religious into account, but I find the hermeneutical-deconstructive-poetical approach insufficient. The authors discussed in this part of the book challenge us to remodel our Christianity, to decide what kind of Christianity we want to think and to live, but can their respective proposals be borne in the long run? Is it good to be so prescriptive? All three authors follow a classical line of scholarship: step one, critique; step two, prescription. Perhaps, this is the nature of hermeneutics. And thank God for it! Nonetheless, the task of asking questions concerning credible Christianity could, I suggest, proceed more carefully and with less haste. When we address the question of Christianity after Christendom, we are ultimately enquiring about a certain mode of being in the world, a particular modality of existence. Perhaps we have already been experiencing it. In that case, we had better examine our experience, the experience we have in the here-and-now, in order to deconstruct illusions and to live in eschatological openness. Perhaps we not only think of Christianity after Christendom, but we also live it. In the final part of the book, the voice of the theologian will be permitted to say a few words to this.

Part Three

Shaken Christianity

What shape does Christianity take after Christendom? The stage for our inquiry was set by the postmodern suspicion of metanarratives in general and the narrative of Christianity in particular, and by the postmodern critical consciousness applied to Christianity (Part I). As part of the philosophical return to the religious, various philosophers have provided novel rereadings of Christianity—a hermeneutical account of Christianity which responds to the contemporary hermeneutics of suspicion (Part II). After taking seriously a critical thesis, we analyzed a set of constructive antitheses. To complete the picture, we therefore require a synthesis. In the third and final part of the book, I will provide a proposal regarding my own sense of the after of Christianity, one which could be deemed heretical in certain circles of contemporary philosophical theology.

In Parts I and II, I closely followed the arguments of particular authors and attempted to go with them as far as possible in order to clarify their point of view and its relevance to our main question. In one way, I will follow the same methodology in Part III. I will engage in a dialogue with one theologian and two philosophers. However, unlike before, my aim here is less to describe, analyze, and interpret as it is to draw inspiration and to think with certain authors while going beyond them—to find my own voice in the debate on Christianity after Christendom.

The question of the after of Christianity not only concerns a rational account of the situation after Christendom but, more importantly, searches for a credible perspective on living Christianity in this situation. In what follows, I will address the credibility and viability of Christianity after Christendom by introducing the concept of *shakenness*. I will offer several variations on this theme. First, I will dialogue with the Flemish theologian Lieven Boeve, who developed, among other things, a theology of *interruption*. What Boeve describes in terms of theological method, I will transpose to the level of application and will ask what kind of Christianity pertains after it has been interrupted. Secondly, I will engage with the French philosopher-theologian Emmanuel Falque, who rehabilitates the notion of experience in theological discourse and designates the experience of finitude—of *being shaken*—as the first word in any credible theology. Finally, after pondering on interruptions and shakings of Christianity and of individuals, I will return to Jan Patočka, a figure familiar to us from our discussion regarding the various senses of the after (Chapter 3). Patočka's concept of *the solidarity of the shaken* will help us to (re)formulate a communitarian aspect of Christianity after Christendom; that is, an ecclesiological existence after the dis-integration of the Christendom church. Introducing one of Patočka's central concepts to the theological debate is a heretical move *sui iuris* as the solidarity of the shaken emerged in a specific historical context and under particular political circumstances,[1] and therefore tends to be discussed

---

[1] In the 1970s, during the rule of the Communist Party in Czechoslovakia (backed up by the presence of the occupying Soviet army), Jan Patočka, a retired philosopher and man of letters from the old world, stood up and became a spokesperson for Charter 77, a civil and human rights movement and one of the few organizations that dared to threaten the hegemony of the Communist regime. Patočka's short but visible public engagement earned him some unwelcome attention from the secret police and ultimately cost the philosopher his life. For more, see Barbara Day, *The Velvet Philosophers* (London: The Claridge Press, 1999), 12–14.

primarily among political philosophers and social theorists.² But I am willing to take this risk. I want the theological voice to be heard. My goal is to show that the experience of being shaken, on both the individual and the collective levels, opens the possibility of reassessing Christianity as a mode of being-in-this-world; a world which is not-Christian but certainly not yet non-Christian.

---

² See a representative collection of essays in Francesco Tava and Darian Meacham (eds.), *Thinking After Europe: Jan Patočka and Politics* (Lanham, MD: Rowman & Littlefield, 2016).

7

Christianity Interrupted: A Theological Experiment by Lieven Boeve

The after of Christianity is not only an issue discussed by philosophers of religion, but also a pressing challenge for theologians. After reviewing some philosophical relectures of Christianity, the time has come to turn our attention to the theological voice, and thus to open the more explicitly theological part of this book. In this chapter, I will enter a dialogue with the Flemish theologian Lieven Boeve, who has been developing a highly original perspective on the state and the task of Christianity in a postmodern context.

Boeve's argument is detailed in three monographs published over the past two decades: *Interrupting Tradition: An Essay on Christian Faith in a Postmodern Context* (2003), *God Interrupts History: Theology in a Time of Upheaval* (2007), and *Lyotard and Theology* (2014). A brief look at these works will give us a sense about the content of the following pages.

Interrupting Tradition is a book-length essay on how to live and communicate Christianity in a shifting context, by which Boeve means the shift from modernity to postmodernity, from a rather Christian monolithic identity to multireligiosity, from a culturally coherent society to one that is radically plural. For Boeve, these and numerous other contextual changes represent challenges which he designates as *interruptions* (a concept we will explore in greater detail later). Against such a background, Boeve arrives at his hypothesis that the only viable option for Christianity is to become an *open narrative*: to embrace the confrontation with otherness while reaffirming the uniqueness of Christianity and its narrative.

This argument is developed and turned into a full-fledged theological method in *God Interrupts History*. Again, the concept of interruption plays a central role, but this time, instead of analyzing the context and the position of Christianity within this context (designated, without any hesitation, as postmodern), Boeve focuses on the question of how to formulate plausible and valid theological claims in a situation we have described as the after of Christianity (although Boeve himself does not use this precise term). His goal is to design a theology which takes seriously the moment of interruption, that is, a theology that continuously reactualizes itself according to its confrontation with the given context. From here comes another concept originally introduced to theology by Boeve: *recontextualization*.

Finally, in *Lyotard and Theology*, Boeve makes it clear that it is the Lyotardian version of postmodernity which he finds most useful for theology in a critical-constructive way. Lyotard's critique of master narratives (which I presented in Chapter 1) is the backbone, although not always explicitly, of Boeve's attempt to recontextualize Christianity after its end. Let us examine this theological project closely and ask whether we can find here a credible theological proposal for navigating Christianity after Christendom.

Context Reinterpreted

Boeve questions a generally accepted thesis about Christianity in a secular age: the so-called secularization thesis which states that more modernization means less religiosity.[1] Of course, Christianity

---

[1] Lieven Boeve, *God Interrupts History: Theology in a Time of Upheaval* (New York, NY: Continuum, 2007), 13–29.

is no longer the leading narrative, and it is far from being a predominant identity marker in our world. Nevertheless, the relative marginalization of Christian influence does not automatically imply the reign of secularism. Boeve suggests a correction: what we have been gradually experiencing is not so much secularization (i.e., less religion), but *detraditionalization*,[2] that is, the retreat of one predominant, privileged tradition. Rather, Christianity finds itself among a plurality of narratives, identities, and fundamental life options (whether religious, secular, political, or cultural). Although Christianity and indeed Boeve's overall perspective are still largely attached to Euro-American centrism, an undeniable *pluralization* points to the limitations of a Westernized perspective. (A South American pope helps to broaden our point of view in this respect quite significantly.) As a consequence of *detraditionalization* and *pluralization*, being or becoming a Christian is a function not of an unquestioned identity transfer between generations, but increasingly of one's personal choice, a conscious decision. Boeve describes this feature under the rubric of *individualization*.[3]

In a nutshell, reducing the contemporary situation to the secular thesis does no justice to the postmodern context. If Christianity is challenged today, the situation is not either/or. Difference and otherness are not merely theoretical concepts developed and discussed in the ivory towers of philosophical departments. Plurality is a reality, the reality of so-called postmodernity, and as such, Boeve suggests, the postmodern context not only presses Christianity to recontextualize but also reveals something that is inherent to the Christian tradition: recontextualization as a continuous process that will never be completed.[4] The postmodern shift is therefore not necessarily a call for the recontextualization of Christianity; rather,

[2] Ibid., 16.
[3] Ibid., 21.
[4] Ibid., 3.

it sheds light on the essence and internal dynamism of the Christian tradition. We need to ponder on this a while.

In *Interrupting Tradition*, Boeve criticizes the cumulative models of tradition development in theology, largely because they present Christianity as a petrified, static, and ahistorical narrative in which nothing new can occur. Cumulative models of tradition function as "the elucidation and explication of what was already implicitly known."[5] From such a perspective, it is obvious that no real relationship between Christianity and its historical context can exist. Historical events and the occurrences of otherness throughout history are "mere" (re-)affirmations or negations of a truth that has already been available (even if slightly obscured). In other words, and to borrow from Heidegger, theology has its positum, and the task of theology is to unfold this given positive content or to translate it according to present needs. The world and history are the arena where this process of the accumulation of tradition takes place, nevertheless, Christianity as such remains fundamentally outside of the historical world.

Boeve juxtaposes this cumulative model of tradition with the concept of recontextualization, that is, with a dynamic perspective that appreciates history and takes it fully into account. Recontextualization implies that:

> Faith and church are not in opposition to the world, they participate in constituting the world and, furthermore, they are in part constituted by the world. Given the fact that God reveals Godself in history and that it is precisely in history that God can be known by us, history ultimately becomes co-constitutive of the truth of faith.[6]

To say this is not the same as to argue that Christianity has no other choice but to adapt itself to the given historical context and change

---

[5] Boeve, *Interrupting Tradition*, 21.
[6] Boeve, *God Interrupts History*, 7.

itself with any paradigm switch. Recontextualization is not the same as accommodation. For Boeve, it is the essential meaning of the Latin verb *tradere*, to hand down a living tradition. Like the doctrine of the incarnation and its truth (the Son of God has become a true human being), the formation of Christian tradition takes place in history and according to contextual standards. Otherwise, Christianity places itself in danger of inauthenticity. Boeve thus concludes that the result of recontextualization is not so much the *more* of tradition (as it is, in fact, in cumulative models) but rather the *differend* tradition.[7]

In other words, and this is crucial, Boeve stresses that the recontextualization of Christianity is both a descriptive and a normative category. The former is clear: recontextualization is about a confrontation with the given historical context; it brings new questions and challenges to Christianity and forces the Christian narrative to open itself. The latter, the normative principle of recontextualization, is more controversial because it calls for "a theological program in which insight into the intrinsic link between faith and context inspires theologians to take contextual challenges seriously, in order to come to a contemporary theological discourse that can claim both *theological validity* and *contextual plausibility*."[8] Hence, recontextualization translates itself into the category of *interruption*.[9] Boeve further elaborates on this intuition from a fundamental-theological perspective and differentiates between the contextual category of interruption and interruption as a theological method.

The contextual interruption of the Christian narrative follows the process of recontextualization described above. Interrupting tradition

---

[7] Boeve, *Interrupting Tradition*, 23.
[8] Boeve, *God Interrupts History*, 3 (italics mine).
[9] It was the German Catholic priest and theologian Johann Baptist Metz who introduced the notion of interruption to theology. See Johann B. Metz, *Glaube in Geschichte und Gesellschaft: Studien zu einer praktischen Fundamentaltheologie* (Mainz: Grünewald, 1977), 150.

forces Christianity to rethink how it is structured, how it presents and communicates faith, and how it understands itself and the world. It is important to note, however, that for Boeve this interruption happens dialectically as the tension between continuity and discontinuity with the Christian tradition as well as continuity and discontinuity with the world. This means that the contextual interruption not only raises challenges to Christianity, but also reveals the particularity of the Christian identity which constantly questions itself from within. In other words, the contextual category of interruption reveals the unfinished nature of Christianity and the task of thinking Christianity through again and again. This brings us to the theological category of interruption.

> Interruption is also capable of pointing to the way in which God reveals Godself in history and the way in which Christians bear witness to this reality in narratives and practices. God's interruption constitutes the theological foundation for a continuous and radical hermeneutic of the context and tradition.[10]

What does Boeve mean exactly? The crucial aspect is *otherness*. We have already seen that Boeve presents context as the other to Christianity and finds this otherness full of potential for becoming a *locus theologicus*. However, what at first sight appears to be wisdom drawn from postmodernity is, for Boeve, also the fundamental truth of Christianity: God and God's revelation is an encounter with otherness *par excellence*. The presupposition of any theological thinking makes room for interruption; even more radically, such thinking is based on such a possibility of being interrupted, this time not merely by the context but by God.

Interruption is therefore a contextual-theological category. The interruption *ad extra*, that is, from outside, forces Christianity to

---

[10] Boeve, *God Interrupts History*, 205.

recontextualize itself *ad intra*, while the interruption *ad intra*, that is, from within the Christian tradition, works as a productively critical force in the world *ad extra*. In short, interruption establishes problematicity, introduces otherness, and causes the narrative to collide with its borders. Hence, interruption is a movement of opening, and, as a theological method, it leads Christianity to becoming an open narrative.

However, before we go on to examine the proposed open narrative of Christianity in detail, there is one more thing to say about the theology of interruption. While Boeve drinks from the fresh waters of postmodern thought, it becomes clear that he is offering an alternative suggestion to, for example, the philosophers with whom we engaged in Part II. Briefly, where Vattimo sees an obvious continuity between Christianity and secularization, Boeve finds a discontinuity. Where Caputo sees a clear continuity between Christianity and deconstruction, Boeve, although drawing inspiration from Lyotard, views the Derridean deconstruction of every particularity as alien: again, where Caputo finds continuity, Boeve confirms discontinuity. Finally, where Kearney proposes a general continuity in anatheistic experience across traditions and fundamental life options, Boeve is undoubtedly at odds with any presupposed general continuities and instead affirms discontinuity between particular narratives.[11]

In fact, Boeve questions presumed continuities on the basis of his analysis of the postmodern context, an analysis which, as we have already noted, undermines the generally accepted thesis of secularization. Boeve favors postmodernity as the situation of plurality, a play of differences, and an affirmation of particularity opposed to the (still too modern) presuppositions of consensus,

---

[11] Lieven Boeve, "Theological Truth in the Context of Contemporary Continental Thought: The Turn to Religion and the Contamination of Language," in *The Question of Theological Truth: Philosophical and Interreligious Perspectives*, ed. Frederiek Depoortere and Magdalen Lambkin (Amsterdam, New York: Rodopi, 2012), 77–100.

harmony, and continuity. He expresses it quite radically (and from here comes Boeve's radical hermeneutics of Christianity): "It is not in the first instance as human beings that Christians are Christians, but it is as Christians that they are human, irreducibly determined by their particular Christian narrativity."[12] Instead of presuming universal structures of human experience, Boeve, with Lyotard at his back, prefers heterogeneity and incommensurability and holds firmly that there is nothing like a meta-perspective. On the contrary, the starting point for thinking Christianity must be its particular narrative. In comparison to the philosophical interlocutors of this book, we can conclude that, for Boeve, the postmodern interruption of Christianity leads to the Christian interruption of postmodernity.

The Christian Open Narrative

What kind of Christianity does Boeve present to his fellows in faith while acknowledging a postmodern context? What kind of narrative shall Christianity develop about God, the world, faith, and tradition? What kind of theological foundation does this narrative provide for a pluralized, detraditionalized, and individualized world—in other words, for the after of Christianity? The shortest definition Boeve would offer for a Christian open narrative runs as follows: "Our narrative is a historically and contextually determined and determinative perspective on reality."[13]

An open narrative is not a single meta-perspective guided by an existing set of laws. Rather, it is a space where the meeting of the irreducible plurality of narratives, and of those who partake in these narratives, is made possible. This means that the structure of

---

[12] Boeve, *God Interrupts History*, 39.
[13] Boeve, *Interrupting Tradition*, 93.

the open narrative combines sensitivity to otherness with critical praxis. Regarding the former, Boeve argues that the open narrative implies an awareness of a particularity that is not overwhelming and all-inclusive. On the contrary, the open narrative discovers both its limits and its discontinuities with other narratives.[14] Regarding the critical praxis of the open narrative, Boeve makes it clear that he thinks about both self-criticism and criticism of the world, that is, of what is outside the narrative borders. One question remains, however: What, if anything, does this very abstract notion of the open narrative contribute to the formation of a credible Christianity after Christendom?

To reiterate, that which is inherent to a Christian open narrative is equally inherent to any other postmodern open narrative, namely, sensitivity to otherness and the practice of critical consciousness. Boeve illustrates this point with reference to Jesus of Nazareth—Jesus' own life story and the story told about Jesus.[15] Boeve views the life of Jesus as an exercise in critical-liberating power on behalf of other humans. Think of Jesus' defense of the women accused of adultery (Jn 7:53–8:11). Instead of reducing the women to an object of juridical dispute which is predetermined by law (*litige*), Jesus opens the (master) narrative. A similar logic is at play in the purification of the temple (Mk 11:15–19), in Jesus' miracles of healing (breaking the closedness of the curse of illness), and in his liberation of the socially ostracized (such as Zacchaeus in Lk 19:1–10). Furthermore, Jesus' preaching of the coming kingdom of God is an open narrative in which parables play the key role.[16] Last but not least, Jesus' open relationship with God, whom he addresses as *abba*, father, seems to confirm Boeve's thesis.

---

[14] Ibid., 95.
[15] Ibid., 120.
[16] Boeve summarizes the instances of open narrative in the parables in *Interrupting Tradition*, 127–31.

In the same way, Boeve interprets the narrative about Jesus of Nazareth, proclaimed the Christ, who conquered death and thus broke the ultimate closedness of human life. The New Testament is full of pluralities that prevent the story of Jesus of Nazareth from being closed into a master narrative,[17] and the development of the Christian tradition throughout two millennia bears witness to the same logic of internal plurality. In other words, Boeve finds both synchronic and diachronic support for his thesis that a credible Christianity is one that holds to an open narrative.

> It would seem possible to maintain theologically that the Christian narrative can only be authentic when it structures itself as an open narrative: a narrative that allows itself to be interrupted time and again by a God who gets involved in history but does not let Godself be captured by it.[18]

In other words, it is not the postmodern context—or any other historical context—which requires Christianity to become an open narrative. The inherent structure of Christianity and its theological narrative urges us to remember that the (hi)story of Christianity is a particular instance of striving for an open narrative. Hence, when Boeve says that "the model of the open narrative is a conceptual exercise designed to explicate what it means for a narrative when it is able to integrate the critical consciousness of our times,"[19] he is formulating this statement as a theologian. Faithful to the Anselmian adagio *fides quaerens intellectum*, Boeve elaborates on the concept of the open narrative in dialogue with the author he sees as the most fruitful and thought-provoking intellectual stimulus of the postmodern world, Jean-François Lyotard (whose harsh criticism of Christianity was discussed in Chapter 1).

---

[17] Ibid., 140–3.
[18] Ibid., 107.
[19] Ibid., 92.

Lyotard certainly does not belong to the group of philosophers associated with the return to religion.[20] Why, then, does Boeve select him as an ideal theological interlocutor? My thesis is that Lyotard provides Christianity with conceptual tools for thinking about difference, otherness, and, in Boeve's application of his thought, even transcendence outside "the hegemonic and self-closing patterns of master narrative,"[21] that is, beyond what other postmodern thinkers and philosophers of religion call the problem of metaphysics:

> Philosophy is not the all-encompassing linkage of phrases according to a hegemonic rule, but is a discourse always in search of its rule. It is thus that [Lyotard] time and again strives to bear witness to the differend.[22]

It is, then, Lyotard's linguistic pragmatics that prove useful for Boeve. Let us recapitulate, briefly, what we learned about Lyotard earlier. The difference between open and hegemonic narratives is encoded in the use of language. Our existence in the world is entangled in language: everything depends on the way we link our phrases. We cannot but link; when a sentence is pronounced, another sentence must follow. And silence itself is a sentence. Lyotard's question is whether we have a freedom in linking (*the differend*) or whether we follow some predetermined patterns of linking (*litige*). And this is the critical point: hegemonic narratives are those that prescribe all linkages between phrases and offer fixed, ready-made identities, and thus demand a strong affiliation with the identity invested by the narrative. Consequently, hegemonic narratives create violent meta-discourses

---

[20] Much of the debate in the so-called continental philosophy of religion clearly seems to prefer Derrida to Lyotard. Hent de Vries's *The Return to Religion*, for example, focuses on Derrida in dialogue with Marion.
[21] Boeve, *Lyotard and Theology*, 71.
[22] Ibid., 72.

that do not allow questioning (or do so only to a very limited extent). As we have seen, Christianity is one of the prime examples offered by Lyotard because it is an overwhelming, all-inclusive, metanarrative of love.

In contrast to closed, hegemonic narratives, the open narrative bears witness to the differend. This means that the open narrative acknowledges: (1) when phrase x is followed by phrase y, all other phrases are actually excluded but virtually possible; (2) the expected linking of phrases can be interrupted, and an unexpected phrase can happen. To put it differently, the open narrative is the memory of those who are not heard. In Boeve's words, the open narrative "does not forget the event." The open narrative is a discourse that is "aware of the fact that there is a differend to be respected, even if such ultimacy is not possible because only one discourse is able to regulate."[23] Structurally speaking, the open narrative does not give up particularity; it is still a concrete narrative with its own rules, expectations, and aims. Hence, nothing is further from the postmodern vision of the differend in Lyotard than the flawed avatars of the relativistic "anything goes." The differend is the experience of conflicting plurality. It is an experience that arises whenever an attempt to close a narrative is made, or whenever injustice or exclusion is induced by something that is said. In sum, the open narrative bears witness to the differend by not forgetting those who are on the margins, who seem to be excluded, who are, in fact, outside the narrative. In some ways, the open narrative as such does not exist. It is a movement, a process, a call to remain open vis-á-vis the plurality and heterogeneity of possible narratives. According to Boeve, Lyotard uses postmodern vocabulary to phrase something inherent and intimately familiar to Christianity; namely, bearing witness to the differend.

---

[23] Ibid., 81.

Christianity: The Realized Differend

What is at stake in the differend and how does it relate to Christianity? Does Christianity not have a regulative idea that informs all linking between phrases? To be a Christian means to be a disciple and hence a follower of a narrative, does it not? This is enough for Lyotard to consider Christianity a hegemonic narrative. Boeve, however, feels Lyotard is being unjust. Despite the temptation for Christianity to close itself off, and despite the numerous historical instances of such closure, Boeve does not agree that Christianity has already found an ultimate, eternal rule for all linking of possible phrases. He argues, on the contrary, that Christianity, its history and development, is a narrative in constant search of a rule, and, even more radically, that Christianity bears witness, on behalf of God, to the event of interruption. Christianity is therefore, in fact, a model for the critique of all closing tendencies. The event of interruption reminds Christianity to remain an open narrative.

What Boeve suggests, then, is that Christian discipleship is the path of openness to interruptions; that it safeguards the possibility of the event that happens in history and in the world. Christianity thus appears as a movement—an unfinished, incomplete movement—which needs to formulate itself in order to communicate its story in the given historical conditions. Like any other narrative, Christianity must link phrases and create its discourse. However, as an instance of the open narrative, Christianity is aware of its falling short in seeking to say something ungraspable:

> Bearing witness to the differend ... means linking in such a way that the inexpressibility of the inexpressible is referred to. Here, therefore, the experience of the differend becomes the sensing of the impossible phrase: the sensing of the impossibility of the phrase

which would succeed in expressing the inexpressible—the phrase which would succeed in articulating the event.[24]

There is something in Christianity which always remains unsayable, yet something must be said. This is where Boeve radically differs from other postmodern reinterpretations of Christianity. For Boeve, there is nothing original, originary, or pure about the unsayable of Christianity. There is no Christianity without religion, no religious experience without particularity. Christianity is an open narrative because it is contaminated by language. And for Boeve, this contamination is something positive, something authentic, something to be embraced and certainly not overcome. The impossible phrase of the open narrative, the impossibility of ultimately closing itself, has the form of a question: Is it happening? Is the event of interruption happening (again)? This is Boeve's idea of Christianity—Christianity as the open narrative of an impossible phrase; Christianity as a realized differend.

Interpreting Christianity and recontextualizing its tradition is analogous to the praxis of reading the Torah in Rabbinic Judaism. The Hebrew Bible is transcribed in words without vowels, and thus the text calls, time and again, for vocalization. The narrative must happen anew and again. Applied to Christianity, the openness of its narrative is not a thing to be achieved but a movement of achieving.

The question we need to ask is whether Boeve's Christianity, inspired by the Jewish philosopher Lyotard, is not paradoxically similar to Caputo's recuperation of Derrida's deconstruction. Boeve would most likely object that in contrast to Caputo's search for a more Hebrew—a purer—Christianity, he takes the particularity of the incarnation seriously and searches for a plausible and legitimate articulation of this event.

Boeve puts forward the following assumption: "The truth of the incarnation indicates, rather, that the particular is constitutive of the

---

[24] Ibid., 87.

truth, essential and indispensable."[25] In other words, the humanity of God's Son is co-constitutive for the truth of the Christian message. The particularity of one concrete person—Jesus of Nazareth—is not an obstacle but the kernel of the Christian narrative. Hence, the incarnation functions as the principle for a credible Christianity, not only in postmodernity but in any given historical circumstances. And this credibility is realized as the always contextualized language and narrative and the imperative of keeping the narrative open:

> For Christians, God's revelation in Jesus Christ forms the hermeneutical key in this regard. … Jesus' particular humanity, concrete history and events, Christian narratives and interpretative frameworks, do not represent a stumbling block on our journey to God, they represent the very possibility of the journey.[26]

This approach to the incarnation distinguishes Boeve's hermeneutical theology from the philosophical hermeneutics of Christianity discussed in the preceding chapter. Jesus of Nazareth is not merely an exemplary instance of some potentially original Christianity which is beyond the realized Christianity. The narrative told by Jesus, a particular historical person, and the narrative about Jesus of Nazareth carried through the centuries is the principle of Christianity and represents the challenge to reformulate the Christian position always anew, although never against the background of some idealized form of pure religion.

Boeve offers a truly radical hermeneutics that defies the setting of a final interpretation—*the* Christianity to follow—because we need to reassess our understanding of Christianity again and again. Hence Boeve's daring chiasmus: "The truth of the incarnation is the incarnation of the truth."[27]

---

[25] Boeve, *God Interrupts History*, 176.
[26] Ibid., 176–7.
[27] Ibid., 175.

Before Hermeneutics

Boeve's theological-epistemological perspective provides a useful critique of the philosophical rereadings of Christianity. Moreover, Boeve's epistemological perspective saves us from the danger of dreaming about a better Christianity and projecting (dangerous) ideals into the past or the future. The problem with Boeve's theological hermeneutics, I suggest, is that it is still hermeneutics.

Boeve's proposal functions well on the level of inculturation (and the attention he dedicates to the concept of recontextualization seems to support this pastoral end). But it seems to me that there is something inherent to the incarnation which sets limits not only to the narrative openness of Christianity but also to the narrative structure as such, and that this something is beyond the epistemological perspective.

For example, when we think of the incarnation as *the incorporation*, the event signals that the center of Christianity is the body, and therefore something prenarrative, something primordial, yet something that is not originary in the sense of a purer faith uncontaminated by language. In fact, the embodiment sets the limits of another contamination, this time the existential contamination of being in the world.

We have this prenarrative, prelinguistic, bodily aspect before we think about it, before we vocalize it, before we turn it into a story; it is something like the pre-reflective *Urdoxa* of the world before we even reflect on our being-in-the-world. It agrees fully with Boeve's justifiable critique of Caputo, Kearney, and others who long for a more original, purer Christianity to which we should return. It also, however, adds a new type of criticism: Boeve's Christianity as a realized differend is a valuable but still, I suggest, highly intellectual concept. When we think of the incarnation in more raw terms, such as with the help of the German notion of *Menschwerdung*, it is possible to take a step before hermeneutics. Before the search for plausibility, legitimacy, and rational acceptance, there comes crude human experience. We should not forget that the question of credibility—the credibility of Christianity—is not merely about the credibility of its propositional statements and truth claims; rather, it should concern the credibility of lived facticity, experience, and being-in-the-world (I will unpack these intuitions in the next chapter).

To give credit to Boeve, he indeed offers a radical hermeneutics of Christianity which is, he suggests, truly radical and not reductionist, unlike the hermeneutics of Kearney, Caputo, and perhaps even Vattimo. We could suggest that Vattimo, because of his explicit appreciation of the Christian particularity, is the closest interlocutor of Boeve's theology. But where they differ is in their understanding of secularization: Vattimo finds continuity between Christianity and the process of modern secularization; Boeve presents a more complex picture. Boeve understands, reads, and interprets Christianity through the lens of recontextualization, a concept that comprises the external (*ad extra*) pressure on the Christian tradition and the internal (*ad intra*) structural movement of the same. The key notion is the category of interruption in its double sense: (1) the interruption of Christianity by otherness (the contextual category), and (2) the interruption of the Other of God, God's revelation, and God's relationship to the world and history (the theological category). Against this background—and combining postmodern critical consciousness with the particularity of Christianity's *Weltanschauung*—Boeve develops his theology of interruption.

And the theology of interruption is the driving force for reinterpreting Christianity in terms of the open narrative which is a model of identity and an affirmation of the tradition that is, according to Boeve, both contextually plausible (i.e., rationally comprehensible and justifiable from the postmodern critical perspective on religion in general and on Christianity in particular), and theologically legitimate (i.e., in agreement with the truth of the Christian tradition). The open narrative of Christianity saves the event of Christianity and protects Christianity from falling (back again) into a closed, hegemonic, and even totalitarian narrative.

Now the question is: What is Christianity for Boeve? The answer, I suggest, is that Christianity is a particular experience of interruption which leads to the open narrative of one's identity while firmly affirming this identity.

What does Boeve's theological engagement with postmodern critical consciousness tell us about the after of Christianity? Boeve's project confirms that in Christianity there is a continuous movement of pointing beyond itself. He calls this movement recontextualization, which is another name for the after of Christianity as we have presented it here. Boeve also makes it clear that Christianity is called to be in touch with the given historical context. Christianity is never without context; it is a worldly and historical religion, a living tradition. Boeve presents a dynamic Christianity which is not only sensitive to otherness but also responsive to the contemporary. Interrupted Christianity lived in an open narrative is a Christianity which is incarnated in the world and in history. It is a Christianity which makes sense of the world and of itself in the world in the form of a narrative identity. It is therefore a highly reflective, self-critical Christianity.

I suggest, however, that Boeve lays too much emphasis on the intellectual side of Christianity—the incarnation as an epistemological principle. His Christianity remains, to say it with Charles Taylor, lived too much in the head (i.e., too much as an overwhelming narrative, although aware of the critical power of the differend). Also, the linguistic structure of existence and the preference for a narrative identity misses, in my opinion, a more basic and down-to-earth structure of the human experience: the crude nature of being-in-the-world, which is a question Christianity cannot avoid. In what follows, I will argue that Christianity is, in fact, a specific mode of being in the world which even contains a prelinguistic component, that is, an aspect which is outside of language. This clash with the narrative is not about exposing something more original, something purer (as some postmodern authors would have it), but about opening something inherently human and true (that is, something in which Christianity, if it is a religion rooted in the world and in history, takes part). I am thinking particularly of the confrontation with finitude and its far-reaching consequences: the shaken experience. I do not hesitate to call it a common grammar of human existence: Christianity not merely as the experience of being open, but, more profoundly, as the experience of being shaken.

8

Being Shaken: The After Movement of Christian Life

Christianity is not a fairy-tale. Although the enduring popularity of shrines and pilgrimage honeypots and their religious-theme-park kitsch may suggest otherwise, and although the mountain of pious literature pumped out by religious organizations would appear to support Nietzsche's critique of the slave mentality, Christianity does not, contrary to the expectations of many, provide a heroic metaphysical happy ending for the human life. On the contrary, Christianity concerns a real experience—the experience of being-in-the-world.

The vocabulary of being-in-the-world carries heavy Heideggerian baggage. And although I will use post-Heideggerian phenomenology as the point of reference here, I will argue that even a particular methodological approach is capable of revealing something more general and universally accessible, although with a constant reference to Christianity.

What is Christianity? I have repeated this question throughout the book and have called numerous authors into the debate. Nonetheless, ultimately there is no other way to come to an answer than to focus on the event of Jesus Christ: the life story *of* Jesus of Nazareth and the story *about* Jesus of Nazareth. And here is the striking thing: the New Testament account of the foundational events of Christianity shows those events to be real, crude, naked experiences: human experiences with no soft landing, no safety net. The train of thought could of course be reversed: if Christianity is to be considered credible, it must concern true, real experience. Some obvious questions immediately arise: Does contemporary theology pay enough attention to the human experience? Is theology, after all, capable of shedding light on that experience? Does theology speak a credible word regarding the human condition in this world? And where should we find the source for this credible theological word?

To answer these questions, I will set into a dialogue an unlikely pair of thinkers: the French phenomenologist Emmanuel Falque, known for his proximity to the field of theology, and the Czech phenomenologist Jan Patočka, who can hardly be identified as a theologically oriented philosopher. The pair will nonetheless make a perfect match to advance my argument. In his article "Philosophie et théologie" (2006), Falque formulated the principle that philosophically and theologically speaking we have no experience of God other than the experience of human being and being human.[1] I claim adherence to this principle. Falque urges the theologian always to start with *the human as such*—human beings as they are and as they find themselves in the world. Patočka, in his own way, names the human experience as *being shaken*. The thesis to be tested in this chapter is that Christianity represents the internalization of this fundamental, individual experience of being human; even more radically, that the core of Christianity, manifested in the situation after Christendom, is the experience of being shaken.

Being shaken is the universally accessible experience of and the reality *tout court* for every single human being, although the narratives concerning this experience may differ according to the religious, cultural, and sociopolitical context. The reason for this is that the experience of being shaken, even though there is no way to reflect on

---

[1] Emmanuel Falque, "Philosophie et théologie: Nouvelles frontières," *Études* 2 (2006): 206. The mantra is repeated in Falque, *Metamorphosis of Finitude*, 6.

it other than in words, concepts, and language, is actually something prereflective, prenarrative, and even extra-narrative.[2] This is why phenomenology provides invaluable insights that remain hidden or at best out of the spotlight in the hermeneutical readings and rereadings of Christianity. To explicate the idea of being shaken, I will thematize the intrinsic link between the human situation of finitude—the essential source of existential shakenness—and Christianity as a specific mode of being-in-the-world that is characterized by unavoidable finitude. In doing this, I set the goal of establishing a common grammar for the voice of theology and existential reflection on the meaning of being human, and thus of articulating what I see as both a rational and a credible approach to Christianity after Christendom.

Grappling with Finitude

Philosophers, particularly phenomenologists, who describe appearances in the world, find nothing strange in saying that we are all human beings, and in immediately adding that as humans we experience finitude. Bluntly, our human situation is the situation of finitude. We have no choice other than to confront ourselves with the inescapable being-toward-death. We fight meaninglessness and search for meaning from within the experience of being stretched between birth and death.

Religion and philosophy are two of the traditional ways of coping with finitude.[3] Philosophical rationalization is swiftly complemented by religious consolation: both ways provide hope and, perhaps,

---

[2] Emmanuel Falque, "Outside Phenomenology?" *Open Theology* 8, no. 1 (2022): 315–30.
[3] "The history of philosophy may have consisted of nothing more than the deepening and universalization of the concept of finitude." Jean-Luc Marion, *Reprise du donné* (Paris: PUF, 2016), 152.

faith to carry on living life (which, ultimately, no one survives). Paradoxically, in their respective ways, philosophical and theological traditions have expended significant effort in seeking to flee from the burden of death and finitude. Starting with Socrates, philosophers have rationalized and reversed the notion of the pressing inescapable reality. Theologians, for their part, have also developed sophisticated but competing strategies for defying the inevitable.[4] The Pelagians, for example, saw suffering and self-policing obedience as virtues that will grant salvation (i.e., eternal life after death); Origen on the other hand understood human sin as grave and irreversible corruption, but that divine mercy proved even greater and therefore salvific. The former attributed too much to the human and too little to God; the latter gave everything to God and too little to the human. The result was the same: flight from finitude, or the recuperation of finitude under the rubric of salvation and its integration into the Christian narrative.

Interestingly, more recent philosophical and theological traditions have exercised a complete about turn and seem to have immersed everything almost unequivocally into death. Existentialism, often very close to nihilism, argues that we are driven toward death and will be nothing: the world is the border (*Schranke*) of our existence and to step out of this strange Platonic cave is to enter the void (*Nichts*). The so-called death of God theologies annihilate the traditional idea of transcendence: the only honest talk of God is silence. The question of God is "so last year"; today, the theme is the *death* of God and our place in the world after experiencing this irreversible loss.

Christianity tends to forget that Jesus of Nazareth—proclaimed and confessed the Christ—experienced, suffered, and went through

---

[4] Emmanuel Falque, *The Guide to Gethsemane: Anxiety, Suffering, and Death*, trans. G. Hughes (New York, NY: Fordham University Press, 2019), 8–9.

finitude. Christmas and Easter—the joy of the birth and the victory of the resurrection—sometimes obscure the fact that *there is*, on the one hand, anxiety vis-á-vis Jesus' own death (Golgotha), and on the other, compassion, or perhaps better, solidarity with those experiencing shakenness in their being (such as the events surrounding the death of Lazarus in Jn 11:1–44). In numerous ways, therefore, Jesus of Nazareth, just like any other human being, was subject to finitude, and being in relationship with the God of Israel did not prevent him from being existentially shaken.

Christ and Finitude

Falque begins his *Guide to Gethsemane*, a philosophical meditation on the death of Christ, with the bold statement that there is no specific Christian meaning to facing finitude. First, we are all, including Christ, human beings.[5] Falque reminds us of the words of the French Catholic poet Charles Péguy: "The Christ once feared to die."[6] Falque's programmatic statement is directed first and foremost against Heidegger, to whom Falque is indebted for his view on finitude, but who at the same time offered an unjustly reductionist interpretation of Christianity. For Heidegger, there is no genuine understanding of finitude in Christianity because, as he argues, Christian theology already interprets finitude from the standpoint of life. In other words, Heidegger suggests that Christianity is less than honest in its account of finitude because it already possesses a solution: the afterlife. For Heidegger, this is like pretending to ask the question but already knowing the answer.

Falque agrees that Christianity has a propensity for erasing finitude. Nonetheless, the problem lies in a misplaced association of finitude

---

[5] Ibid., 7.
[6] Ibid., 34.

with the concept of sin. If sin is presented as the effective cause of finitude, naturally there follows a need to overcome finitude as a moral evil. On the symbolic level, the absence of God indeed equals death. But on the ontological-existential level, Falque demands that sin be uncoupled from finitude.[7] The key is a proper understanding of the concept of sin. Instead of the mainstream view that sin means disobedience (in the moral sense), Falque argues that sin is "the auto-enclosure of the self by the self."[8] A second aspect of sin is not accepting the self as oneself. Here, Falque refers to Gen 3:5 where the serpent tempts the human, saying "You will be like God." The combination of these two points leads Falque to conclude that the true nature of sin is in fact the nonacceptance of finitude and therefore a turning away from the human condition. Sinful transgression is adhering to the illusion that finitude is a kind of imperfection in being human. Theologically speaking, the rejection of finitude—an ever-present temptation—is an expression of a distorted image of God in the human being. Hence, theology cannot undo the precariousness of being with any simple answers but must deal with the human condition as given.

Falque self-critically admits that Christianity has significantly deviated from placing finitude in the center of its thought. Interestingly enough, he finds a particular philosophical cause for this, namely the Cartesian pre-emption of the infinite, which infected not only modern philosophy but also theology. The idea that the infinite is somehow originary and that it is possible to draw some knowledge about finitude from the concept of the infinite is, in Falque's opinion, deeply flawed: "The contemporary theologian, like the philosopher, needs to take finitude as the first given. Finitude does not summarize a doctrine, but simply sums up the most ordinary existence of all human beings."[9]

---

[7] Ibid., 11–12.
[8] Ibid., 12.
[9] Falque, *Metamorphosis of Finitude*, 13.

Falque clarifies his position by distinguishing between finitude and the polar opposites of the finite and the infinite. In short, finitude is not the same as the finite. The finite/infinite dyad refers to the limits of human existence and thus represents the ontic. As Descartes put it in his *Meditations*, "I manifestly understand that there is more reality in infinite than in finite substance, and that therefore the perception of the infinite in me must be in some way prior to that of the finite: the perception of God, in other words, prior to that of myself."[10] For Falque, this is a dubious *postulat secret* that is present in both philosophy and theology. Why should any notion of the perfect God precede my finite being? What is our ordinary experience? True, on the one hand, we have a sense of certain limitations of being human (with the moment of death as the ultimate limit). But on the other, we cannot but start from the situation of being in the world; that is, from within our finitude—the facticity of being-there (*Dasein*). Hence, Falque argues that finitude refers to the ontological: the unsurpassable and the first given.[11] Finitude is not the limitation of being but the horizon of being. Our experience, before rational reflection takes place, is that *there is* finitude, which resists rationalization, aestheticization, consolation, and so on, because it is always "my" finitude. In other words, no one can take my place; no one can remove the burden of finitude from my shoulders: "Finitude is happy simply with 'Being-there,' facing death, and is definitively anchored in an existence that is devoid, at least to begin with, of an elsewhere."[12]

Falque names this situation *the impassable immanence*, which implies grappling with finitude on the horizon of time and space (being-in-the-world) without a hasty—theological—flight from

---

[10] René Descartes, *Meditations on First Philosophy*, trans. M. Moriarty (Oxford: Oxford University Press, 2008), 33.
[11] Falque, *Guide to Gethsemane*, 16.
[12] Ibid.

the ontological condition of being human to some supernatural fulfillment.[13]

One can easily object that Falque applies Heidegger's reading of finitude as normative.[14] It is certainly true that the Heideggerian line of thought plays an important role in the articulation of Falque's point, but I suggest that here, Heidegger's depiction of finitude—the analytics of *Dasein*—is used as the entry point for exploring the structure of human experience,[15] particularly the experience of Jesus Christ, who is not excluded from experiencing finitude and so bears witness to being shaken.

From the Christian perspective, Jesus Christ is the model and paradigmatic example of being. That is, the image of the incarnated Son of God is the instance *par excellence* of what it means to live the impassable immanence—finitude. Christ grapples with finitude simply as a human as such:

> Could we not say that Christ would also for his part really have lived through anxiety when faced with *mort tout court*, not as an accident of Creation, or a product of the supposed Fall, but as the total and definitive assumption of human finitude given to us by God.[16]

"*Eli, eli, lama sabachtani*," the cry from the cross, is not so much a kenotic word concerning the weakness of God (as hermeneutical

---

[13] Falque, *Metamorphosis of Finitude*, 15–20.
[14] For a critique of Falque's privileging of Heidegger's conception of finitude, see, for example, Barnabas Aspray, "Transforming Heideggerian Finitude? Following Pathways Opened by Emmanuel Falque," and Victor Emma-Adamah, "The Sense of Finitude in Emmanuel Falque: A Blondelian Engagement," Both in *Transforming the Theological Turn: Phenomenology with Emmanuel Falque*, ed. M. Koci and J. W. Alvis (London: Rowman & Littlefield, 2020), 163–74 and 175–86 respectively.
[15] I offered an extensive evaluation of various critiques addressed to Emmanuel Falque, including a critique of his preference for Heidegger, in Martin Koci, "Phenomenology and Theology Revisited: Emmanuel Falque and His Critics," *Revista Portuguesa de Filosofia* 76, no. 2/3 (2020): 903–26.
[16] Falque, *Guide to Gethsemane*, 47.

rereadings of Christianity would suggest). The real meaning of this shocking event is human and is revealed when the methodological maxim "We have no other experience of God but human experience" is applied.[17]

"My God, my God, why have you forsaken me?" (Mt 27:46) explicates the situation of being in the world, the precarious situation of being human: being shaken. The proper way to introduce kenosis into this debate is to understand it as the kenosis of meaning, and thus the possibility of being confronted with nothing—the meaninglessness of the impassable immanence. Kenosis means to be shaken; and to be shaken is to be human as such. But this shakenness by no means affirms meaninglessness. Being shaken does not equate to resignation to the death sentence pronounced over life. On the contrary, being shaken reaches out to interrogate finitude. This is why I prefer different wording from Falque's language of assumption regarding Christ's finitude. The words and deeds of Jesus of Nazareth—his being in the world—*explicate* the given of finitude. Christ makes finitude visible. One must immediately add, nonetheless, that he also brings this shakenness of finitude into a relationship to God, and hence introduces the possibility of transforming finitude. Christ embodies the experience of being shaken, but his life story (and the subsequent story about Christ's story, which makes Christian history) is the blueprint for an interpretation of the experience of being shaken. Phenomenology precedes and meets hermeneutics.

Christianity introduces something original to living finitude and reflecting on it. In contrast to Heidegger and Descartes, the Christian grappling with being is embodied. What for philosophers operates mostly on the level of consciousness, for Christianity is all about the flesh, the body—the incarnation—personal existence as the carrier

---

[17] Falque, *Metamorphosis of Finitude*, 15.

of finitude.[18] Grappling with finitude—being shaken—is not merely about meditation and the inner life of the soul. It is a crude life searching for a way of living. The Christian internalization of being shaken makes Christianity less a system of faith and more a mode of being—a way of existence in the world.

The foundational event of Christianity does not flee from finitude; the New Testament testimonies about Jesus of Nazareth do not avoid it. The events of the first Easter—Golgotha, the cross, the passion of Christ—make finitude truly visible. But we should not forget that the life story of Jesus of Nazareth begins with his birth, and everyone stretched between birth and death is old enough to die. The incarnation fully embraces finitude. There are many other instances of the reality of finitude in Scripture. The story of Lazarus is one: Lazarus who is raised from death by Christ but not deprived of his finitude (Jn 11). The whole story is, in fact, a lesson about the impassable immanence. How else are we to explain Jesus' initial refusal to go and see Lazarus? Why do Lazarus's sisters insist that "If you were here, our brother would not have died?" The story explicates the fact of finitude and reveals the situation of being shaken.

> Only the *positiveness of finitude*, understood as realized within temporality by the future (death), and independent of all considerations of the finite (the insufficiency of man), or of the infinite (the plenitude of God), can tell us what there is of the Being-there of man (*Dasein*).[19]

It should be clear by now that we are not primarily concerned with the psychological fear of our inevitable death (although that is always present). Grappling with finitude points to an existential struggle, it touches the very being of being human, and opens the space

---

[18] Falque, *Guide to Gethsemane*, 64–7.
[19] Falque, *Metamorphosis of Finitude*, 18.

of shaking. Grappling with finitude is not merely "being scared" (*erschrecken*); it means, and the event of Christ confirms this, "being shaken" (*erschüttern*).

The Christian Experience of Being Shaken

Again, Christianity is not a fairy-tale. On the contrary, Christianity manifests the crudeness of being in the world, but without remaining enclosed in itself. Christianity constantly points beyond itself, to the movement of the after of Christianity. Yet this movement happens from within finitude. The after of Christianity constitutes a middle way between the extremes of fleeing from finitude and adoring the human situation of being toward death. And I cannot put enough emphasis on the word *way*. Does it sound paradoxical, or perhaps even heretical? Christianity and finitude—are those not opposites? For Nietzsche, who accused Christianity of exchanging the life that happens in this world for a second-rate reward in heaven, this would most likely be the case. The same would undoubtedly apply to Marx's critique of Christianity as a painkiller, a kind of sedative, an opiate, useful for surviving this doomed world until we leave it at death (and, according to the Christian message, join the afterlife). However, although the critique of the so-called masters of suspicion has some value for Christendom, for its self-reflection, and should not be readily dismissed, it misses the core of Christianity, namely engaging with the experience of being shaken. This is the human condition, Falque says, a condition that is fully adopted and embraced by Christianity.

I will now return to my dialogue with Jan Patočka, a phenomenologist who was always at great pains not to be mistaken for a theologian. Patočka is aware of the pitfalls and blind spots of Christendom and is not a million miles from the critique mentioned above. He has no room for belief in immortality, in a life that succeeds this life, and resolutely dismisses this possibility as a cheap metaphysical happy ending.[20] Furthermore, it is not entirely clear what Patočka has to say about the question of God. He is certainly not interested in entering the debate about the existence of God: he sees these discussions as flawed metaphysical speculations. Although this should not be taken as a decisive statement about the plausibility or implausibility of faith in a personal transcendent agent, it is a logical position for a philosopher who confesses that he "must always remain walking on earth … without accepting any orders from God."[21] Nor is Patočka interested in Christianity's moral-ethical legacy. The Social Gospel is insufficient. In Kierkegaardian fashion, Patočka stands in direct opposition to a religion of enlightened reason and moral order which constrains the individual within an anonymous community.[22]

Despite all this criticism, or perhaps because of it, Patočka considers Christianity one of the most important movements in the world. When I associate the concept of movement with Patočka's view on Christianity, I am not thinking about a random group of people tied together by a certain set of convictions, beliefs, and goals. The movement Patočka has in mind is an existential movement, an Aristotelian entelechy moving from point A to point B and experiencing the change—both the internal and the external change. In his own words: "Christianity remains thus far the greatest, unsurpassed but also un-thought-through élan that enabled humans to struggle against decadence."[23] In this sense, Christianity is a movement, perhaps *the* movement, of human existence.

---

[20] Patočka, "Čtyři semináře k problému Evropy," 403.
[21] Patočka, "Theologie a filosofie," 19.
[22] For more on the negative delineation of Patočka's Christianity, see Ludger Hagedorn, "Beyond Myth and Enlightenment: On Religion in Patočka's Thought," in *Jan Patočka and the Heritage of Phenomenology: Centenary Papers*, ed. E. Abrams and I. Chvatík (Dordrecht: Springer, 2011), 245–62.
[23] Patočka, *Heretical Essays*, 108 (translation modified).

In what we may now consider a somewhat politically incorrect approach, Patočka considers Christianity the only religion worth his attention.[24] However, one needs to bear in mind that the reason for this Christo-centrism is not theological (supersessionism, exclusivism), or political (imperialism, colonialism), but philosophical in nature. Christianity, as Patočka understands it, equips the human being to accept, do battle with, and, most importantly, move within the world while being shaken.

I used to read Patočka's surprising thoughts on Christianity as an attempt to respond to Heidegger's challenge that we have not yet started thinking,[25] and to suggest, therefore, that Christianity may be helpful in disclosing the real potential of (philosophical) thinking because it is oriented toward individual existence situated in the world of appearances and yet takes seriously the need to think through—to offer interpretations—anew and again; to think through what remains unthought.[26] I am convinced about the validity of this train of thought, but now see the need to enlarge this perhaps overly intellectual perspective with a perspective that turns our attention to the embodied—to the crude reality of being in the world.

Patočka's vocabulary of caring for the soul associated with Christianity is deceptive: as if the movement of Christianity was in the line with the traditional point of view that privileges the spiritual over the embodied. And indeed, one of the meanings of caring for the soul is an intellectual, intentional practice: "Care for the soul

---

[24] In earlier work, I contended that Patočka does not place Christianity on a pedestal, above other religions. I was wrong. Erin Plunkett rightly argues that Christianity, for Patočka, is indeed the only religion worthy of consideration. Erin Plunkett, "Review of *Thinking Faith after Christianity* by Martin Koci," *Phenomenological Reviews* 7 (2021): 53.
[25] Martin Koci, "Christianity after Christendom: Rethinking Jan Patočka's Heresy," *The Heythrop Journal* 63, no. 4 (2022): 717–30.
[26] John D. Caputo has recently developed a similar interpretation of faith as a form of thinking and thinking as a form of faith. See John D. Caputo, "Thinking with Faith, Thinking as Faith: What Comes after Onto-theo-logy?" *Open Theology* 8, no. 1 (2022): 237–47.

means that truth is something not given once and for all, nor merely a matter of observing and acknowledging the observed, but rather a lifelong inquiry, a self-controlling, self-unifying intellectual and vital practice."[27] In this sense, Christianity represents a certain school of thinking: an intellectual activity of reflecting on the world in its inherent problematicity. Perhaps, one can say that to be Christian means to materialize the vocation of thinking. Yet, when this is said, an obvious question arises: Thinking what? Is the practice of Christian thinking as realized care not merely *l'art pour l'art*, a useful intellectual exercise but one with no practical relevance? On the contrary, as we have argued several times already, the sense of the after of Christianity contains a truly concrete experience—the experience of finitude, the human condition of being there in the world, that is, being situated in time and space. Thus, thinking meets being. And being (situated in the world) precedes thinking. In short, the answer to the question is: Thinking being shaken.

Care for the soul is care for the self that is realizing its finitude. And finitude comes before reflection. In other words, Patočka urges us to start thinking from the human per se, from within the human condition of being shaken. And here we find the importance of Christianity, which he sees less as a religion and more as a movement of being which internalizes this experience. This is the principal reason Patočka does not hesitate to claim, quite boldly, that Christianity is unsurpassed and unique—for Christianity knows about finitude; it feels finitude and it lives and thinks through being shaken.

Patočka's later writings circle around this religionless and perhaps even heretical understanding of Christianity, although he makes much effort to speak somewhat figuratively, without, for example, explicitly naming Christ. But Patočka's intention is not to write theology.

---

[27] Patočka, *Heretical Essays*, 82–3.

Rather, he is sincerely interested in conveying what he finds valuable for the battle against decadence; something he finds in Christianity, even though his time was no less post-Christian than ours. Kenosis and conversion are two (theological) terms of high importance in this respect.

Kenosis and Conversion

Kenosis has been a highly favored term in recent philosophical reflections on religion. I have already mentioned Vattimo, Caputo, and Kearney, for whom kenosis plays an important role in, respectively, conceptualizing a weak God, constructing a radical theology after metaphysics, and displaying a preference for the possibility rather than the actuality of God. I could have mentioned other representatives of kenotic philosophy and theology, such as the death of God theologies or radical political theologies. The point here is not to discuss these schools of thought but to raise awareness of the vast debate concerning kenosis. Does Patočka belong to any of these camps?

Traditional teaching on kenosis finds its keystone in the hymn from the Apostle Paul's letter to the Philippians:

> Who, though he was in the form of God, did not regard equality with God something to be grasped. Rather, he emptied himself, taking the form of a slave, coming in human likeness; and found in human appearance, he humbled himself, becoming obedient to death, even death on a cross.
> (Phil 2:6-8)

The Son of God accepts the role of the ultimate slave and is executed by the most humiliating method available at the time. And indeed, kenosis as humiliation—descending from the high of glorious divinity—is the mainstream understanding of the concept: God humbled himself and refused to use his omnipotence to prevent the cruel fate of Jesus of Nazareth.[28]

The philosophical debate concerning kenosis lays great weight on the process of God's emptying, on the weakening of God, who makes Godself nothing and many times ends up as nothing. Caputo says that God does not exist but insists; Kearney allows a God who may be, but a God who is kenotically emptied; Vattimo's understanding of God's kenosis leaves him without God, although with charity realized in the Christian community.

Patočka changes the focus by interpreting kenosis existentially. He does not name Jesus of Nazareth explicitly because he is interested—phenomenologically—in the structure of experience—the meaning of kenosis. *Keneo* and *heauton ekenosen*—to empty and to empty oneself—refer to the individual life, to the human per se. For Patočka, kenosis manifests the depth of being in the world; it is the touch of crude life at its absolute limit.[29] Kenosis is the experience of nothing; the experience that there is nothing to hold onto. Patočka explains this enigmatic perspective with the help of a biblical reference we have met before, from the Gospel of Matthew (and its allusion to Psalm 22):

> Why have you forsaken me? The answer lies in the question. What would have happened if you had not forsaken me? Nothing would have happened. Something happens only when you forsake me. … He has forsaken me so that there would be nothing, no thing that I could still hold on to.[30]

For Patočka, the question says it all. Kenosis is this question. But before the question arises in the mind, there is experience, the human condition, a peculiar situation of being in the world: my situation, the situation no one can take in my place. Despite all the relationships,

---

[28] Emilio Brito, "Kenosis," in *Encyclopedia of Christian Theology*, ed. J.-Y. Lacoste (New York, NY: Routledge, 2005), 853–6.
[29] Patočka, "Čtyři semináře o problému Evropy," 392.
[30] Ibid., 413.

despite all the being-with, including, for a religious person, being-with God, the self finds itself on its own. Ontologically, nothing can change this; nothing can prevent it; nothing can save the self from bumping into this emptying experience of existential nothing. Now we see it: kenosis is grappling with finitude. It is the experience of being shaken. It is "my" experience of being shaken.

Christ's kenosis does not, therefore, primarily communicate the story of a humiliated God. In the first instance, Christ experiences engagement with finitude and finds himself fully in the peculiar situation of being human, the human condition as such: being shaken. The event of the crucifixion is, then, a revelatory event: the manifestation of the ontological condition of being shaken.

The experience of Jesus of Nazareth manifests the structure of human experience and shows that there are no easy solutions and no exit from human finitude. Christianity manifests the pressing character of being shaken and engages with it. Patočka appreciates Christianity because it does not deviate from the hard fact of being. It goes to the crux (literally) and carries the weight of being in the world. Yet, there is more. In contrast to modern existential philosophies, the result is not despair and anxiety. Engaging with being shaken, recognizing the human condition, accepting and incorporating it, opens the space for a step forward: conversion.

Because Christianity grapples with finitude and incorporates the experience of being shaken, Christian conversion represents an existential possibility for every single human being without undoing the ontology of being human. Christianity remains standing on the earth, yet this does not prevent it, to use Patočka's words, from introducing a transubstantiation of life.[31] Here Patočka continues in his heretical thinking, this time directed not only toward Christianity

---

[31] Patočka talks about the concept of transubstantiation in, for example, Jan Patočka, "Prostor a jeho problematika," in *Sebrané spisy Jana Patočky, Fenomenologické spisy III/2*, vol 8/2 (Praha: Oikoymenh, 2016), 49–50.

but toward philosophy itself. For Patočka, Christianity is the conversion of philosophy. Not a religious conversion, a turn to God or to some doctrine of faith, or anything like that. What Patočka means is that Christianity can teach or remind philosophy about the weight of finitude and consequently about the meaning of being as being shaken. Of course, after all the philosophy of the twentieth century and its death-drives and *Sein zum Tode*, Patočka's suggestion could come as something of a surprise. Does Christianity bring anything new in this respect?

We need to understand Patočka's call to conversion in its proper chronological setting. Patočka understands the creation of philosophy—ancient Greek philosophy—as the beginning of history. It was the Socratic question that opened the possibility of turning from the clutches of fate and myth to an historical life of individual and collective existence. Philosophy is the first historical conversion. Philosophy is care for the soul.

However, philosophy (and again Patočka is thinking of ancient philosophy, although we could also apply his critique to a number of later philosophical schools) and its caring for the soul has a tendency to elevate the spiritual at the expense of the carnal, the embodied—the human per se. Thus, for Socrates, death is not to be feared as it represents liberation of the soul from the imprisonment of the body. The scene from Plato's dialogue *Phaedo* which depicts Socrates' passing away from this life and this world should not be compared to Christ's crucifixion.[32] And this is Patočka's point: philosophy (both ancient and modern) flees too often from finitude. It may allow for a certain intellectual shaking (doubting, problematizing, asking pertinent critical questions), but forgets about the existential—ontological—condition of being shaken.

Christianity represents the second conversion—the conversion of philosophy that remembers faithfulness to the world. Christianity

---

[32] Krzysztof Michalski, *The Flame of Eternity: An Interpretation of Nietzsche's Thought* (Princeton, NJ: Princeton University Press, 2007), 75–89.

incorporates the experience of being shaken. Even more radically, being shaken is at the center of Christianity as much as it is the inherent experience of the Christ event. The drama of personal existence is made explicit in Christianity and its foundational narrative which emancipates the human person from the determination of myth/religion, from the *sophia tou kosmou* of metaphysics, from the primacy of rational insight. Christianity, however, redirects attention to the inner life of individual existence and its internal conflict.[33] Nonetheless, this movement of grappling with being shaken is never finished. Which is why Christianity remains not only great and unsurpassed but also un-thought-through. The challenge reactualizes itself in the given historical conditions anew and again. In a certain sense, Christianity is always after Christianity.

The Lived Experience of Being Shaken

What remains of Christianity after Christianity? In a personal communication with his friend Josef Souček, a prominent Czech Protestant theologian of the time, Patočka once wrote that the important thing was "not only to live faith, but also to think it."[34] Hence, or so we can draw from thinking with and beyond Patočka, Christianity returns to where it began: the after of Christianity is back and it is a philosophical way of life (*vita philosophica*) without all the confessional baggage that obscured its real potential.

"Could Patočka's authentic Christianity be, after all, something like this? A process in which there is no ultimate, absolute end to reach, but where the goal would be reached in every moment?"[35] Perhaps. And for this reason, numerous interpreters find difficulty in

---

[33] Patočka, *Heretical Essays*, 107–8.
[34] For more on this unpublished correspondence, see my *Thinking Faith after Christianity*, 1.
[35] Ivan Chvatík, "Rethinking Christianity," 324.

linking Patočka's rapprochement with Christianity with any kind of theological thinking or, God forbid, theological practice. In Patočka, the incarnation translates itself as *Seinsereignis*. It therefore has philosophical not theological significance. The resurrection translates itself as the transformation of the *nihil* into the search for meaning. Again, this is a philosophical reading of Christianity and by no means a theological proposition. At best, standard interpretations hold: Christianity is a certain school of thinking, a way of reflecting on our being in the world.[36] The task of thinking Christianity philosophically and the challenge to do so seems to be a plausible conclusion.

Hence, the after of Christianity is about contemplating the world from the perspective of the human per se; from a default position of the Godless world as it is mirrored in our general experience of finitude without contamination from the metaphysical structure of religion. Some theologians would designate such a theory of Christianity as heretical and confessionally unorthodox because this Christianity seems to resign on Revelation. Other theologians may find Patočka's position totally acceptable, with nothing heretical or even surprising to say. After all, the events of the incarnation, the crucifixion, and the resurrection bear witness to a serious dealing with human experience on the part of Christianity. And philosophers, as highlighted above, are not interested in Patočka's potential contribution to theology. If there is anything heretical, it is the effort to turn Patočka into a Christian thinker (as Derrida, for example, once attempted to do).[37] Patočka's prime interest was hardly to help the theologian, but philosophers and theologians can perhaps agree that Patočka's challenge lies in the task of thinking the condition of being shaken, and Christianity is instrumental

---

[36] Ultimately, the situation is the same in the scholarship dedicated to a particular philosophical figure such as Jan Patočka and the overall field of the so-called continental philosophy of religion: the archivist mentality seems to run the discourse. I critically addressed this problematic in Martin Koci, "After the Theological Turn: Towards a Credible Theological Grammar," *Open Theology* 8, no. 1 (2022): 114–27.

[37] Koci, *Thinking Faith after Christianity*, 192–8.

in this respect. Philosophy reflects on this under the rubric of finitude and its possible transformation, in which Christianity plays only an illustrative role. Theology reflects on the same matter under the rubric of transcendence as the actual transformation, and Christianity remains the essential driving force here. In one way or another, Christianity, as a philosophical way of life, has a specific content of *thinking being shaken*.

Whichever approach we prefer, I find myself feeling uneasy about one thing: philosophers and theologians alike seem too often to privilege the intellectual structures of *thinking* Christianity after Christendom. To recall Charles Taylor's diagnosis from his *Secular Age*, Christianity remains too much in the head. And for Patočka, perhaps, Christianity is indeed about the intellectual, spiritual aspect of being in the world—caring for the soul as grappling with finitude and being shaken. However, the intention of this book and this chapter is not to provide a new canonical interpretation of Patočka or any other (philosophical) interpreter of Christianity after Christendom. The point is to think with those authors to discover a new horizon for living Christianity and thus to allow a theological voice to be heard.

The grammar of finitude (Falque) explicates the experience of being shaken (Patočka). Christianity incorporates this experience. And I shall say it again: being shaken is an experience—the experience of the peculiar human situation of being in the world. No idea, no concept, no theory (although we need all these to reflect on this experience) has the power to remove the given reality of finitude and its effects and affects materialized in the experience of being shaken. We are shaken before we reflect on being shaken. Our search for a credible Christianity after Christendom cannot, therefore, be satisfied with merely adopting *the task of thinking*—it must be complemented with *the vocation of living*.

Grappling with finitude—being shaken—is a lived facticity, although not one that is necessarily consciously recognized and embraced by all. Christianity is the sense for the human situation as far it is following the program of *imitatio Christi*. Before it is a religion, before it is a body of doctrine, before it is a ritual, Christianity is the incorporation of being shaken—the movement of being shaken. The religion, the doctrine, prayers, and rituals, the ecclesiastical structures, everything that Christianity is and that makes it visible is in service to the inherent movement of Christianity—grappling with being shaken.

The Christian does not have to be a philosopher or intellectual to care for the soul. Christians experience the fundamental condition of being human as spiritual people.[38] And the notion of being spiritual by no means stands in opposition to the embodied. On the contrary, Christianity is an embodied mode of being—the movement of a constant after; after being shaken. Embracing the ontological condition of being human—being shaken—is the meaning of the after of Christianity. In this sense, it becomes clear that Christianity after Christendom is not, therefore, the coming of something completely new in the chronological sense, as if Christianity comes *after* religion. The after is inherently historical and linked to the never-completed structure of Christianity—the need to think through the unthought.

Christianity as a mode of being is constantly *after* Christianity and chasing a credible Christian existence in the world. This is much more than a repetition of Christianity after its proclaimed end, regardless of its narrative thickness. The after of Christianity is the condition of the possibility of coming to conversion in a situation that is not-Christian but not yet non-Christian. In line with numerous philosophical interpretations, Christianity is indeed less a religious structure and more a philosophical way. Nonetheless, I wish to add that it is a real *vita philosophica*: a way of life, a way of inhabiting the world; a mode of being.

---

[38] Jan Patočka, "The Spiritual Person and the Intellectual," in *Living in Problematicity* (Praha: Oikoymenh, 2007), 51–69.

9

The Solidarity of the Shaken: Christian Community after Christendom

"Christianity remains thus far the greatest, unsurpassed but also un-thought-through élan that enabled humans to struggle against decadence." Patočka proclaims these words in his *Heretical Essays*,[1] and I have been intrigued and fascinated by this single sentence for many years. What is Patočka doing here? Does his proposition contain a programmatic statement? Is this philosopher, who otherwise never helps a theologian, inadvertently pronouncing a theological idea? I remain puzzled. However, the nature of my questioning of this enigmatic sentence does not seek to find the most precise reading of Patočka. Rather, I am challenged, by Patočka, to search for a credible meaning from my own theological perspective.

In the previous chapter, with Patočka's help, I argued a case for interpreting Christianity as a particular mode of being—being-in-the-world. We have seen that Christianity is neither the consolation nor the rationalization of the human condition. Rather, Christianity incorporates, sanctifies, and transforms the human condition in its crude seriousness. Christian discipleship is thus not about heroic resistance to this world but about grappling with the weight of being (shaken). Consequently, for Christianity, nothing can be taken for granted: questions of faith must be real questions, not a means of pretending to be involved in an existential drama yet

---

[1] Patočka, *Heretical Essays*, 108.

already knowing the answers. Christianity is a way of being in the world which starts with walking the earth.

Having established this approach to the human as such as the starting point of Christianity, the human condition of being fundamentally shaken when confronted with finitude cannot be avoided. However, being shaken, a grammar in common with the human condition, does not concern individuals only. When linked to Christianity, we must also enter the level of intersubjective relations—the community. The aim of this chapter is to reinterpret the Christian community which finds itself in the midst of existential upheaval and disorientation, and which seeks meaning even after the end of Christianity as the privileged provider of total meaning. Hence, I will enlarge the perspective from the individual-existential to the intersubjective-communal aspect of being shaken.

I will continue the dialogue with Patočka's phenomenological philosophy and will introduce one of the most visited concepts from his unfinished oeuvre: the solidarity of the shaken. Nonetheless, my intention is not to merely comment on one philosopher and the concept he developed. The goal of this final chapter is to apply the solidarity of the shaken to our thinking on the after of Christianity and present it as a potential foundation for the Christian community after Christendom. If a credible Christianity is about being the movement of existence, a credible Christian community must embody this movement and live it.

The Solidarity of the Shaken

In the original sense of Roman law, solidarity refers to an individual's responsibility for the whole (*in solidum*). I do not stand on my own and I am not for myself. The "I" is liable for the others. The question is: Who are the others? History suggests that they are usually those who are like us. Hence, solidarity is traditionally derived from solidity, that is, community on the firm ground of a shared identity. The most solid foundation blocks are ethnicity, social background, and culture: it is not difficult to imagine solidarity among, for example, fellow Romans, comrades in the revolution, or Christian brothers and sisters.

Solidarity appears to be a narrow term. A certain unity—solidity—precedes solidarity. And solidarity is effective in a community that has a solid foundation. The question "What do we have in common?" often precedes any reflection on solidarity. Historically, Christians have often raised this question, "What do we—Christians—share with Jews?" Yes, we share the Hebrew Bible. What about with Muslims? We share a belief in one God—monotheism. With Pagans, or as we say today, nonbelievers, we at least have the common ground of reason. On the one hand, Christianity finds certain solid foundations for its solidarity when understood as an openness toward others because those who are the others are, to a certain extent, like us. On the other hand, history also shows that what we share with others is sometimes not enough—or just enough to oppress, expel, or murder them. Asking the question of solid foundations, the question of what we have in common, can lead, and historically has indeed led, to tragic consequences. Why solidarity, then? What is the point of this reflection?

In contrast to a solid solidarity, Patočka introduces a groundless solidarity, and thus offers a completely different picture.[2] This solidarity centers itself on the conflict inherent in every human being and does not provide any common ground that can be defined in any positive sense. It literally shares nothing, that is, the consciousness of being no-thing. Not ethnicity, not fraternity; there is no *a priori*

---

[2] For a general introduction to Patočka's concept of the solidarity of the shaken, see Martin Palouš (ed.), *The Solidarity of the Shaken: Jan Patočka's Philosophical Legacy in the Modern World* (Washington, DC: Academica Press, 2019).

content, or an affiliation to the proposition: "It is a solidarity brought about by existential upheaval and disorientation, not by sharing something but, in a sense, by sharing nothing. It is solidarity beyond solidity."[3] This is the solidarity of the shaken.

What is this groundless solidarity without solidity? Patočka says, somewhat enigmatically, that the solidarity of the shaken brings together those "who are capable of understanding what life and death are all about and what history is about."[4] This is not a proclamation of gnostic knowledge or quasi-elitism. For Patočka, to know what history is about is to be aware of chaos, non-sense, problematicity. It is about facing existential disorientation. Life, death, and history appear as crucial catchwords in this respect. However, it is also about noticing that this is not merely the experience of some enlightened individuals, but a general human experience. In other words, the solidarity discussed by Patočka is not a solidarity in moral or social-political terms, although the unfolding implication of this solidarity is to keep the political space open. There is no collective liability for a debt, or a sovereign decision imposed on others. Rather, Patočka thinks of solidarity in terms of ontology and existence. It is an open narrative that is not exclusive or predetermined. It is not a solidarity for a clanship or confraternity and therefore not for those who are not like us. The solidarity of the shaken is a solidarity of those who are in a world full of heterogeneity.

The solidarity of the shaken is therefore the solidarity of those who bear the weight of finitude—the proper experience of human existence. Finitude, as argued earlier, is a universal and thus collective experience—the experience of being shaken. Moreover, it seems to me that the situation after the end of metaphysics, after the death of God, after the disintegration of Christianity; the situation full of dramatic

---

[3] Ludger Hagedorn, "Solidarity beyond Exclusion," *Baltic Worlds* 8, no. 1/2 (2015): 89.
[4] Patočka, *Heretical Essays*, 134.

upheavals and disorientation, where meaning slips away; the human condition of being thrown into the world—all this can be described under the rubric of being shaken. This very experience, which is not merely an individual experience, affects "us" as the whole, that is, on the level of community. Being shaken calls for solidarity. Solidarity in finitude drives us outside an enclosed individual existence. It drives us to the others and to otherness. Grappling with finitude—being shaken—is what opens the *with* the others, *in* the world, *coram et cum Deo*.

Alternative Spiritual Authority

The solidarity of the shaken is Patočka's answer to the crisis of humanity which bursts out in modernity. It is a response to the accumulation of forces that caused the conflicts, wars, totalitarianisms—the political, cultural, and civilizational disasters. Against this background, Patočka formulates a radical request: "The solidarity of the shaken ... can and must create a spiritual authority, become a spiritual power that could drive the warring world to some restraint, rendering some acts and measures impossible."[5] No wonder Patočka's concept provokes discussion of the political aspects of the solidarity of the shaken. Moreover, his personal actions toward the end of his life were inherently political and inspired not merely reflection but also an embodied practice of dissidence.[6] Nevertheless, what interests us here in Patočka's solidarity of the shaken is its relationship to Christianity. And, interestingly enough, Patočka introduces the concept of the solidarity of the shaken not only in the context of modern technological civilization but also in dialogue with Christianity.

---

[5] Ibid., 135.
[6] See Aspen Brinton, *Confronting Totalitarian Minds: Jan Patočka on Politics and Dissidence* (Prague: Charles University Press, 2021).

Often, the solidary of the shaken is set in sheer contrast to the Christian community, and thus presented as an alternative to ahistorical, metaphysical, and overwhelming unity with Christ.[7] And indeed, one can read Patočka's demand for a new spiritual authority, for developing a new spiritual power, as the final judgment addressed to a Christianity that ultimately failed to be this positive force for restraint. In other words, one possible answer to our question "What comes after Christianity?" is the solidarity of the shaken.

In this perspective, Christianity's deemed failure lies in its recursing to a pre-existent truth. That is, in having answers before the questions are asked, or to repeat Heidegger's critique: Christianity applies the interpretation from the perspective of life (eternal). *Ergo*, the challenge is to overcome Christianity by means of the situational solidarity of the shaken. Nietzsche's critique of dogmatic, metaphysical Christianity, which turned out to be an unquestioned Platonism for the masses, proves instrumental in describing what must be left behind: the solid, ahistorical meaning of the grand narrative of Christianity.

Well, a theologian must admit that Patočka's criticism could be valid, at least when we consider the mainstream version of Christianity and the dry, intellectually uninteresting Christianity Patočka probably witnessed at close hand in his day.[8] No wonder he prophetically announces its end. A careful reading of *Heretical Essays* will uncover numerous ways in which Patočka supports his own thesis, the most important, perhaps, being his call to philosophically complete Christianity that it may become a truly historical force.[9] For

---

[7] The perspective that juxtaposes Patočka's solidarity of the shaken with Christianity and suggests that the former supersedes the latter is presented in Michaela Belejkaničová, "Solidarity of the Shaken: From Experience (Erlebnis) to History," *Studies in East European Thought* 73, no. 3 (2021): 287–307.

[8] Patočka, for example, engaged in a written polemic with Neo-Thomism, for which he expressed very little understanding. See Jan Patočka, "Mezinárodní filosofická konference tomistická," in *Sebrané Spisy Jana Patočky, Češi I.*, Vol. 12 (Praha: Oikoymenh, 2006), 463–7.

[9] Patočka, *Heretical Essays*, 101–2.

philosophical interpreters of Patočka's work, the situation appears clear. Patočka distances himself from Christianity as an ahistorical deadweight that has not caught up with the peculiarity of the world as it appears to us. In my earlier *Thinking Faith after Christianity*, I sought to problematize this clear-cut reading of Patočka as a theology-free thinker. On the other hand, I do not buy into the occasional attempts to read Patočka as a Christian thinker; a thinker with the intention of reviving Christianity.[10] I am convinced that Patočka's thought has relevance for theology, but I should make it clear that what follows is not Patočka's theology, but a theology written with Patočka looking over my shoulder. To say it even more explicitly, the point of my argument is not to provide a literary reading and philosophical exegesis of Patočka's writing. My interest is not so much what Patočka says or wanted to say. I am searching for what I can think in dialogue with Patočka's thought. Hence, the point is not to prove that Patočka establishes the solidarity of the shaken as a potential philosophical completion of Christianity, but to argue that a confrontation with Patočka's existential phenomenology opens up a promising path for not only thinking but also living the after of Christianity. The solidarity of the shaken is not an alternative to Christianity; it is an alternative perspective on the after of Christianity, that is, the situation in which Christianity remains operative but can never pretend to be the same as it used to be.

Christianity as the Solidarity of the Shaken

I would like to repeat the words which are a refrain in this chapter and could perhaps be read as a golden thread of the entire book: "Christianity remains thus far the greatest, unsurpassed but also

---

[10] See especially the sections dedicated to a discussion of the interpretation of Patočka provided by Caputo and Derrida: Koci, *Thinking Faith after Christianity*, 188–98.

un-thought-through élan that enabled humans to struggle against decadence."[11] What is Patočka suggesting when he says that Christianity is un-thought-through, or, as he puts it elsewhere in *Heretical Essays*, that Christianity must be philosophically completed? Could we say that the solidarity of the shaken is, perhaps, this completion? The argument of this chapter suggests that the answer is negative. Talking about Christianity in terms of the solidarity of the shaken is rather about the transformation, recontextualization, and liberating power of philosophical concepts when they enter the field of theology.

Nonetheless, what strikes me is the tacit trinitarian logic inscribed into the solidarity of the shaken—a logic which means nothing to the philosophical author of the concept, but which is still a logic that corresponds to the general contours of the solidarity of the shaken when assessed from a theological perspective. Theologically, then, the trinitarian structure of Christianity is the blueprint for this kind of solidarity: God the Father suffers from not dying the death of the Son but receives and experiences the death of the Son spiritually—being moved by the event of Christ, transformed in a way, because no parent can remain still or numb to the ordeals of their child. God the Father experiences solidarity with the one who is existentially shaken. God the Father is being shaken in communion with the shaken one. The Spirit is this shakenness. Being in the Spirit means experiencing and partaking in this existential shakenness of the Son received by the Father.

Christianity as a community—the church—is the space of the realized solidarity of the shaken among the disciples who imitate (*imitatio*) the trinitarian solidarity. Being shaken is there. *Dasein ist erschüttert*. The solidarity of the shaken is the positive fruit of existential shakenness: being with one another in the world; being with Christ not as a pre-existent objective truth but the truth of life

---

[11] Patočka, *Heretical Essays*, 108 (translation modified).

which is itself shaken. And this shakenness is not a game. It is for real. This profound shakenness questions the meaning of existence but also fully embraces life. Yes, this remains as a challenge and a task entrusted to Christianity: the constant after carrying the movement of history.

Community formation is therefore a logical consequence of the experience of being shaken. When the "I" of irreducible persona is shaken, when this ability to search for meaning from within history is awoken, embraced, and put into action, this gives rise to solidarity with others and from others who fight the meaninglessness of a precarious world. True, to paraphrase Heidegger, one is always shaken as an individual. Nobody can be shaken in place of "me," and nobody can, in fact, take on my shakenness. But this is the point, isn't it? One is always shaken as an individual but never alone. To be shaken is to be *shaken-with*.

Borrowing Patočka's vocabulary, the solidarity of the shaken is a solidarity of those who are distressed by the day, by the bright, clear, and all too obvious truths of a triumphalist Christianity with all its absolute claims and demands. The solidarity of the shaken remembers, or tries to remember, that the sky went dark when Jesus of Nazareth was hanging on the cross (Mt 27:45; Mk 15:33; Lk 23:44). The solidarity of the shaken bears witness to the loss of meaning, a loss that is not fatal but moving. Those who partake in this solidarity, as Patočka dares to express, "know what matters in history." And Patočka adds: "History is nothing other than the shaken certitude of pre-given meaning."[12] What sounds presumptuous turns out to be a humble yet courageous confession: to live historically, to be in the world, means to stand vis-á-vis meaninglessness. It is the confrontation with the nonsense that sometimes precedes and sometimes conquers the sense. And those who are shaken do not forget about the obscure

---

[12] Ibid., 118.

and dark side of the world and the dark side of life. The solidarity of the shaken means sharing those things that are chaotic, unpleasant, uncanny; sharing them with others, for we all, in one way or another, grapple with finitude.

From Shaken Christianity Toward a Christianity of the Shaken

Shaken Christianity takes the opposite approach to the theology of interruption. Starting with the human per se, shaken Christianity undermines wishful thinking that grounds the Christian community in a particular, revealed identity—the narrative thickness that precedes community formation. In contrast to Boeve and his argument that the particularity of being Christian precedes the universality of being human, I support Falque's thesis that there is no other experience of God but the human experience.

I suggest, however, that Christian solidarity of the shaken is not based on sharing a particular narrative of previously defined truth claims, beliefs, and morals. Following Patočka and bringing him into proximity with Lyotard, it would be amiss to subscribe to the somewhat easy solutions offered by historical metanarratives (which have a clear tendency to include everything in their totalizing visions of the world and to provide answers even before the questions have been asked). What is at stake is an opening to actual historical happening. This is what Lyotard calls *the differend*. Patočka prefers the concept of *living in problematicity*. One way or another, the order of things is reversed. In the center of Christianity stands a shaken narrative of being human *tout court* announced and lived by the prophet of shakenness—Jesus of Nazareth. It is this human experience of being shaken to which Christians, not by the privilege of the relation but by their human vocation, are called to bear witness.

It is equally possible to bring Patočka's notion of being shaken into dialogue with Nancy. The deconstruction of Christianity, as argued earlier, is the internal movement of Christianity; something inherently inscribed into the Christian DNA and thus embodied in the Christian community. Although for Nancy deconstruction results in the self-effacement of Christianity, I suggest that we understand this process not in chronological terms but as the cyclical, constant return of the after of Christianity—the coming of Christianity after Christendom. The solidarity of the shaken is an outcome of the movement of deconstruction because it does not leave Christians with empty hands: a community is formed on this basis. True, Nancy and Patočka would probably agree that this community is not about safeguarding a set of doctrines. In this sense, it is a community without solidity which shares *nothing*. However, because the solidarity of the shaken engages with no-thing, it touches upon everything, for the solidarity of the shaken embodies living in problematicity firmly rooted in the world.

Are we repeating here Kearney's anatheistic gesture? Have we arrived at Caputo's Christianity without religion? I do not think so. It is true that the community gathered around the situation of being shaken is a community asking questions; and asking again and again. That is the core of living in problematicity. However, the goal of those questions is not to arrive at the originary *religious* experience. Rather, the Christian setting means a radical democratization of sharing a general *human* experience of being shaken, and from there it is possible to draw conclusions for particular contexts. The solidarity of the shaken is a universal experience, as the anatheistic experience supposes itself to be. However, the similarity contains a greater dissimilarity. Anatheism is formulated from a certain meta-ethical/religious standpoint, and thus searches for the general anatheistic structure in religions, cultures, and arts. By contrast, the solidarity of the shaken is drawn from the internal conflict in every human being, and this conflict is always reinterpreted according to particular religious and philosophical traditions. Christianity is the place which "internalizes" the conflict; it creates a place of the sanctification of this peculiar human condition. The solidarity of the shaken is thus, first and foremost, an ontologically grounded existential experience. The reflection provided by the Christian tradition comes only later.

In this sense, I must reject any association of the solidarity of the shaken with Caputo, whose sense of deconstruction aims to peel away all culturally conditioned and contextually particular layers of Christianity in order to arrive at the undeconstructible. But what is this undeconstructible core? The longing for justice in an unjust world? An insistence on praying in a Godless universe? Naming the unnamable? Keeping the process going? I am aware that I am not doing justice to Caputo's intellectual world here,[13] but my point is different: the solidarity of the shaken is not the undeconstructible. It is a universal ontological concept—the peculiar situation of human existence—but this universality by no means neglects particularity. And Patočka, as a good phenomenologist, never leaves the world even though he speaks, hesitantly and humbly, about God. The solidarity of the shaken is for real. And the community based on this shared experience of being shaken in an unjust world and Godless universe is a real embodied community.

The work and thought of Vattimo on Christianity as the community of realized charity thus looks to be closest to Patočka. Vattimo indeed develops a hermeneutical ecclesiology; one could even say an explicit Christian ecclesiology for the world after secularization and the death of God. There is one fundamental difference, however: Vattimo, standing in the Christian tradition, prescribes charity as the credible shape of the Christian community. Patočka's solidarity of the shaken does not prescribe because it is without solidity—without any

---

[13] The plasticity of Caputo's radical theological thought is well captured in Schrijvers and Koci (eds.), *The European Reception of John D. Caputo's Thought*.

predetermined content. The solidarity of the shaken does not drive the community to a common goal, such as loving relationships that are open and mutually respectful (and we should remember that definitions of what counts as open and respectful are always particular and contextually conditioned). Rather, it builds upon grappling with the experience of nothing—finitude, which is a real universal experience (*Erfahrung*) although lived (*Erlebnis*) in particular ways. The solidarity of the shaken forces the gathered community to come to decisions, but these decisions are always embedded in actual historical conditions. In other words, intersubjective love is more an effect of the solidarity of the shaken than it is the cause.

The solidarity of the shaken is therefore the realization of living in problematicity, another concept which occupies a prominent place in Patočka's later writings. We can translate it as an active questioning of the given state of being, a radicalized phenomenological method which puts every single claim about the essence of the world under question. Living in problematicity does not mean doubting everything according to a kind of postmodern suspension of all truths. Rather, it is patience directed at a constant attempt to embrace history with all its riddles. It is a commitment to never give up on searching for meaning, however difficult this enterprise may be.

Being shaken and experiencing this shakenness with others in the solidarity of the shaken means being able to see the world as a place of problematicity. And those who come to this insight are well equipped to fight, to borrow from Patočka, against decadence. In this sense, the church as the community of the shaken is indeed the corrective to a world without God. However, this critical correction has nothing in common with the triumphalism of preceding "Christian" centuries. The ecclesiology of being shaken comes after Christianity; it is Christianity after Christendom.

Being shaken is not a pleasurable position, but it is for real. There is no need for despair, however. Everything we have written so far leads to the following recognition: the solidarity of the shaken is lived in the community of those who despite or perhaps because of their experiences are ready to invest in life. The solidarity of the shaken is an ever-actualized *trotzdem*—a movement of transcendence, a step further along the existential path. Christianity that practices the solidarity of the shaken, Christianity as the movement of this solidarity grounded in human experience, represents a merciless critique of myths and metaphysical happy endings. The after of Christianity clears out all illusions and triumphalist tendencies and relinquishes all comforting but false metanarratives. Does that sound difficult? Almost unbearable? We must proceed carefully. It would be a grave mistake to understand the challenge of the *after* in quasi-Sartrean terms and to conclude that what remains is a tragic sense of existence, albeit one shared by a community that once used to be a great identity marker—religion *par excellence*. If what remains is nothing but despair and anxiety without exit, an existential burden, a loss of orientation, we would be right to turn our backs on such a Christianity.

Nevertheless, this is not where the after of Christianity as the embodied solidarity of the shaken is about to take us. Being shaken is not an end in itself. It is an existential situation lived, internalized, and cultivated through Christianity as the solidarity of the shaken. This solidarity does not fix its sights on wounds and traumas. On the contrary, it opens its eyes to the wonder; it enables the struggle against decadence by wondering (again). The solidarity of the shaken is the beginning of thinking about and striving for what has yet to come. In this sense, the solidarity of the shaken touches something original, but without recourse to the false ideal of the originary. It allows, rather, the disciples of Jesus of Nazareth to experience here and now the epiphany of meaning as the first generation of Christians experienced it. In other words, the after of Christianity makes it possible to experience something new as new.

Yet, the after of Christianity is not merely an intellectual activity. The solidarity of the shaken creates a space of lived freedom—the freedom to take decisions, including decisions about faith and belief, but taken in the world. The community of the shaken does not prescribe, force, or predetermine these decisions. It invites them. Perhaps the notion of invitation is the right way to describe the entire movement: everyone is invited to take part. This is the message of Christianity as the solidarity of the shaken, which grapples with the essential human experience without needing to rationalize the experience and immediately translate it into an intellectual register. At the same time, no one is forced to accept the invitation. The church of the shaken is the incarnation of Christianity after Christendom.

In Conclusion

Christianity after Christendom is a constant coming to terms with this challenge to be an historical, existentially engaged, and in-this-world embodied community. To return to where we began: "Christianity remains thus far the greatest, unsurpassed but also un-thought-through élan that enabled humans to struggle against decadence."[14] These words are challenging and demand that we critically open new horizons of thinking and living Christianity. Responding to this challenge does not result in the end of Christianity—in its abolishment, destruction, or deprivation. On the contrary, the Christian community after the disintegration of Christendom is a positive program; it is a call to develop a creative-critical response to the given historical conditions. The proposal of this chapter is therefore nothing like the emancipation of Christianity from a certain lower mode of existence and its elevation (*Aufhebung*) to a better, more complete form. What

[14] Patočka, *Heretical Essays*, 108.

stands at the center is not emancipation but liberation: the liberation of Christianity by means of philosophical reflection on human being in the world.

However, before any kind of confusion or misunderstanding arises, we must immediately add that this liberation is by no means a process of purification. The most important lesson of Christianity as the realized solidarity of the shaken is that there is no need to return to any original, authentic, if later degraded version. Liberation does not undo the deemed ballast of the human layer(s) in Christianity. Such a strategy would be another travesty of a solid, metaphysical, dogmatic, and ahistorical meaning, albeit cloaked in beautiful and bountiful metaphors.

Thinking the after of Christianity, thinking through Christianity, with the help of philosophy (is there any other way to think Christianity, by the way?) means making—sometimes even forcing—Christianity to be more acquainted with the human, the all too human. The after of Christianity has no aversion to the dirt of being in the world. On the contrary, Christianity embraces the factual reality of being human *tout court*. If the legacy of Jesus of Nazareth is to be taken seriously, there is no other way. Yet this way is far from univocal. Perhaps we have the direction and see the horizon but there are many crossroads.

There is the end of Christianity as an ahistorical metanarrative that claims to explain the totality of being and beings. There is the deconstruction of Christianity, although this deconstruction is without overcoming, without destruction, without the travesty of making Christianity more attractive by deeming it purer and closer to the originary. The striving for authenticity is an historical task: a constant asking about meaning and searching for credible and plausible answers. Understanding Christianity as the carrier of the solidarity of the shaken, a universal accessible human experience, and forming Christianity as the community of those who are shaken, regardless of their intellectual capacities—to reflect on this fundamental life experience creates the space for conversion to the truth of Christianity, which is the constant after, the pointing beyond itself. In short, the movement of transcendence.

But one can certainly ask: Isn't Christianity all this already? Perhaps, yes. The counter question is: Doesn't Christianity, in the course of its history, constantly forget this? The end of Christianity, the factual after of Christianity in the temporal sense, makes us aware that the presence of Christianity is self-evident. However, the after of history (*die Historie*) reveals the after of Christianity as the historical religion (*die Geschichte*). The solidarity of the shaken is, however, not merely speaking in prohibitions and warnings. It is a positive program of remaining uncertain and thus of undoing all temporary idols and myths. Being shaken also means being questioned and being questioned. In other words, to live in problematicity is to live an examined life, a life worth living in a peculiar place called the world. Of course, Christianity can withdraw from its critical potential, as it often did, and enact a parody on the eternal return of the same. Or Christianity can embrace the possibility of being shaken, as it has ever been, at least since the days of Jesus of Nazareth, who assumed the experience of being shaken with everyone and everything around. This task is given not only to individuals. It is a challenge for the entire community—the universal church of the shaken.

Conclusion

The English author G. K. Chesterton is said to have said that a heresy is not a lie but a truth gone mad.[1] I agree that a heresy is a passion for a truth otherwise diminished or practically forgotten. The word heresy appears in the subtitle of this book, and now it is perhaps clear why that is so. Each chapter has provided a different, heretical perspective on Christianity after Christendom, discussing the ends and prospects of Christianity in terms which are hardly compatible with the orthodox-ecclesial version of institutionalized Christianity. On the other hand, we have seen that some authors, even open atheists (or at best agnostics), cannot forget Christianity and instead bring it back time and again into discussion. For this reason, the heretical perspectives presented here function as a double-edged sword that strikes both the Christian audience (which perhaps takes Christianity in its current state for granted) and the secular audience (which is perhaps wrongly convinced that Christianity belongs in the past).

The debate with philosophers in Part I revealed the postmodern end of sovereign Christianity and its narrative, pointed out the deconstruction of the reign of Christian metaphysical principles, and touched upon the internal tension between the movement

---

[1] In fact, what Chesterton once wrote was that "Every heresy is a truth taught out of proportion." Elsewhere, he explains how heretics pick up an idea which is *a* truth and turn it into *the* truth. The aphorism "A heresy is a truth gone mad" therefore represents the compression of a number of Chesterton's sayings into a single pithy phrase. For more on this, see Dale Ahlquist, "Pope Francis Quotes Chesterton! But What Was the Quotation?" *Crisis* 19, March 2014, https://www.crisismagazine.com/2014/pope-francis-quotes-chesterton-but-what-was-the-quote (accessed August 31, 2022).

of being Christian and the static nature of religious structures. In other words, Christianity is still with us even though its presence is utterly problematic. What has gone is Christendom. The challenge is therefore to think Christianity after Christendom.

The Catholic philosophers discussed in Part II, philosophers who undoubtedly have certain theological aspirations, attempt to reinterpret Christianity in this situation that can also be described as not-Christian but certainly not entirely non-Christian. Taking the postmodern ends of Christendom as the given condition and focusing on the "signs of the times," Christianity is demythologized, deprived of its religious structure, and reread as a particular instance of universal religious experience. All these attempts to provide a new hermeneutics of Christianity, and perhaps even to offer new foundations for (hermeneutical) theology after Christendom, are intellectually rich and thought provoking but, I suggest, insufficient. They are truly heretical perspectives that venerate the truth but forget about some other truths.

Part III therefore provided an alternative perspective on Christianity after Christendom. I argue for a Christianity which embraces the world and history; a Christianity as an embodied community—traditionally called the church—based on the solidarity of the shaken, that is, on a solidarity that is founded on our common human condition. I search for a Christianity which is not first and foremost attached to a set of propositions (on the epistemological level) or narrative thickness (on the hermeneutical level) but is based on grappling with finitude—our common human grammar (on the existential level). According to this perspective, I understand Christianity as a mode of being—a specific way of living in and inhabiting the world and responding to history. Christianity after Christendom naturally has its hermeneutical, epistemological, and religious aspects, but all these are dependent on what precedes, and that is the existential-experiential movement.

What is heretical about all this? Perhaps nothing. Perhaps everything. The first heresy I dare to associate with the perspective presented in this book is the heresy of allowing a theological voice to be heard in the context of the so-called continental philosophy of religion. I discussed numerous philosophers; in fact, with only one exception, the previous chapters discussed philosophers exclusively. And in philosophy, especially in the philosophy of religion, Christianity is often taken as hostage for a certain archival and genealogical academic work in order to explain our ethical, political, and social concepts.

The recent literature is full of the return to religion and even theological turns in philosophy (sometimes used as a sign of the times, sometimes pejoratively as hijacking the true task of philosophy). The truth is, those who identified themselves as philosophers scrupulously reject the theological, even though they are discussing themes, problems, and questions drawn from the world of religions. The conclusion of the book is not the best place to open a controversial and highly complex debate.[2] What seems to be given, however, is a reversal of the traditional distribution of tasks. *Philosophia ancilla theologiae* belongs to the past. Today, philosophers borrow concepts and vocabulary from theologians. This practice, however, does not necessarily result in the secularization of theology or its straightforward de-theologization. Rather, I am of the view that we are witnessing the transformation of theological concepts such as faith, charity, hope, God, religion, and Christianity, and I am grateful to philosophers for performing such a transformation.

The responsibility of theology is to take the transformed ideas back—not to exercise a sovereign claim on the stolen heritage but to learn from philosophical-theological encounters about rigor and

---

[2] I have done this elsewhere. See Koci, "After the Theological Turn," 114–27.

credibility of thought. It is precisely in this context that I dare to talk as a theologian (a philosophical theologian who claims allegiance to the continental philosophical tradition) who hopes that reflections on Christianity after Christendom will have a theological impact.

The second heresy formulated here (mostly in Part III) is a clear theological preference given to the book of "the world" over the book of "Revelation." This seems to be at odds with traditional Christianity, but I am of the view that the truth of this "heresy" is rather, in fact, at odds with Christendom. The reflection on the *after* as presented in this book is not about sociological analysis.[3] Rather, I suppose that Christendom is a certain mode of thinking and organization which lost credibility; it is a superstructure which underwent self-deconstruction. What remains after Christendom is Christianity.

And Christianity that fights for its credibility is called, I suggest, to be integrated in and faithful to the world. This worldly vocation does not contradict the biblical notion that the followers of Christ "do not belong to the world" (Jn 17:14). Christianity is perhaps indeed "not of this world," but this is not to say it is "out of the world." Christianity undoubtedly finds itself in the world and is constantly coming into the world. And it is from within the world that Christianity always points beyond itself and thus reveals the principal truth of the category of the after: Christianity, and even much less Christendom, is never an end in itself.

Now it becomes clearer that the book of Revelation is not a gnostic knowledge but the hermeneutical key to the book of the world and the ultimate template for understanding the human condition and the meaning of well-being. To put it differently, the book of Revelation is the explication of the universal human experience of being in the world. Revelation makes the story of "the shaken being" explicit and

---

[3] The various sociological and political aspects of the church in a culture that is no longer Christian are covered in detail by Chantal Delsol, *La Fin de la Chrétienté* (Paris: Les Éditions du Cerf, 2021).

outlines the meaning of "being shaken." The universal grammar is filled with a particular language, narrative, and hermeneutics, but it is important to underline that this particularity is not an obstacle to but the necessary condition for understanding the universal. And as Christians we are right to say that this particular view of things is the true explication of the human condition.

Thomas Aquinas—the doctor of the church—would most likely find himself uneasy with our train of thought. When he searched for common ground while proposing his argument for a credible Christianity, he decided to rely on reason. The Angelic doctor was convinced that all humans—Christians and Pagans, Jews and Muslims—share one and the same rationality and that a certain logical argumentation can serve as the grammar in common. Modernity and postmodernity challenged the supposition of a single rationality shared by all, and even if there is such a thing, it is hardly possible to reach a consensus about the content of this rationality. The case of finitude, I suggest, is different.

The point could be illustrated in the context of my debate with the Flemish theologian Lieven Boeve, who, inspired by Lyotard, proposes a radical hermeneutics of Christianity and argues that our Christian identity (like any other identity) is structured narratively. Richard Kearney says something similar and holds that we cannot escape narratives. Yet Boeve, in contrast to Kearney, who proposes a kind of universalist narrative of anatheism, is convinced that we have no other option but to address ourselves from within a particular tradition, that is, from within a particular story. In other words, for Boeve, hermeneutics comes first. Therefore, the challenge for Christianity after Christendom (i.e., after the loss of the credibility of the Christian master narrative) is to create an open narrative. I have to say that Boeve and Kearney are partly right. The truth of their position pertains to the intellectual, reflected Christian identity. They offer a useful way *to think* about Christian identity in a postmodern world.

I suggest, however, that the ontology of finitude precedes the narrative structure. First, we have the experience of being shaken vis-a-vis the human condition, and only then do we reflect upon this experience. The experience of having finitude precedes the interpretation of finitude. We have this experience—our being is shaken—even without conducting any intellectual reflection. Every single human being participates in the grammar of finitude. In turn, the grammar of finitude is indeed the universal grammar in common. In other words, phenomenology precedes hermeneutics. And from there, it seems reasonable that before we ponder on the open narrative, we should engage with Christianity as the shaken narrative. In fact, Christianity shakes every narrative about being in the world because it is less about assigning an interpretation to the human condition than about a specific mode of being human in the world.

In sum, I argue that the core of Christianity is not its narrative structure but the experience of being-in-the-world. When we bump into "the impassable immanence" of the human condition, that is, when we are confronted with the inevitable experience of finitude, the limitations of narrative(s) are clearly exposed. The point is that Christianity, before it is a reflexive account that delivers a narrative, has the world—a life world. Hence, Christianity is a mode of being-in-the-world. And as a mode of being, Christianity is dynamic, full of life, and mobile, and the central movement of Christian being in the world is care for the experience of being shaken. This is the primary meaning of the *after* of Christendom.

Christianity after Christendom is not a chronological moment but an ever-actualizing movement. The after is a positive response to Nancy's somewhat negative program of the deconstruction of Christianity and Christianity's self-effacement. It is also an attempt to respond to Charles Taylor's rightful charge that our Christianity is lived too much in our heads. Theologically speaking, Christian history (telling the story about Jesus of Nazareth) is set in motion by "the Word was made flesh" (Jn 1:14). Nonetheless, this event—this "Big Bang" of Christianity—is not only an expression that the Son of God became man, but also the condition of possibility of any theology. The prologue to the fourth Gospel suggests more than the unification of God and human being. It points toward the notion that the incarnational principle of Christianity "connotes the precarious conditions of human beings who are subject to death."[4] To say it once again with Falque, "we have no other experience of God but *that of human beings*."[5] The primary locus of this experience is our bodily existence—the visible, touchable, experiential body in the world; and the world is just a different name for *time* and *space*. It would be natural to extend this book in other directions: discussing the theme of the body, the incarnation, and embodiment in the context of Christianity after Christendom; it would also be helpful to explore the concept of the world as a theological problem and perhaps even to develop a systematic theology of the world and the spirituality of being-in-the-world.[6] These ambitious projects are beyond the scope of this little book, but they certainly remain on the horizon of any future thinking about Christianity after Christendom.

To reiterate: the grammar of finitude reveals what it means to be shaken (*erschüttern*): to be shaken intellectually (the suspension of meaning regarding one's death); to be shaken bodily (the corruption of the carrier of our existence, the container we have, and the body we are); and last but not least to be shaken existentially (experiencing anxiety as the human, all too human reaction to the condition of being in the world). Christianity, following the Christ, is called to embrace finitude

---

[4] Jean-Yves Lacoste, "Incarnation," in *Encyclopedia of Christian Theology, Vol. 3*, ed. J.-Y. Lacoste (New York, NY: Routledge, 2005), 763.
[5] Falque, *Metamorphosis of Finitude*, 97.
[6] I outlined the early contours of this project in Martin Koci, "The World as a Theological Problem," *Journal for Continental Philosophy of Religion* 2 (2020): 22–46.

and to be in the world as Christ was, physically and authentically, in the world. My thesis about Christianity after Christendom can therefore be summarized as follows: Being Christian is a mode of being in the world which is concerned with the care for being shaken. And this care is just another name for the movement of the constant after.

In this book, I raised the criticism that contemporary philosophers and theologians offer visions of Christianity after Christendom that are too intellectual. I seem now to be proposing another philosophical theology. How should I respond to this self-inflicted critique? What does it mean to say that Christianity is a movement—an existential movement?

Christianity after Christendom is not about the reform of Christianity; it is not a search for a more radical, hermeneutical, or cultural theology. Rather, I prefer to translate the after of Christianity as a *conversion*. And this conversion is not about a switch from one set of opinions to another; the conversion of the after is not epistemic. This conversion is linked to the grammar of finitude, the universal human condition that is transformed. It is critical to understand this argumentative move correctly, so I will underline what this conversion is not: it is not a conversion in the sense of a sovereign victory over finitude; it is not a flight from finitude (and thus from the world and history) into the open arms of the Redeemer, the Savior who comes from on high. On the contrary, Christian conversion equips the human being to convert finitude as the unavoidable part of life and to fight the danger of nihilism that can stem from an unprocessed, perhaps even suppressed experience of finitude. In short, conversion stands here for grappling with finitude.

Christianity after Christendom is therefore about an existential conversion which, in contrast to calls for mystical and deeply spiritual Christianity, is *human, all too human*. This existential conversion proceeds from within the experience of being shaken. Christianity is the internalization of the experience of being shaken and even though we use philosophical vocabulary to describe it, the Christian dynamic of grappling with finitude and the existential processing of the shaken being is accessible to everyone. In other words, it is not necessary to conduct any kind of intellectual reflection in order to embrace the Christian movement of being. Moreover, Christianity is directed not at mere individual inwardness but at the realization of the potential of human freedom as a community. From there, we can move to our thinking on the solidarity of the shaken. Christian conversion opens up the membership of the community of the church. I attempt to argue that the model and the realization of this community is to be found in the community of those who are brought together by their common human condition, that is, the shakenness of being-in-the-world.

The saving power comes from within the world. Because of—rather than despite—Christianity's attachment to this world, we can talk about hope in salvation, but without running into all-too-easy solutions or naive metaphysical happy endings. One old theological phrase reads: what has been assumed (by the Son of God) has been saved.

What is Christianity? It is impossible to give a univocal answer. The array of thinkers discussed in this book bears witness to the equivocity of the question. What is the after of Christianity? Jan Patočka suggests that in the post-European epoch, "all the pillars of the community, traditions, and myths [are] shaken."[7] This book attempts to show that Christianity is going through this experience now. Nonetheless, I argue that this is not a loss but a challenge. And perhaps this challenge will resonate less with ecclesial communities than with the world.

Christianity, I suggest, appears in the world as an existential path. Christianity comes to the world again and again in order to reactualize the repetition of its after. This book is perhaps more about being-in-the-world, about inhabiting the world, than it is an apologetic for the importance of Christianity. Yet, even if there

---

[7] Patočka, *Heretical Essays*, 39.

is no apologetic effort hidden between the lines, there is surely an invitation to see Christianity, in its movement of the after, as the force of caring for life and for the community. Perhaps I have failed to add anything to Christianity as a confessional religion. I have not produced a better, purer, or more attractive Christianity. I have not conceived an ideal vision of Christianity. Nor have I proposed a radical reform, de-mythologization, or deconstruction in a postmodern fashion. Instead, I wanted to understand—to understand not only what Christianity might be, as Derrida requests, but what Christianity already in some ways is and has ever been.

Certainly, this book leaves us with more questions than answers: How do we read the Bible from the peculiar situation of being shaken? How do we celebrate the liturgy of the shaken? How do we not only think Christianity but also live it? How will the Christian life of being shaken manifest itself? How do we proclaim to the world this message—this gospel—of being shaken? In what ways, if any, have we already been reading the Bible as a testimony about grappling with the shakenness of being? In what sense, if any, have we already been celebrating liturgy from within our being shaken? In what sense, if any, have we already been forming the church as the community of the shaken? I should perhaps have offered answers to these questions. Or perhaps it is good that these questions remain after writing and reading this book. Why so? A suitable, albeit partial answer is to appeal to Heidegger, who famously responded to Marx that before we are ready to change the world, we need to understand the world we are thrown into, the world we all have before we ponder on our experience in the world. This philosophical truism is also pertinent to theological reflection. The center of gravity of this book is the "happening" of the after as an orientation to the situation we have been thrown into. To understand the challenges naturally points in the direction of further explorations in both the philosophical and the theological register. First, however, we need to understand better what *being shaken* means. We can then develop a systematic-theological reflection on the *how* of Christianity after Christendom, a Christianity of being shaken.

Then, and only then, will we be faithful to the challenge of John D. Caputo, who is perhaps best positioned to respond to Derrida's critique: "Every theology worthy of the name must come after the theology that up to now has staked its claim to that name." To which Caputo adds: "Every God worthy of the name must come after the God that up to now has held sovereign sway over that name."[8] I dare to humbly complement the story and say that every Christianity worthy of the name must come after the Christianity of hegemonic Christendom, and that a genuine Christianity reveals itself, precisely in its coming, as Christianity after Christendom.

---

[8] John D. Caputo, "Theology, Poetry, and Theopoetics," in *The Art of Anatheism*, ed. R. Kearney and M. Clemente (Lanham, MD: Rowman & Littlefield, 2017), 43.

Bibliography

Ahlquist, Dale. "Pope Francis Quotes Chesterton! But What Was the Quotation?" *Crisis* 19 (March 2014). https://www.crisismagazine.com/2014/pope-francis-quotes-chesterton-but-what-was-the-quote (Accessed August 31, 2022).

Aspray, Barnabas. "Transforming Heideggerian Finitude? Following Pathways Opened by Emmanuel Falque." In *Transforming the Theological Turn: Phenomenology with Emmanuel Falque*, edited by M. Koci and J. W. Alvis, 163–74. London: Rowman & Littlefield, 2020.

Barber, Michael. "Richard Kearney's *Anatheism* and the Religious and Theoretical Provinces of Meaning." *Revista Portuguesa de Filosofia* 2, no. 3 (2020): 973–1008.

Belejkaničová, Michaela. "Solidarity of the Shaken: From Experience (Erlebnis) to History." *Studies in East European Thought* 73, no. 3 (2021): 287–307.

Berger, Peter L. *The Sacred Canopy: Elements of a Sociological Theory of Religion*. New York, NY: Anchor, 1990.

Bloechl, Jeffrey. "Christianity and Possibility: On Kearney's *The God Who May Be*." *Metaphilosophy* 36, no. 5 (2005): 730–40.

Boeve, Lieven. "Bearing Witness to the Differend: A Model for Theologizing in the Postmodern Context." *Louvain Studies* 20 (1995): 362–79.

Boeve, Lieven. *God Interrupts History: Theology in a Time of Upheaval*. New York, NY: Continuum, 2007.

Boeve, Lieven. "God, Particularity and Hermeneutics: A Critical-Constructive Theological Dialogue with Richard Kearney on Continental Philosophy's Turn (in)to Religion." *Ephemerides Theologicae Lovanienses* 81, no. 4 (2005): 305–33.

Boeve, Lieven. *Interrupting Tradition: An Essay on Christian Faith in a Postmodern Context*. Translated by B. Doyle. Louvain: Peeters, 2003.

Boeve, Lieven. "J.-F. Lyotard's Critique of Master Narratives: Toward a Postmodern Political Theology." In *Liberation Theologies on Shifting Grounds: A Clash of Socio-Economic and Cultural Paradigms*, edited by G. De Schrijver, 296–314. Leuven: Peeters, 1998.

Boeve, Lieven. *Lyotard and Theology: Beyond the Christian Master Narrative of Love*. London: Bloomsbury, 2014.

Boeve, Lieven. "Theological Truth in the Context of Contemporary Continental Thought: The Turn to Religion and the Contamination of Language." In *The Question of Theological Truth: Philosophical and Interreligious Perspectives*, edited by Frederiek Depoortere and Magdalen Lambkin, 77–100. Amsterdam, New York: Rodopi, 2012.

Bradbury, Ray. *Fahrenheit 451*. London: Transworld, 1967.

Brinton, Aspen. *Confronting Totalitarian Minds: Jan Patočka on Politics and Dissidence*. Prague: Charles University Press, 2021.

Brito, Emilio. "Kenosis." In *Encyclopedia of Christian Theology*, edited by J.-Y. Lacoste, 853–6. New York, NY: Routledge, 2005.

Bultmann, Rudolf. *New Testament and Mythology and Other Basic Writings*. Translated by S. C. Ogden. London: SCM, 1985.

Caputo, John D. *Deconstruction in a Nutshell: A Conversation with Jacques Derrida*. New York, NY: Fordham University Press, 1998.

Caputo, John D. *Demythologizing Heidegger*. Bloomington, IN: Indiana University Press, 1993.

Caputo, John D. *The Folly of God: A Theology of the Unconditional*. Salem, OR: Polebridge Press, 2016.

Caputo, John D. *Hoping against Hope: Confessions of a Postmodern Pilgrim*. Minneapolis, MN: Fortress Press, 2015.

Caputo, John D. *In Search of Radical Theology: Expositions, Explorations, Exhortations*. New York, NY: Fordham University Press, 2020.

Caputo, John D. *The Mystical Element in Heidegger's Thought*. Athens, OH: Ohio University Press, 1978.

Caputo, John D. *On Religion*. London: Routledge, 2002.

Caputo, John D. "Only as Hauntology Is Religion without Religion Possible: Response to Hart." In *Cross and Khôra: Deconstruction and Ethics in the Work of John D. Caputo*, edited by M. Zlomislic and N. DeRoo, 109–17. Eugene, OR: Pickwick Publishers, 2010.

Caputo, John D. *The Prayers and Tears of Jacques Derrida: Religion without Religion*. Bloomington, IN: Indiana University Press, 1997.

Caputo, John D. "Richard Kearney's Enthusiasm: A Philosophical Exploration of the God Who May Be." *Modern Theology* 18, no. 1 (2002): 87–94.

Caputo, John D. "The Sense of God: A Theology of the Event with Special Reference to Christianity." In *Between Philosophy and Theology: Contemporary Interpretations of Christianity*, edited by L. Boeve and C. Brabant, 27–41. Farnham, MD: Ashgate, 2010.

Caputo, John D. "Spectral Hermeneutics: On the Weakness of God and the Theology of the Event." In *After the Death of God*, edited by J. W. Robbins, 47–85. New York, NY: Columbia University Press, 2007.

Caputo, John D. "Theology, Poetry, and Theopoetics." In *The Art of Anatheism*, edited by R. Kearney and M. Clemente, 43–7. Lanham, MD: Rowman & Littlefield, 2017.

Caputo, John D. "The Theopoetic Reduction: Suspending the Supernatural Signified." *Literature and Theology* 33, no. 3 (2019): 248–54.

Caputo, John D. "Thinking with Faith, Thinking as Faith: What Comes After Onto-theo-logy?" *Open Theology* 8, no. 1 (2022): 237–47.

Caputo, John D. *Truth*. London: Penguin, 2013.

Caputo, John D. *What Would Jesus Deconstruct? The Good News of Postmodernism for the Church*. Grand Rapids, MI: Baker Academic, 2007.

Caputo, John D. "Where Is Richard Kearney Coming From? Hospitality, Atheism and Ana-deconstruction." *Philosophy and Social Criticism* 47, no. 5 (2021): 551–69.

Caputo, John D., Kevin Hart, and Yvonne Sherwood, "Epoché and Faith: An Interview with Jacques Derrida." In *Derrida and Religion: Other Testaments*, edited by Y. Sherwood and K. Hart, 27–50. New York, NY: Routledge, 2005.

Cavanaugh, William T. *The Myth of Religious Violence: Secular Ideology and the Roots of Modern Conflict*. Oxford: Oxford University Press, 2009.

Chabbert, Marie. "The Eternal Return of Religion: Jean-Luc Nancy on Faith in the Singular-Plural." *Angelaki* 26, no. 3/4 (2021): 207–24.

Chvatík, Ivan. "Rethinking Christianity as a Suitable Religion for the Postmodern World. An Attempt to Reconstruct the Most 'Heretical' Idea of Jan Patočka." *Phenomenology* 4 (2010): 315–25.

Davis, Phillip E. "St Lyotard on the Differend/Difference Love Can Make." In *The Postmodern Saints of France: Refiguring "the Holy" in Contemporary French Philosophy*, edited by C. Dickinson, 123–38. London: T&T Clark, 2013.

Day, Barbara. *The Velvet Philosophers*. London: The Claridge Press, 1999.

D'Costa, Gavin. *Christianity and the World Religions: Disputed Questions in the Theology of Religions*. Oxford: Willey-Blackwell, 2009.

Deegan, D. L. "The Ritschlian School of the Essence of Christianity and Karl Barth." *Scottish Journal of Theology* 16, no. 4 (1963): 390–414.

Deibl, Jakob Helmut. *Geschichte – Offenbarung – Interpretation: Versuch einer theologischen Antwort an Gianni Vattimo*. Frankfurt: Lang, 2008.

Deibl, Jakob Helmut. *Menschwerdung und Schwächung: Annäherung an ein Gespräch mit Gianni Vattimo*. Vienna: Vienna University Press, 2013.

Delsol, Chantal. *La Fin de la Chrétienté*. Paris: Les Éditions du Cerf, 2021.

Depoortere, Frederiek. *Christ in Postmodern Philosophy: Gianni Vattimo, René Girard, and Slavoj Žižek*. New York, NY: T&T Clark, 2008.

Depoortere, Frederiek. "Gianni Vattimo's Concept of Truth and Its Consequences for Christianity." In *Theology and the Quest for Truth: Historical- and Systematic-Theological Studies*, edited by F. Depoortere and M. Lamberights, 241–58. Leuven: Peeters, 2006.

Derrida, Jacques. *Circumfession*. Translated by G. Bennington. Chicago, IL: The University of Chicago Press, 1993.

Derrida, Jacques. "Faith and Knowledge: The Two Sources of 'Religion' at the Limit of Reason Alone." In *Acts of Religion*, edited by G. Anidjar, 40–101. New York, NY: Routledge, 2002.

Derrida, Jacques. *Rogues: Two Essays on Reason*. Translated by P.-A. Brault and M. Naas. Stanford, CA: Stanford University Press, 2005.

Descartes, René. *Meditations on First Philosophy*. Translated by M. Moriarty. Oxford: Oxford University Press, 2008.

Devisch, Ignaas and Aukje van Rooden. "Deconstruction, Dis-Enclosure and Christianity." *Bijdragen* 69, no. 3 (2008): 249–63.

Dickinson, Colby. *Continental Philosophy and Theology*. Boston, MA: Brill, 2018.

Dickinson, Colby. "Ending Christian Hegemony: Jean-Luc Nancy and the Ends of Eurocentric Thought." *Open Theology* 8, no. 1 (2022): 14–27.

Dickinson, Colby. *The Fetish of Theology: The Challenge of the Fetish-Object to Modernity*. Cham: Springer, 2020.

Dickinson, Colby. *Theological Poverty in Continental Philosophy: After Christian Theology*. London: Bloomsbury, 2021.

Dickinson, Colby. *Theology and Contemporary Continental Philosophy: The Centrality of a Negative Dialectics*. Lanham, MD: Rowman & Littlefield, 2019.

Drakulic, Slavjenka. *Café Europa: Life after Communism*. London: Penguin, 1999.

Eagleton, Terry. *Reason, Faith, and Revolution: Reflections on the God Debate*. New Haven, CT: Yale University Press, 2009.

Ebeling, Gerhard. *Das Wesen des christlichen Glaubens*. München: Siebenstern, 1967.

Emma-Adamah, Victor. "The Sense of Finitude in Emmanuel Falque: A Blondelian Engagement." In *Transforming the Theological Turn: Phenomenology with Emmanuel Falque*, edited by M. Koci and J. W. Alvis, 175–86. London: Rowman & Littlefield, 2020.

Falque, Emmanuel. *The Guide to Gethsemane: Anxiety, Suffering, and Death*. Translated by G. Hughes. New York, NY: Fordham University Press, 2019.

Falque, Emmanuel. *The Metamorphosis of Finitude: An Essay on Birth and Resurrection*. Translated by G. Hughes. New York, NY: Fordham University Press, 2012.

Falque, Emmanuel. "Outside Phenomenology?" *Open Theology* 8, no. 1 (2022): 315–30.

Falque, Emmanuel. "Philosophie et théologie: Nouvelles frontières." *Études* 2 (2006): 201–10.

Feuerbach, Ludwig. *The Essence of Christianity*. Cambridge: Cambridge University Press, 2011.

Fodor, James. *Christian Hermeneutics: Paul Ricoeur and the Refiguring of Theology*. Oxford: Clarendon Press, 1995.

Fritz, Peter J. "Capitalism—or Christianity: Creation and Incarnation in Jean-Luc Nancy." *Political Theology* 15, no. 5 (2014): 421–37.

Fritz, Peter J. "On the V(I)Erge: Jean-Luc Nancy, Christianity, and Incompletion." *The Heythrop Journal* 44, no. 4 (2014): 620–34.

Gauchet, Marcel. *The Disenchantment of the World: A Political History of Religion*. Translated by O. Burge. Princeton, NJ: Princeton University Press, 1999.

Grenz, Stanley J. *A Primer on Postmodernism*. Grand Rapids, MI: William B. Eerdmans, 1996.

Gritten, Anthony. "Event." In *The Lyotard Dictionary*, edited by S. Sim, 70–3. Edinburgh: Edinburgh University Press, 2011.

Guarino, Thomas G. *Vattimo and Theology*. London: T&T Clark, 2009.

Hagedorn, Ludger. "Beyond Myth and Enlightenment: On Religion in Patočka's Thought." In *Jan Patočka and the Heritage of Phenomenology: Centenary Papers*, edited by E. Abrams and I. Chvatík, 245–62. Dordrecht: Springer, 2011.

Hagedorn, Ludger. "Solidarity beyond Exclusion." *Baltic Worlds* 8, no. 1/2 (2015): 87–90.

Halík, Tomáš. *Der Nachmittag des Christentums: Eine Zeitansage*. Freiburg: Herder, 2022.

Harris, Matthew E. "Nietzsche's 'Death of God,' Modernism and Postmodernism in the Twentieth Century: Insights from Altizer and Vattimo." *The Heythrop Journal* 62, no. 1 (2021): 53–64.

Heidegger, Martin. *Off the Beaten Track*. Translated by J. Young and K. Haynes. Cambridge: Cambridge University Press, 2002.

Heidegger, Martin. *Sein und Zeit*. Tübingen: Verlag, 1993.

Husserl, Edmund. *Ideen zur einer reinen Phänomenologie und Phänomenologische Philosophie: Allgemeine Einführung in die reine Phänomenologie*. Berlin: De Gruyter, 1994.

John Paul II. *Familiaris consortio*. https://www.vatican.va/content/john-paul-ii/en/apost_exhortations/documents/hf_jp-ii_exh_19811122_familiaris-consortio.html (Accessed June 30, 2022).

Kearney, Richard. "Ana-theism: God after God." In *Phenomenology and the Theological Turn*, edited by J. McCurry and A. Pryor, 8–11. Pittsburg, PA: Duquesne University, 2012.

Kearney, Richard. "Anatheism, Nihilism, and Weak Thought: Dialogue with Gianni Vattimo." In *Reimagining the Sacred: Richard Kearney Debates God*, edited by R. Kearney and J. Zimmermann, 128–48. New York, NY: Columbia University Press, 2015.

Kearney, Richard. *Anatheism: Returning to God after God*. New York, NY: Columbia University Press, 2010.

Kearney, Richard. "A Game of Jacks: Review Essay of John D. Caputo's Recent Works." *Philosophy and Social Criticism* 47, no. 5 (2021): 570–86.

Kearney, Richard. *The God Who May Be: A Hermeneutics of Religion*. Bloomington, IN: Indiana University Press, 2001.

Kearney, Richard. *On Stories*. London: Routledge, 2002.

Kearney, Richard. *Sam's Fall*. London: Spectre, 1996.

Kearney, Richard. *Strangers, Gods and Monsters: Interpreting Otherness*. London: Routledge, 2005.

Kearney, Richard. *Touch: Recovering Our Most Vital Sense*. New York, NY: Columbia University Press, 2021.

Kearney, Richard, and Emmanuel Falque. "Anatheist Exchange: Returning to the Body after the Flesh." In *Richard Kearney's Anatheistic Wager: Philosophy, Theology, Poetics*, edited by C. van Troostwijk and M. Clemente, 88–109. Bloomington, IN: Indiana University Press, 2018.

Klun, Branko. "Incarnation and 'De-Carnation' in the Hermeneutics of Gianni Vattimo." *Acta Philosophica* 29, no. 1 (2020): 161–77.

Koci, Martin. "After the Theological Turn: Towards a Credible Theological Grammar." *Open Theology* 8, no. 1 (2022): 114–27.

Koci, Martin. "Christianity after Christendom: Rethinking Jan Patočka's Heresy." *The Heythrop Journal* 63, no. 4 (2022): 717–30.

Koci, Martin. "Phenomenology and Theology Revisited: Emmanuel Falque and His Critics." *Revista Portuguesa de Filosofia* 76, no. 2/3 (2020): 903–26.

Koci, Martin. *Thinking Faith after Christianity: A Theological Reading of Jan Patočka's Phenomenological Philosophy*. Albany, NY: State University of New York Press, 2020.

Koci, Martin. "The World as a Theological Problem." *Journal for Continental Philosophy of Religion* 2 (2020): 22–46.

Krastev, Ivan. *After Europe*. Philadelphia, PA: University of Pennsylvania Press, 2017.

Lacoste, Jean-Yves. *From Theology to Theological Thinking*. Charlottesville, VA: University of Virginia Press, 2014.

Lacoste, Jean-Yves. "Incarnation." In *Encyclopedia of Christian Theology, Vol. 3*, edited by J.-Y. Lacoste, 763–66. New York, NY: Routledge, 2005.

Lascaris, André. "Can I Say 'We'? An Encounter between the Good Samaritan and Three Postmodern Philosophers." In *Who Is Afraid of Postmodernism? Challenging Theology for a Society in Search of Identity*, edited by S. Van Erp and A. Lascaris, 16–33. Münster: LIT Verlag, 2005.

Lyotard, Jean-François. *The Differend: Phrases in Dispute*. Translated by G. Van Den Abbeele. Manchester: Manchester University Press, 1988.

Lyotard, Jean-François. *The Hyphen: Between Judaism and Christianity*. Translated by P.-A. Brault and M. Naas. London: Polity Press, 1999.

Lyotard, Jean-François. *The Postmodern Condition: A Report on Knowledge*. Translated by G. Bennington and B. Massumi. Minneapolis, MN: University of Minnesota Press, 1984.

Lyotard, Jean-François. *The Postmodern Explained: Correspondence 1982–1985*. Translated by J. Pefanis and D. Barry. Minneapolis, MN: University of Minnesota Press, 1993.

Lyotard, Jean-François. *Postmodern Fables*. Translated by G. Van Den Abbeele. Minneapolis, MN: University of Minnesota Press, 1997.

Malpas, Simon. *Jean-François Lyotard*. New York, NY: Routledge, 2003.

Marion, Jean-Luc. *The Idol and Distance: Five Studies*. Translated by T. A. Carlson. New York, NY: Fordham University Press, 2001.

Marion, Jean-Luc. *Reprise du donné*. Paris: PUF, 2016.

Meganck, Erik. "God Returns as Nihilist *Caritas*: Secularization According to Gianni Vattimo." *Sophia* 54, no. 3 (2015): 363–79.

Meganck, Erik. "*Philosophia Amica Theologiae*: Gianni Vattimo's 'Weak Faith' and Theological Difference." *Modern Theology* 31, no. 3 (2015): 377–402.

Metz, Johann B. *Glaube in Geschichte und Gesellschaft: Studien zu einer praktischen Fundamentaltheologie*. Mainz: Grünewald, 1977.

Michalski, Krzysztof. *The Flame of Eternity: An Interpretation of Nietzsche's Thought*. Princeton, NJ: Princeton University Press, 2007.

Nancy, Jean-Luc. *Adoration: The Deconstruction of Christianity II*. Translated by J. McKeane. New York, NY: Fordham University Press, 2013.

Nancy, Jean-Luc. *After Fukushima: The Equivalence of Catastrophes*. Translated by C. Mandell. New York, NY: Fordham University Press, 2015.

Nancy, Jean-Luc. *Being Singular Plural*. Translated by R. Richardson. Stanford, CA: Stanford University Press, 2000.

Nancy, Jean-Luc. *Corpus*. Translated by R. Rand. New York, NY: Fordham University Press, 2008.

Nancy, Jean-Luc. *Dis-enclosure: The Deconstruction of Christianity*. Translated by B. Bergo. New York, NY: Fordham University Press, 2008.

Nancy, Jean-Luc. "In the Midst of the World; or, Why Deconstruct Christianity?" In *Re-treating Religion: Deconstructing Christianity with Jean-Luc Nancy*, edited by A. Alexandrova, I. Devisch, L. Ten Kate, and A. Van Rooden, 1–21. New York, NY: Fordham University Press, 2012.

Nancy, Jean-Luc. *The Sense of the World*. Translated by J. S. Librett. Minneapolis, MN: University of Minnesota Press, 1997.

Nancy, Jean-Luc, and the editors. "On Dis-enclosure and Its Gesture, Adoration: A Concluding Dialogue with Jean-Luc Nancy." In *Re-treating Religion: Deconstructing Christianity with Jean-Luc Nancy*, edited by A. Alexandrova, I. Devisch, L. Ten Kate, and A. Van Rooden, 304–44. New York, NY: Fordham University Press, 2012.

Newheiser, David. *Hope in a Secular Age: Deconstruction, Negative Theology, and the Future of Faith*. Cambridge: Cambridge University Press, 2019.

Palouš, Martin, ed. *The Solidarity of the Shaken: Jan Patočka's Philosophical Legacy in the Modern World*. Washington, DC: Academica Press, 2019.

Pascal, Blaise. *Pensées*. Translated by A. J. Krailsheimer. New York, NY: Penguin, 1995.

Patočka, Jan. "Le christianisme et le monde naturel." *Istina* 38, no. 1 (1993): 16–22.

Patočka, Jan. "Čtyři semináře k problému Evropy." In *Sebranné spisy Jana Patočky, Vol. 3. Péče o duši, III: Kacířské eseje o filosofii dějin; Varianty a přípravné práce z let 1973-1977; Dodatky k Péči o duši I a II*, edited by I. Chvatík and P. Kouba, 374–423. Praha: Oikoymenh, 2002.

Patočka, Jan. "The Danger of Technicization in Science according to E. Husserl and the Essence of Technology as Danger according to M. Heidegger (Varna Lecture)." In *The New Yearbook for Phenomenology and Phenomenological Philosophy XIV. Religion, War and the Crisis of Modernity: A Special Issue Dedicated to the Philosophy of Jan Patočka*, edited by L. Hagedorn and J. Dodd, 13–22. London: Routledge, 2015.

Patočka, Jan. *L'Europe après l'Europe*. Translated by Erika Abrams. Lagrasse: Verdier, 2007.

Patočka, Jan. *Heretical Essays in the Philosophy of History*. Translated by Erazim Kohák. La Salle, IL: Open Court, 1996.

Patočka, Jan. *Liberté et sacrifice*. Translated and edited by Erika Abrams. Grenoble: J. Millon, 1990.

Patočka, Jan. "Mezinárodní filosofická konference tomistická." In *Sebrané Spisy Jana Patočky, Češi I., Vol. 12*, edited by K. Palek and I. Chvatík, 463–7. Praha: Oikoymenh, 2006.

Patočka, Jan. *Plato and Europe*. Translated by Peter Lom. Stanford, CA: Stanford University Press, 2002.

Patočka, Jan. "Prostor a jeho problematika." In *Sebrané spisy Jana Patočky, Fenomenologické spisy III/2, vol 8/2*, edited by I. Chvatík and P. Kouba, 11–71. Praha: Oikoymenh, 2016.

Patočka, Jan. "The Spiritual Person and the Intellectual." In *Living in Problematicity*, edited by E. Manton, 51–69. Praha: Oikoymenh, 2007.

Patočka, Jan. "Theologie a filosofie." In *Sebranné spisy Jana Patočky, Vol. 1. Péče o duši, I: Stati z let 1929–1952; Nevydané texty z padesátých let*, edited by I. Chvatík and P. Kouba, 15–21. Praha: Oikoymenh, 1996.

Petříček, Miroslav. "Jan Patočka and Phenomenological Philosophy Today." In *Jan Patočka and the Heritage of Phenomenology: Centenary Papers*, edited by E. Abrams and I. Chvatík, 3–6. Dordrecht: Springer, 2011.

Plunkett, Erin. "Review of *Thinking Faith after Christianity* by Martin Koci." *Phenomenological Reviews* 7 (2021): 53.

Raffoul, François. "The Self-Deconstruction of Christianity." In *Re-treating Religion: Deconstructing Christianity with Jean-Luc Nancy*, edited by A. Alexandrova, I. Devisch, L. Ten Kate, and A. Van Rooden, 46–62. New York, NY: Fordham University Press, 2012.

Ratzinger, Joseph. "Europe in the Crisis of Cultures." *Communio: International Catholic Review* 32, no. 2 (2005): 345–56.

Rorty, Richard, Gianni Vattimo, and Santiago Zabala. "What Is Religion's Future after Metaphysics?" In *The Future of Religion*, edited by S. Zabala, 55–81. New York, NY: Columbia University Press, 2005.

Rose, Marika and Anthony P. Smith. "Hexing the Discipline: Against the Reproduction of Continental Philosophy of Religion." *Palgrave Communications* 5, no. 2 (2019). http://doi: 10.1057/s41599-018-0207-4 (Accessed June 30, 2022).

Roy, Olivier. *Is Europe Christian?* Translated by C. Schoch. London: C. Hurst & Co, 2019.

Sands, Justin. "Confessional Discourses, Radicalizing Traditions: On John Caputo and the Theological Turn." *Open Theology* 8, no. 1 (2022): 38–49.

Schillebeeckx, Edward. *Interim Report on the Books Jesus and Christ*. Translated by J. Bowden. New York, NY: Crossroad, 1981.

Schrijvers, Joeri. *Between Faith and Belief: Toward a Contemporary Phenomenology of Religious Life*. Albany, NY: State University of New York Press, 2016.

Schrijvers, Joeri. "Metamorphosis or Mutation? Jean-Luc Nancy and the Deconstruction of Christianity." *Angelaki* 26, no. 3/4 (2021): 162–77.

Schrijvers, Joeri. *Ontotheological Turnings? The Decentering of the Modern Subject in Recent French Phenomenology*. Albany, NY: State University of New York Press, 2011.

Schrijvers, Joeri and Martin Koci, eds. *The European Reception of John D. Caputo's Thought: Radicalizing Theology*. Lanham, MD: Lexington Books, 2022.

Simmons, Aaron J. *God and the Other: Ethics and Politics after the Theological Turn*. Bloomington, IN: Indiana University Press, 2011.

Smerick, Christina M. *Jean-Luc Nancy and Christian Thought: Deconstruction of the Bodies of Christ*. Lanham, MD: Lexington Books, 2018.

Steinbock, Anthony J. *Phenomenology and Mysticism: The Verticality of Religious Experience*. Bloomington, IN: Indiana University Press, 2007.

Tava, Francesco and Darian Meacham, eds. *Thinking After Europe: Jan Patočka and Politics*. Lanham, MD: Rowman & Littlefield, 2016.

Taylor, Charles. *A Secular Age*. Cambridge: The Belknap Press, 2007.

Ten Kate, Laurens. "Outside in, Inside out." *Bijdragen* 69, no. 3 (2008): 305–20.

Tracy, David. *Plurality and Ambiguity: Hermeneutics, Religion, Hope*. Chicago, IL: The University of Chicago Press, 1987.

Treanor, Brian. "The Anatheistic Wager: Faith after Faith." *Religion and the Arts* 14, no. 5 (2010): 546–59.

Vattimo, Gianni. *After Christianity*. Translated by Luca D'Isanto. New York, NY: Columbia University Press, 2002.

Vattimo, Gianni. *Belief*. Translated by Luca D'Isanto. Cambridge: Cambridge University Press, 1999.

Vattimo, Gianni. "Nihilism as Postmodern Christianity." In *Transcendence and Beyond: A Postmodern Inquiry*, edited by J. D. Caputo and M. J. Scanlon, 44–8. Bloomington, IN: Indiana University Press, 2007.

Vattimo, Gianni. *Not Being God: A Collaborative Autobiography*. New York, NY: Columbia University Press, 2009.

Vattimo, Gianni. "Towards a Nonreligious Christianity." In *After the Death of God*, edited by J. W. Robbins, 27–46. New York, NY: Columbia University Press, 2007.

Vattimo, Gianni. "A Prayer for Silence." In *After the Death of God*, edited by J. W. Robbins, 89–113. New York, NY: Columbia University Press, 2007.

Vattimo, Gianni. *Of Reality: The Purposes of Philosophy*. Translated by R. T. Valgenti. New York, NY: Columbia University Press, 2016.

Vattimo, Gianni. *The Transparent Society*. Cambridge: Polity Press, 1992.

Vattimo, Gianni and Santiago Zabala. *Hermeneutic Communism: From Heidegger to Marx*. New York, NY: Columbia University Press, 2011.

Vries, Hent de. *Philosophy and the Turn to Religion*. Baltimore, MD: The Johns Hopkins University Press, 1999.

Ward, Graham. *Theology and Contemporary Critical Theory*. London: Macmillan, 2000.

Index

being-in-the-world 11, 45, 48, 65, 74, 87, 166, 167, 168, 171, 193, 216, 219
being shaken 37, 39, 148–9, 169, 171–221
Berger, Peter L. 73
Bible 79–80, 83, 220
Boeve, Lieven 13, 16–19, 62, 137, 148, 151–69, 202, 215
Bradbury, Ray 27
Bultmann, Rudolf 68

Caputo, John D. 12, 64, 69–70, 93–113, 134, 138–44, 157, 164, 166–7, 183, 186, 203–4, 221
church 16, 25, 38, 64, 84, 107–10, 141–2, 154, 200, 205, 207–9, 212, 219–20
conversion 17, 52–3, 59–60, 111, 185–8, 192, 209, 218–19

Dasein 52, 90, 177–8, 180, 200
Derrida, Jacques 1, 84–6, 93–7, 100–22, 161, 164, 190
Descartes, René 50, 177, 179

Eagleton, Terry 65
Ebeling, Gerhard 68

Falque, Emmanuel 2, 9, 116, 172–81, 191, 202, 217

Gauchet, Marcel 73

Halík, Tomáš 1, 45
Hegel, G.W.F. 17, 44, 77, 121
Heidegger, Martin 7, 33, 44, 50, 54–7, 69, 71–2, 74, 77–8, 80, 85–6, 91, 93–4, 118, 121–2, 140, 175, 178–9, 198, 201, 220

heresy 25, 36, 47–9, 211–14
hospitality 116–17, 129, 131–42
Husserl, Edmund 12, 50–1, 54, 121, 128

incarnation 38–9, 76–8, 80, 89–90, 108–10, 155, 164–8, 179–80, 190, 207, 217
interruption 13, 27, 31, 42, 125, 148, 151–2, 155–8, 163–4, 167–8, 202

Judaism 27, 133, 164

Kant, Immanuel 44, 87
Kearney, Richard 115–38, 140–4, 157, 166–7, 185–6, 203, 215
kenosis 32, 76–8, 80, 85–90, 140, 179, 185–7
Kierkegaard, Soren 55, 99, 108, 127, 182

Lacoste, Jean-Yves 8, 217
Levinas, Emmanuel 85, 115, 117–18, 125–6
Lyotard, Jean-François 15–29, 35, 53, 62, 65, 73, 84, 108, 119, 129, 132, 151–2, 157–8, 160–4, 202, 215

Marion, Jean-Luc 47, 74, 106, 116, 126, 161, 173

Nancy, Jean-Luc 31–45, 53, 62–3, 203, 216
Nietzsche, Friedrich 44, 47, 55, 69, 71–4, 77–80, 87, 91, 140, 171, 181, 198
nihilism 32, 55, 69, 73–4, 88, 91, 134, 143, 174, 218

otherness 13, 102–3, 108, 115,
    117–18, 122, 126–9, 131–2,
    152–4, 156–61, 167–8, 197

Pascal, Blaise 116–17, 135
Patočka, Jan 47–60, 65, 172, 181–205, 219
phenomenology 12, 99, 110, 112,
    121, 126, 171–3, 179, 199,
    216
postmodernism 14, 20–2, 28, 36, 62,
    88, 120, 140

Ratzinger, Joseph 117, 119, 135
recontextualization 6, 85, 94, 152–5,
    166–8, 200
resurrection 39, 124, 175, 190

revelation 28, 42, 82, 86, 98, 156, 165,
    167, 190
Sein 57, 74, 108, 188
secularization 1, 13, 41, 45, 73–80,
    84, 87–8, 140, 144, 152–3, 157,
    167, 213
solidarity of the shaken 148, 193–219

Taylor, Charles 61, 168, 191, 216
Torah 27, 164

Vattimo, Gianni 45, 71–91, 110, 124,
    134, 139–44, 157, 167, 185–6,
    204

weak thought 71, 78–80, 84, 87, 141

www.ingramcontent.com/pod-product-compliance
Lightning Source LLC
Chambersburg PA
CBHW071826300426
44116CB00009B/1458